AVENGING SPIDER-MAN

MY FRIENDS CAN BEAT UP YOUR FRIENDS

WRITER
ZEB WELLS

#1-3

ARTIST
JOE MADUREIRA

COLOR ARTIST
DOMMO AYMARA

COVER ART
JOE MADUREIRA WITH **ARON LUSEN** (#1)
& FERRAN DANIEL (#2-3)

#4

PENCILER
GREG LAND

INKER | **COLORIST**
JAY LEISTEN | **WIL QUINTANA**

COVER ART
GREG LAND WITH **JUSTIN PONSOR**

#5

PENCILER
LEINIL FRANCIS YU

INKER
GERRY ALANGUILAN

COLORIST
SUNNY GHO

COVER ART
LEINIL FRANCIS YU
WITH **JASON KEITH**

LETTERER: VC'S JOE CARAMAGNA ASSISTANT EDITOR: ELLIE PYLE

ASSOCIATE EDITOR: ALEJANDRO ARBONA EDITOR: STEPHEN WACKER

EXECUTIVE EDITOR: TOM BREVOORT

Collection Editor: Jennifer Grünwald • Assistant Editors: Alex Starbuck & Nelson Ribeiro • Editor, Special Projects: Mark D. Beazley
Senior Editor, Special Projects: Jeff Youngquist • Senior Vice President of Sales: David Gabriel
SVP of Brand Planning & Communications: Michael Pasciullo • Book Design: Jeff Powell

Editor in Chief: Axel Alonso • Chief Creative Officer: Joe Quesada • Publisher: Dan Buckley • Executive Producer: Alan Fine

AVENGING SPIDER-MAN: MY FRIENDS CAN BEAT UP YOUR FRIENDS. Contains material originally published in magazine form as AVENGING SPIDER-MAN #1-5. First printing 2012. Hardcover ISBN# 978-0-7851-5778-6. Softcover ISBN# 978-0-7851-5779-3. Published by MARVEL WORLDWIDE, INC., a subsidiary of MARVEL ENTERTAINMENT, LLC. OFFICE OF PUBLICATION: 135 West 50th Street, New York, NY 10020. Copyright © 2011 and 2012 Marvel Characters, Inc. All rights reserved. Hardcover: $24.99 per copy in the U.S. and $27.99 in Canada (GST #R127032852). Softcover: $19.99 per copy in the U.S. and $21.99 in Canada (GST #R127032852). Canadian Agreement #40668537. All characters featured in this issue and the distinctive names and likenesses thereof, and all related indicia are trademarks of Marvel Characters, Inc. No similarity between any of the names, characters, persons, and/or institutions in this magazine with those of any living or dead person or institution is intended, and any such similarity which may exist is purely coincidental. Printed in the U.S.A. ALAN FINE, EVP - Office of the President, Marvel Worldwide, Inc. and EVP & CMO Marvel Characters B.V.; DAN BUCKLEY, Publisher & President - Print, Animation & Digital Divisions; JOE QUESADA, Chief Creative Officer; TOM BREVOORT, SVP of Publishing; DAVID BOGART, SVP of Operations & Procurement, Publishing; RUWAN JAYATILLEKE, SVP & Associate Publisher, Publishing; C.B. CEBULSKI, SVP of Creator & Content Development; DAVID GABRIEL, SVP of Publishing Sales & Circulation; MICHAEL PASCIULLO, SVP of Brand Planning & Communications; JIM O'KEEFE, VP of Operations & Logistics; DAN CARR, Executive Director of Publishing Technology; SUSAN CRESPI, Editorial Operations Manager; ALEX MORALES, Publishing Operations Manager; STAN LEE, Chairman Emeritus. For information regarding advertising in Marvel Comics or on Marvel.com, please contact Ron Stern, SVP of Business Affairs and Marketing, at jdokes@marvel.com. For Marvel subscription inquiries, please call 800-217-9158. Manufactured between 4/30/2012 and 5/28/2012 (hardcover), and 4/30/2012 and 10/1/2012 (softcover), by R.R. DONNELLEY, INC., SALEM, VA, USA.

10 9 8 7 6 5 4 3 2 1

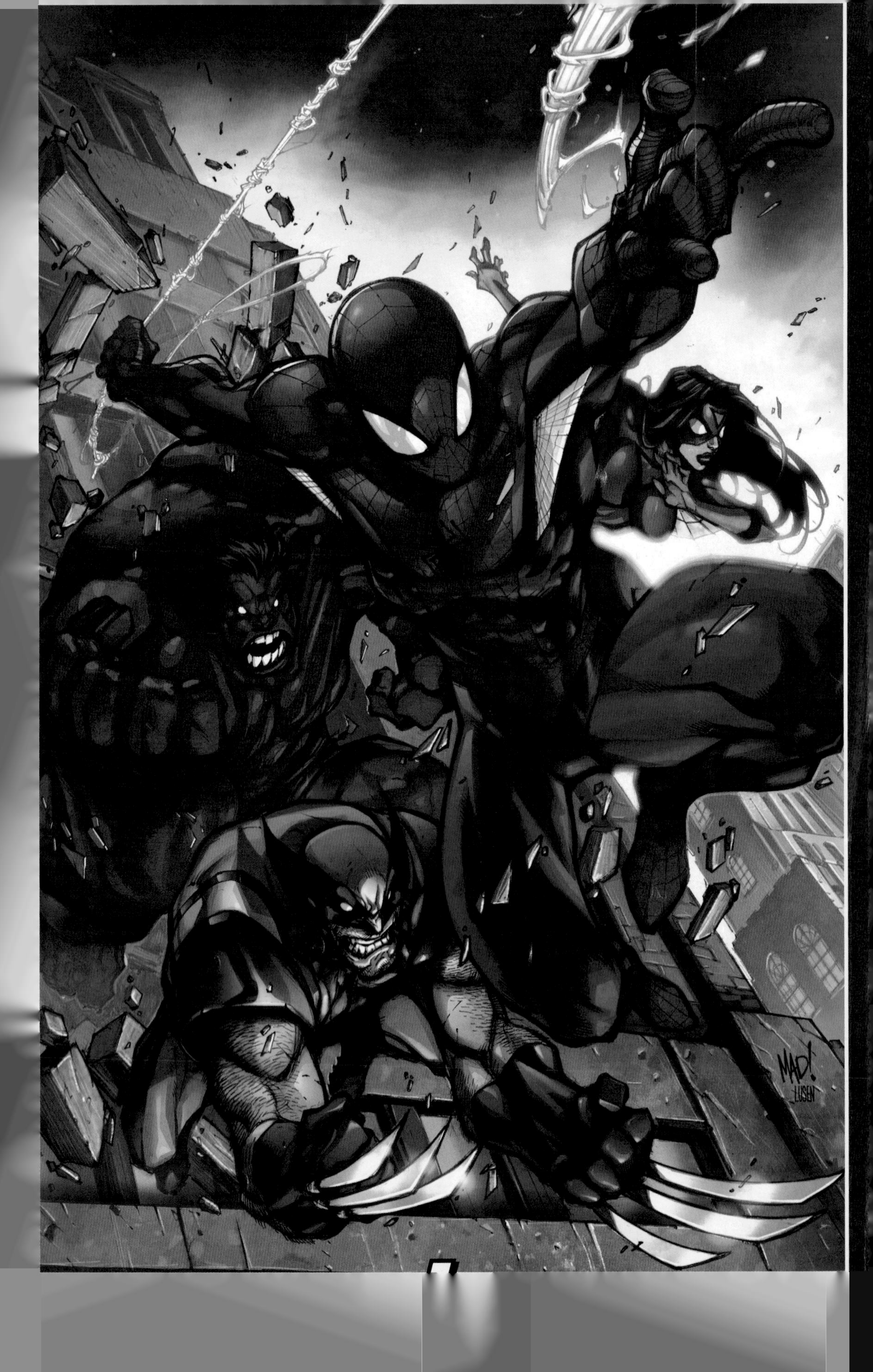
MAD!
LUSEN

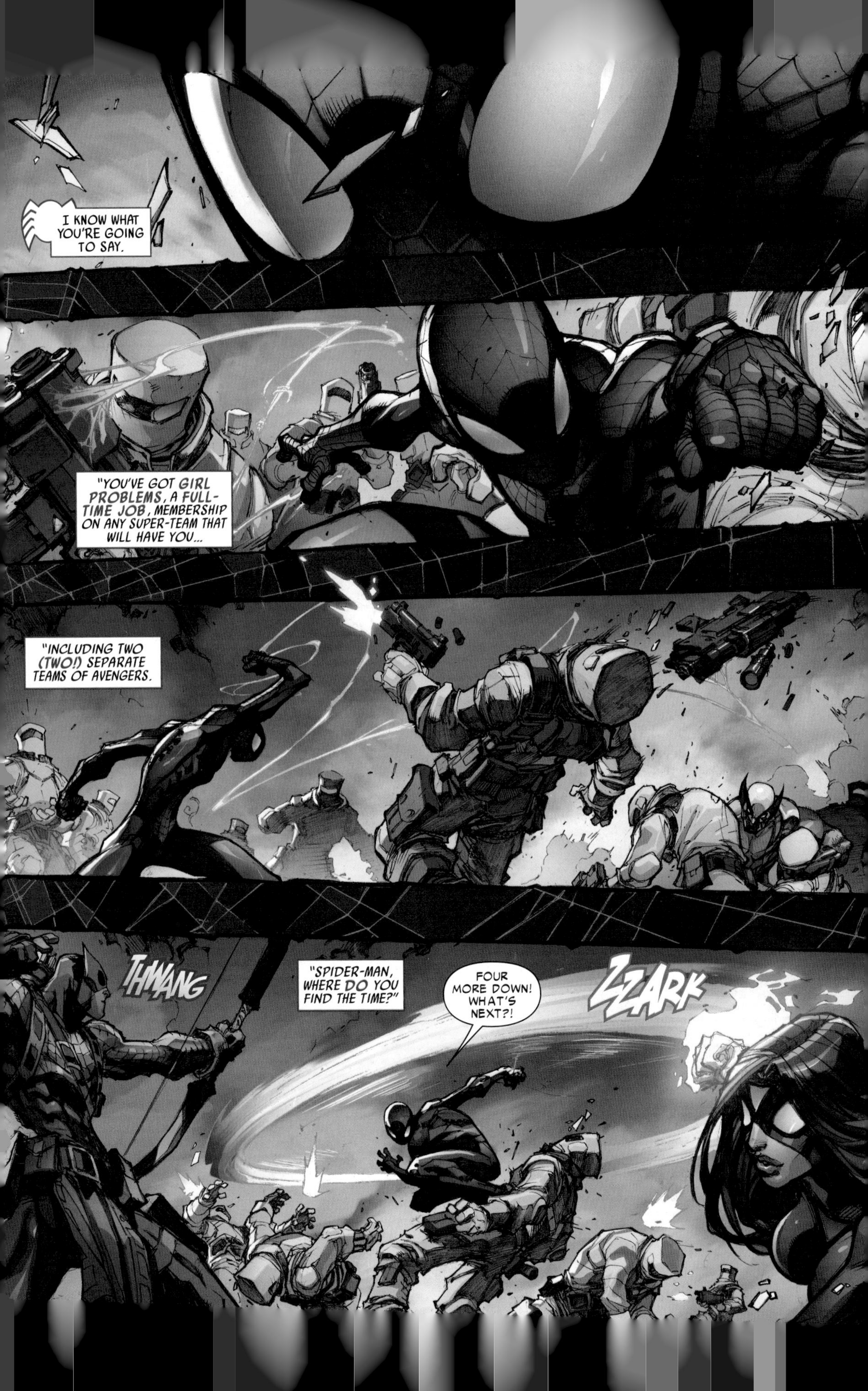
I KNOW WHAT YOU'RE GOING TO SAY.
"YOU'VE GOT GIRL PROBLEMS, A FULL-TIME JOB, MEMBERSHIP ON ANY SUPER-TEAM THAT WILL HAVE YOU...
"INCLUDING TWO (TWO!) SEPARATE TEAMS OF AVENGERS.
THWANG
"SPIDER-MAN, WHERE DO YOU FIND THE TIME?"
FOUR MORE DOWN! WHAT'S NEXT?!
ZZARK

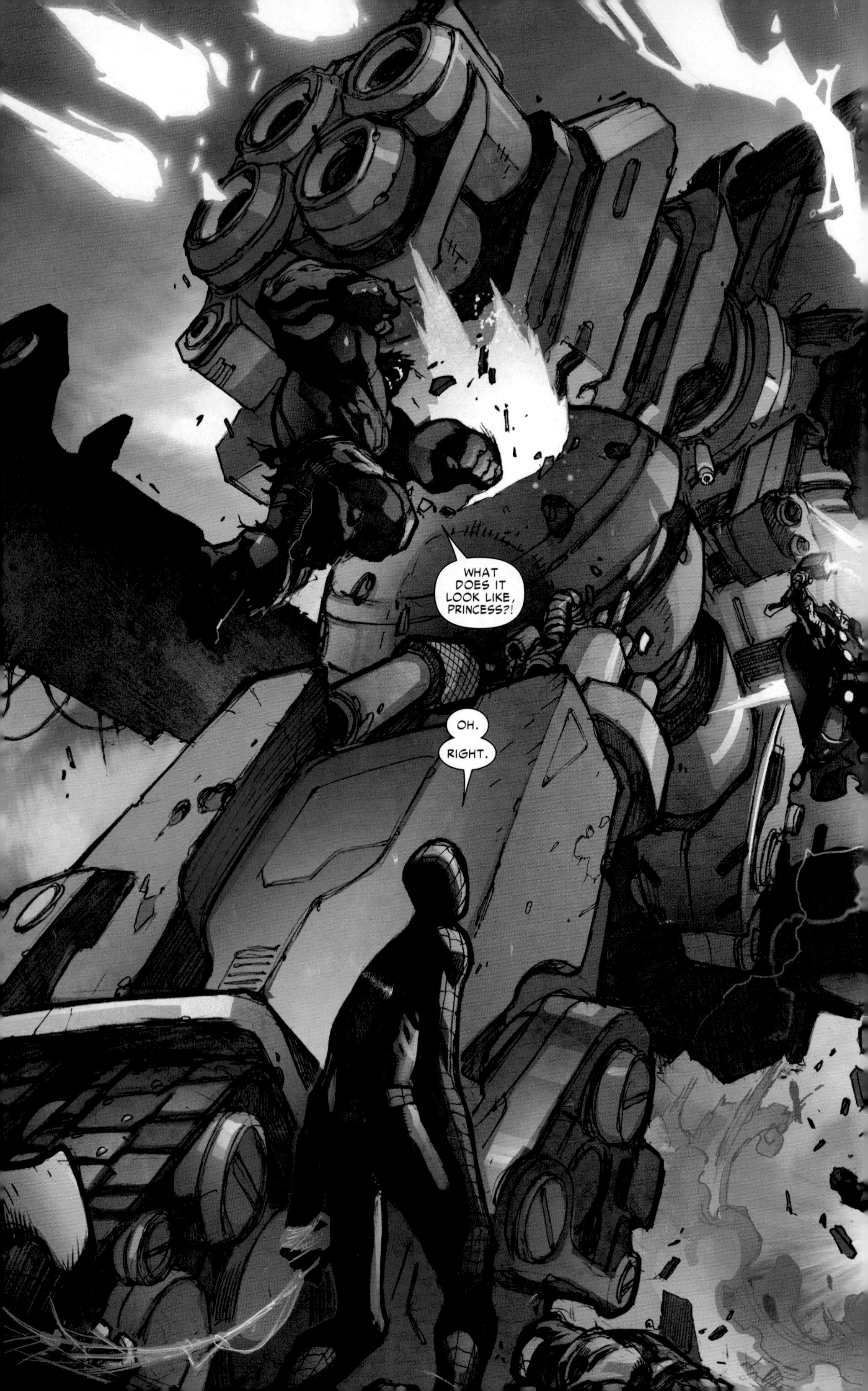
WHAT DOES IT LOOK LIKE, PRINCESS?!
OH.
RIGHT.

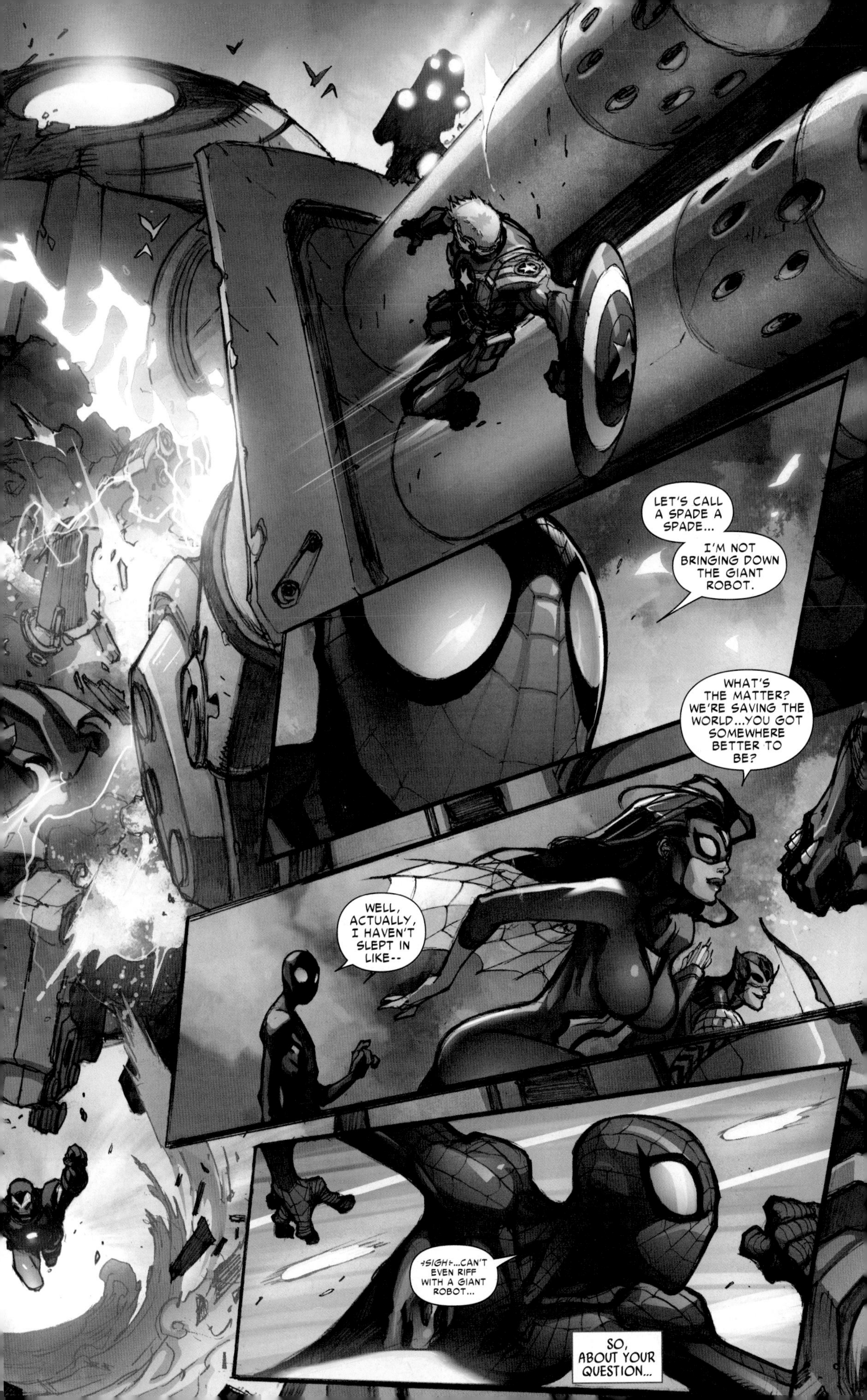
LET'S CALL A SPADE A SPADE...
I'M NOT BRINGING DOWN THE GIANT ROBOT.
WHAT'S THE MATTER? WE'RE SAVING THE WORLD...YOU GOT SOMEWHERE BETTER TO BE?
WELL, ACTUALLY, I HAVEN'T SLEPT IN LIKE--
SIGH...CAN'T EVEN RIFF WITH A GIANT ROBOT...
SO, ABOUT YOUR QUESTION...

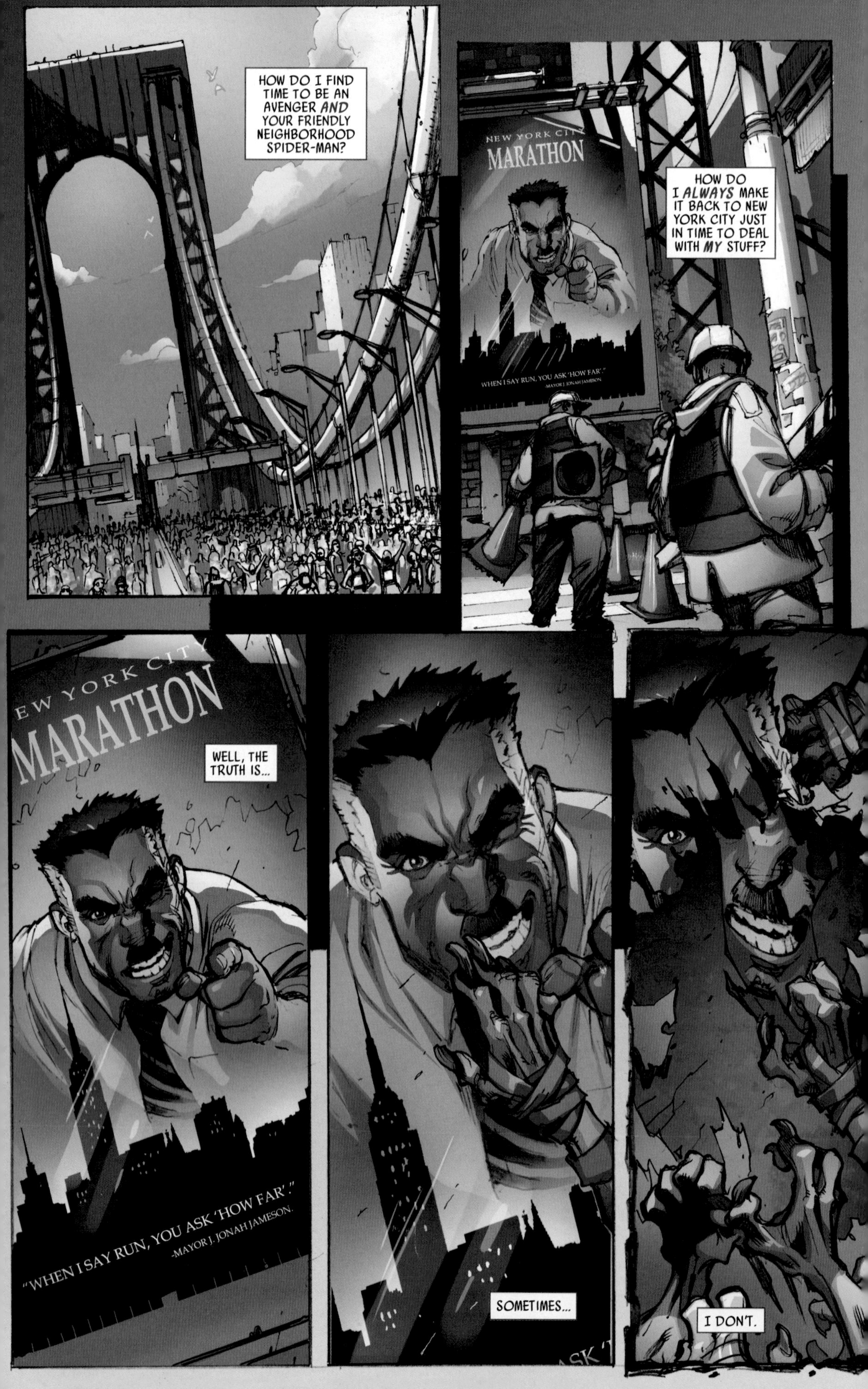
HOW DO I FIND TIME TO BE AN AVENGER AND YOUR FRIENDLY NEIGHBORHOOD SPIDER-MAN?
NEW YORK CITY MARATHON
"WHEN I SAY RUN, YOU ASK 'HOW FAR'." -MAYOR J. JONAH JAMESON
HOW DO I ALWAYS MAKE IT BACK TO NEW YORK CITY JUST IN TIME TO DEAL WITH MY STUFF?
NEW YORK CITY MARATHON
WELL, THE TRUTH IS...
"WHEN I SAY RUN, YOU ASK 'HOW FAR'." -MAYOR J. JONAH JAMESON.
SOMETIMES...
I DON'T.

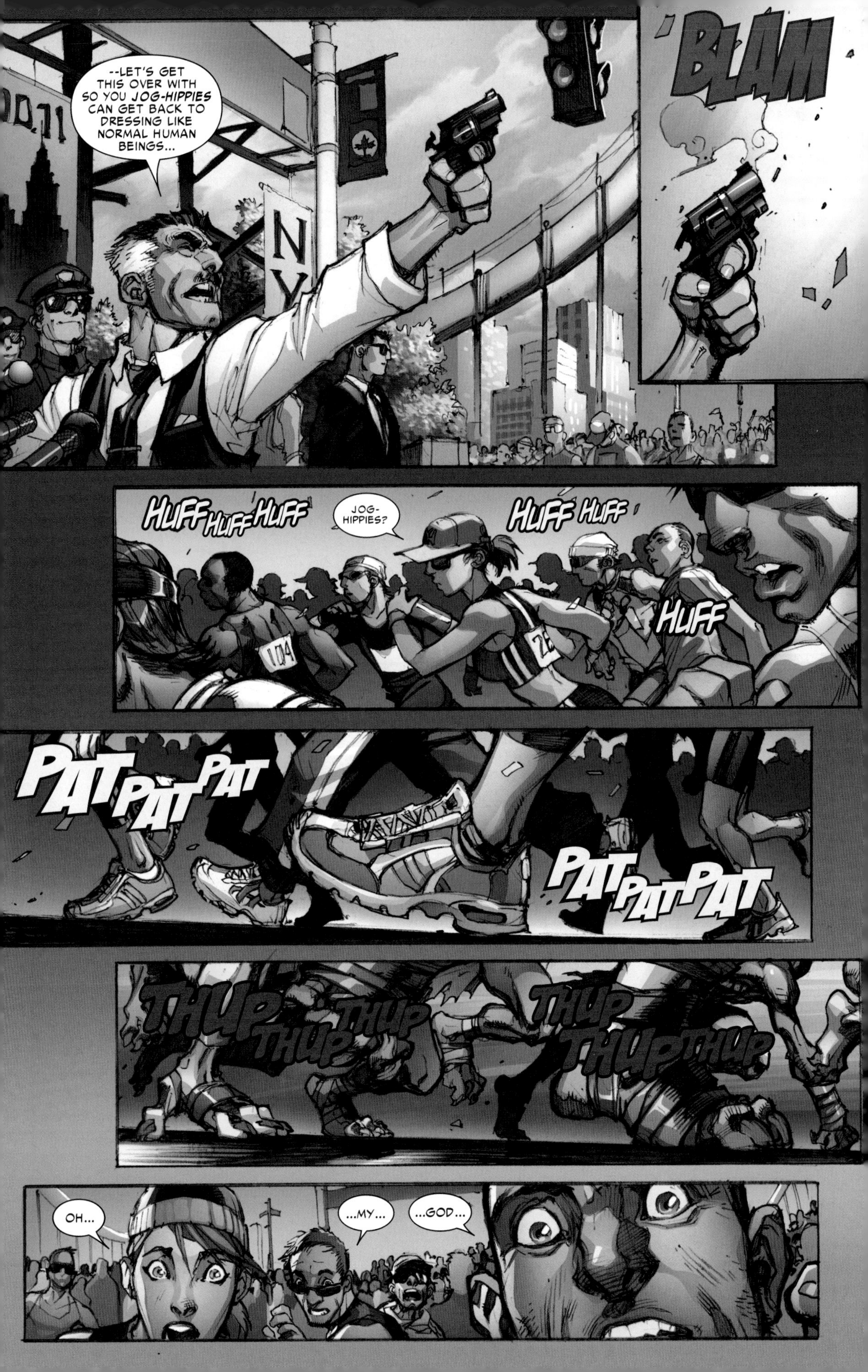
--LET'S GET THIS OVER WITH SO YOU JOG-HIPPIES CAN GET BACK TO DRESSING LIKE NORMAL HUMAN BEINGS...
NY
BLAM
HUFF HUFF HUFF
JOG-HIPPIES?
HUFF HUFF
HUFF
PAT PAT PAT
PAT PAT PAT
THUP THUP THUP
THUP THUP THUP
OH...
...MY...
...GOD...

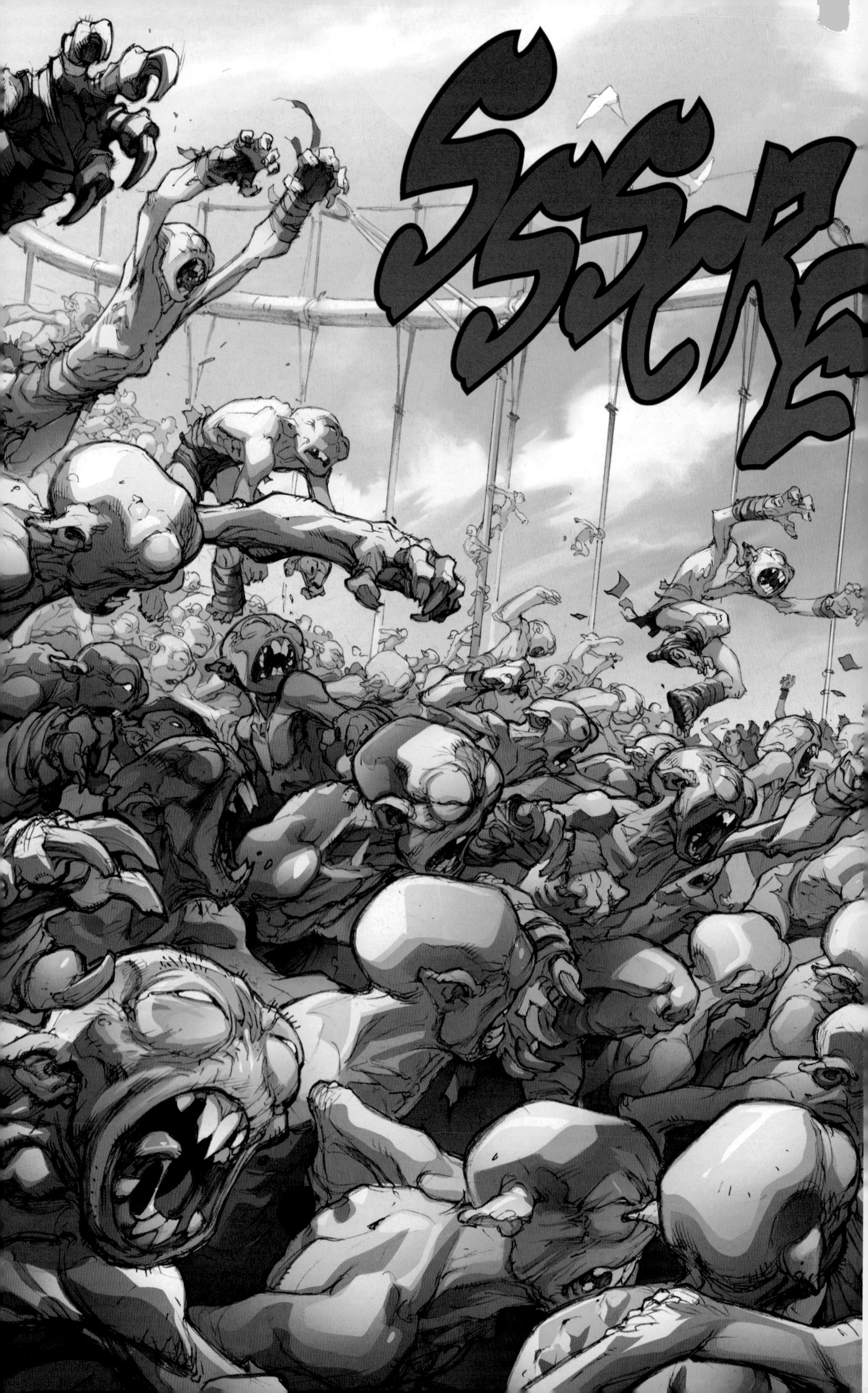

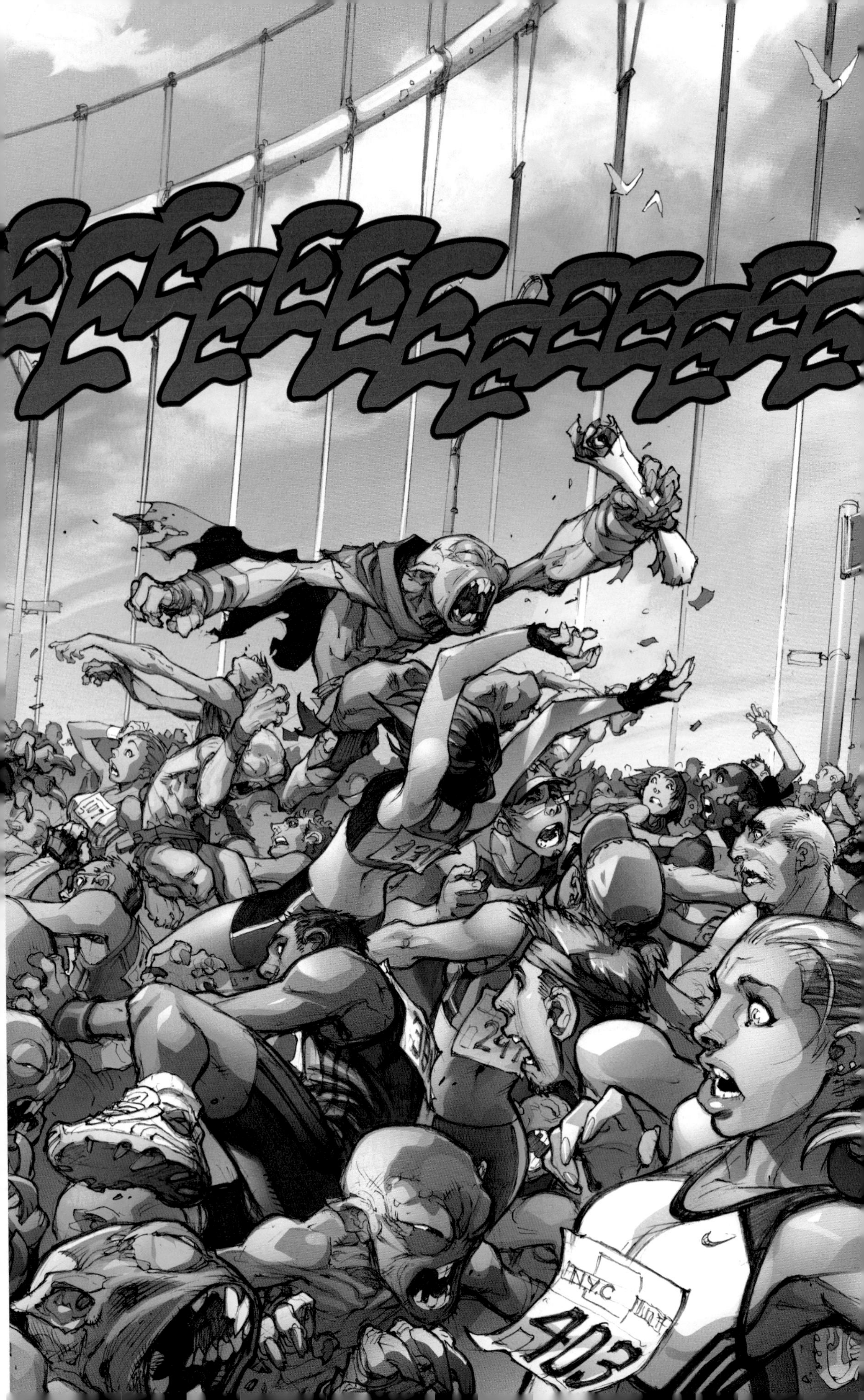
EEEEEEEEEEEEEEEEEEEE
N.Y.C
403

While attending a demonstration in radiology, high school student Peter Parker was bitten by a spider which had accidentally been exposed to radioactive rays. Through a miracle of science, Peter soon found that he had gained the spider's powers… and had, in effect, become a human spider! From that day on he was the…

AVENGING SPIDER-MAN

AVEN
SPIDEI

WRITER: ZEB WELLS

COLOR ART: FERRAN DANIEL

PRODUCTION ASSIST: **MANNY MEDEROS**

ASSISTANT EDITOR: **ELLIE PYLE**

EDITOR IN CHIEF: **AXEL ALONSO**

CHIEF CREATIVE OFFICER: **JOE QUESADA**

VARIANT COVER ARTISTS: **RAMOS & DELGADO; CAMPBELL & DELG**

BLANK VARIANT BY

General Thaddeus "Thunderbolt" Ross was a decorated war hero who fiercely hunted the Hulk. After several futile years of chasing the original Green Goliath, Ross sought vengeance and made a pact for power with the evil Intelegencia. Imbued with the powers of super-strength, energy absorption and gamma radiation… he now seeks redemption as…

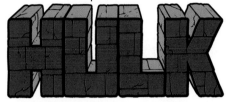

GING R-MAN

ARTIST: JOE MADUREIRA

LETTERER: VC's JOE CARAMAGNA

EDITOR: **STEPHEN WACKER** EXECUTIVE EDITOR: **TOM BREVOORT**

PUBLISHER: **DAN BUCKLEY** EXECUTIVE PRODUCER: **ALAN FINE**

O; JOE QUESADA, DANNY MIKI, & RICHARD ISANOVE

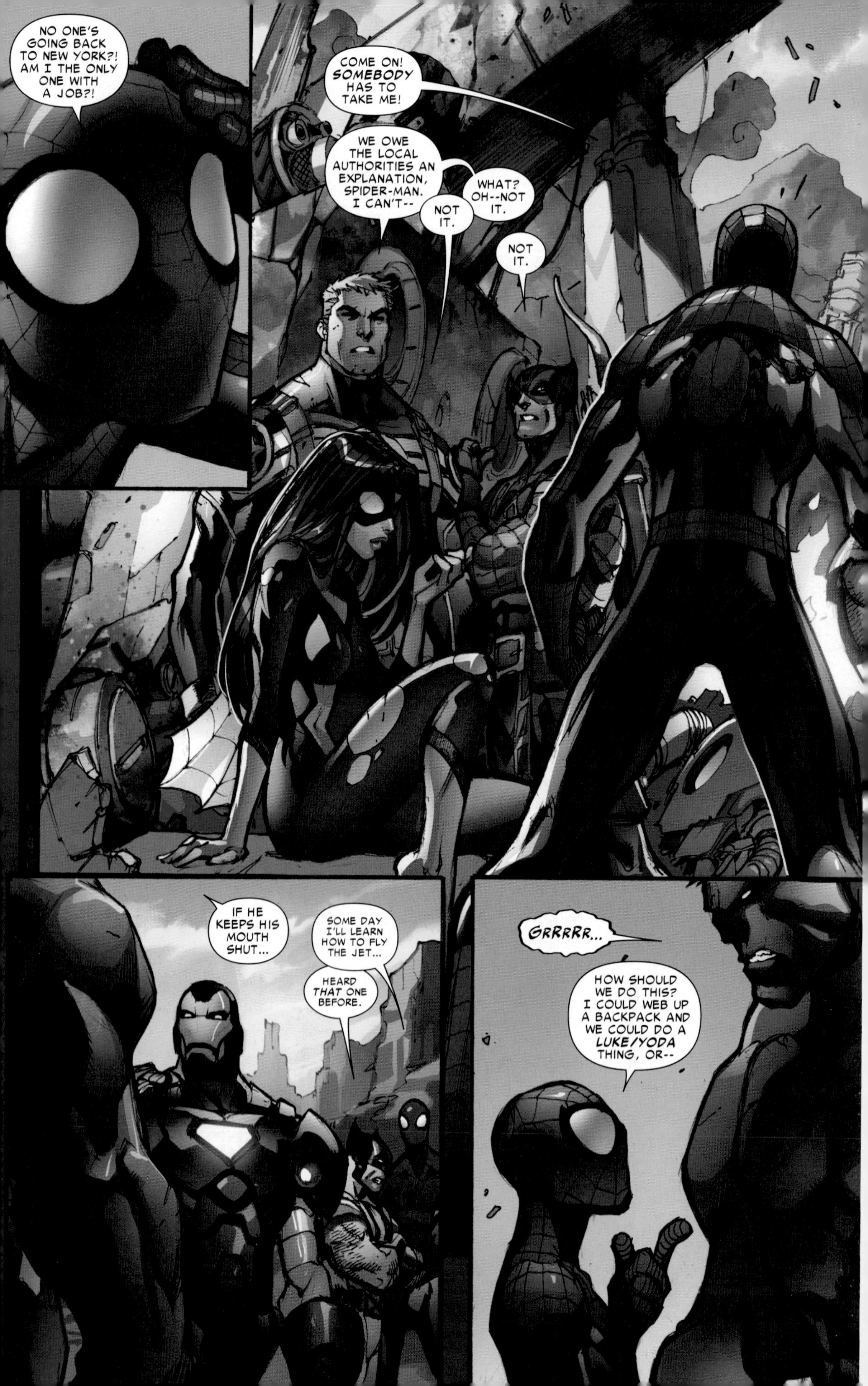
NO ONE'S GOING BACK TO NEW YORK?! AM I THE ONLY ONE WITH A JOB?!
COME ON! SOMEBODY HAS TO TAKE ME!
WE OWE THE LOCAL AUTHORITIES AN EXPLANATION, SPIDER-MAN. I CAN'T--
NOT IT.
WHAT? OH--NOT IT.
NOT IT.
IF HE KEEPS HIS MOUTH SHUT...
SOME DAY I'LL LEARN HOW TO FLY THE JET...
HEARD THAT ONE BEFORE.
GRRRRR...
HOW SHOULD WE DO THIS? I COULD WEB UP A BACKPACK AND WE COULD DO A LUKE/YODA THING, OR--

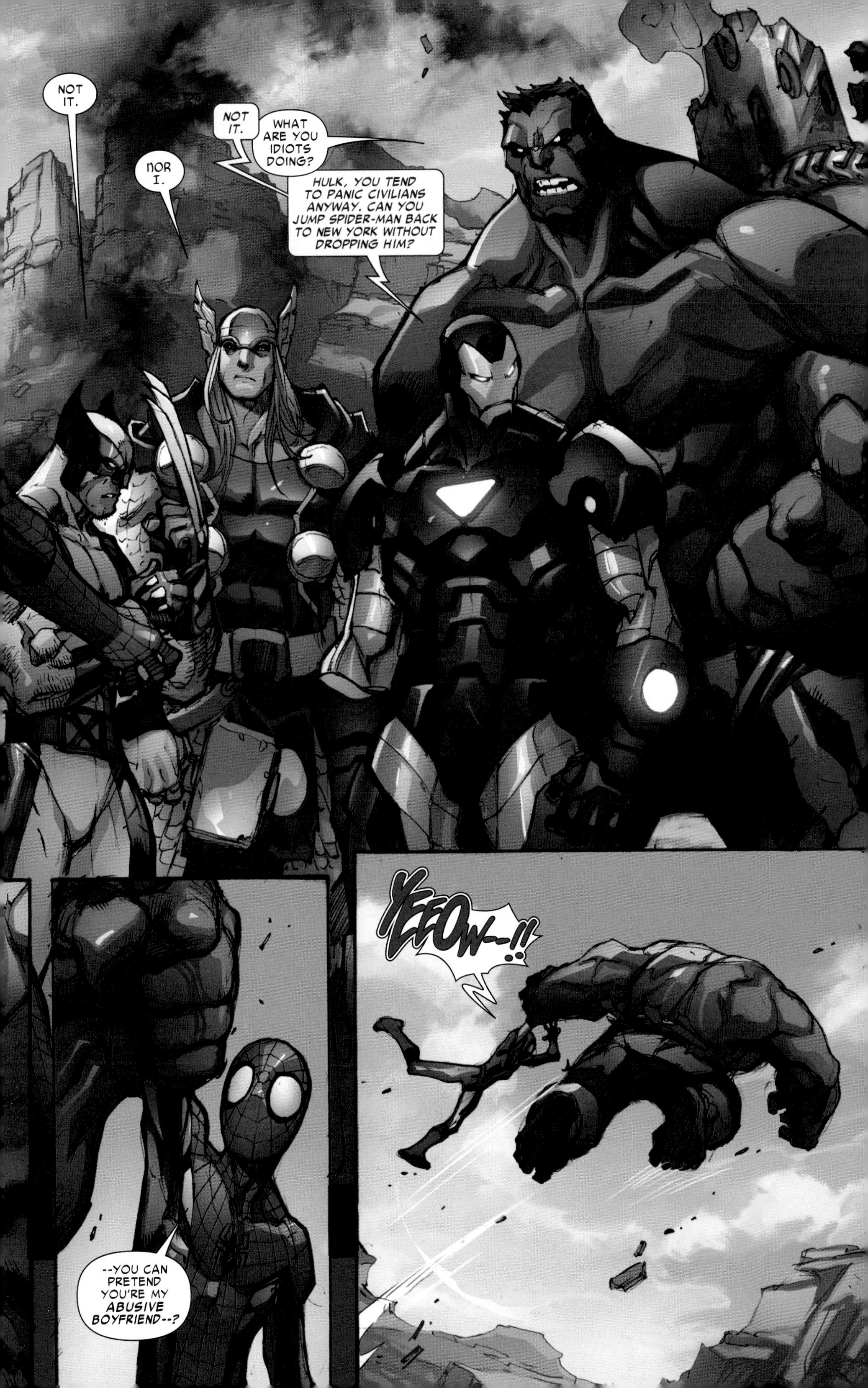
NOT IT.
NOT IT.
NOR I.
WHAT ARE YOU IDIOTS DOING?
HULK, YOU TEND TO PANIC CIVILIANS ANYWAY. CAN YOU JUMP SPIDER-MAN BACK TO NEW YORK WITHOUT DROPPING HIM?
--YOU CAN PRETEND YOU'RE MY ABUSIVE BOYFRIEND--?
YEEOW--!!

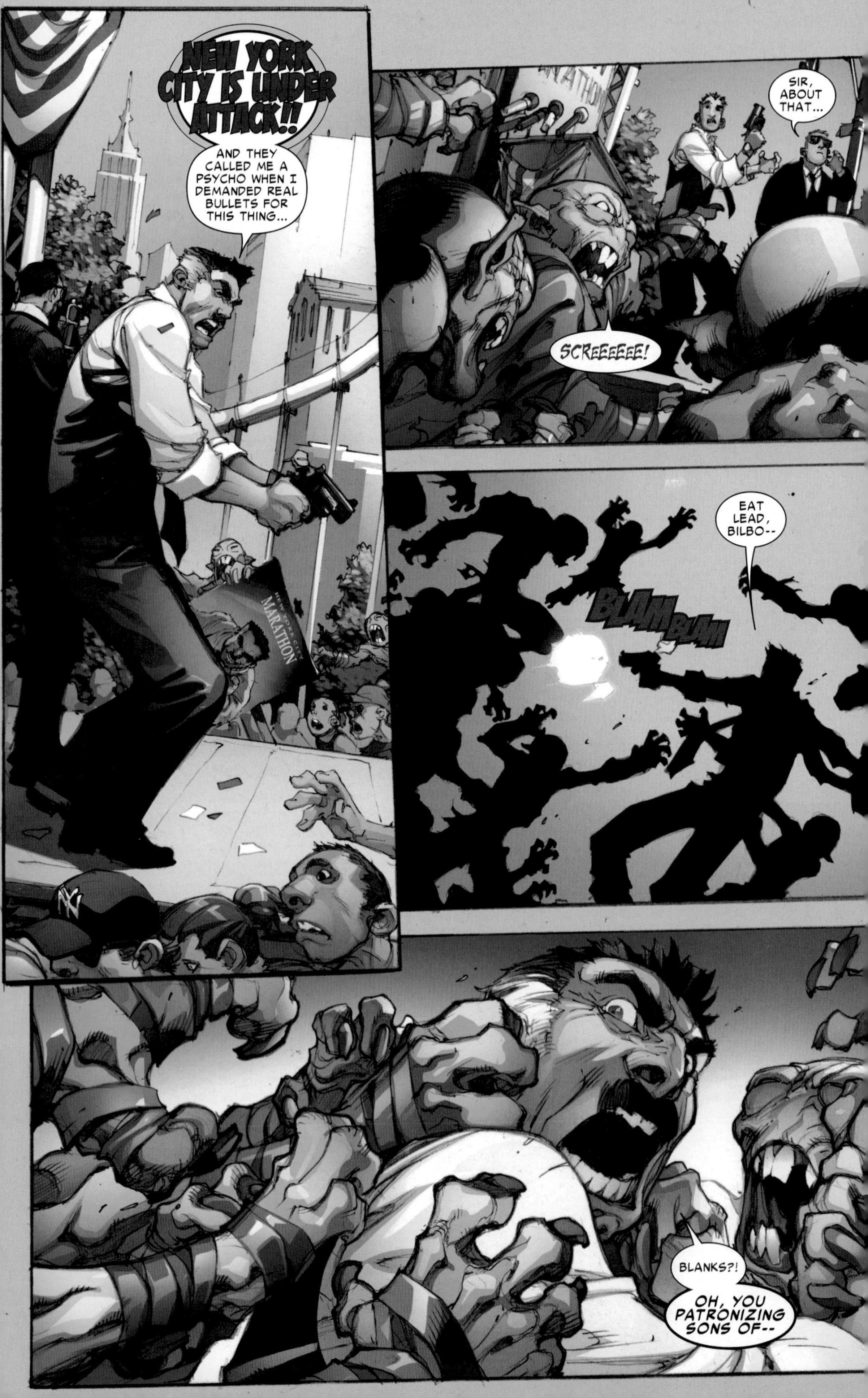
NEW YORK CITY IS UNDER ATTACK!!
AND THEY CALLED ME A PSYCHO WHEN I DEMANDED REAL BULLETS FOR THIS THING...
NEW YORK CITY MARATHON
SIR, ABOUT THAT...
SCREEEEEEE!
EAT LEAD, BILBO--
BLAM BLAM
BLANKS?!
OH, YOU PATRONIZING SONS OF--

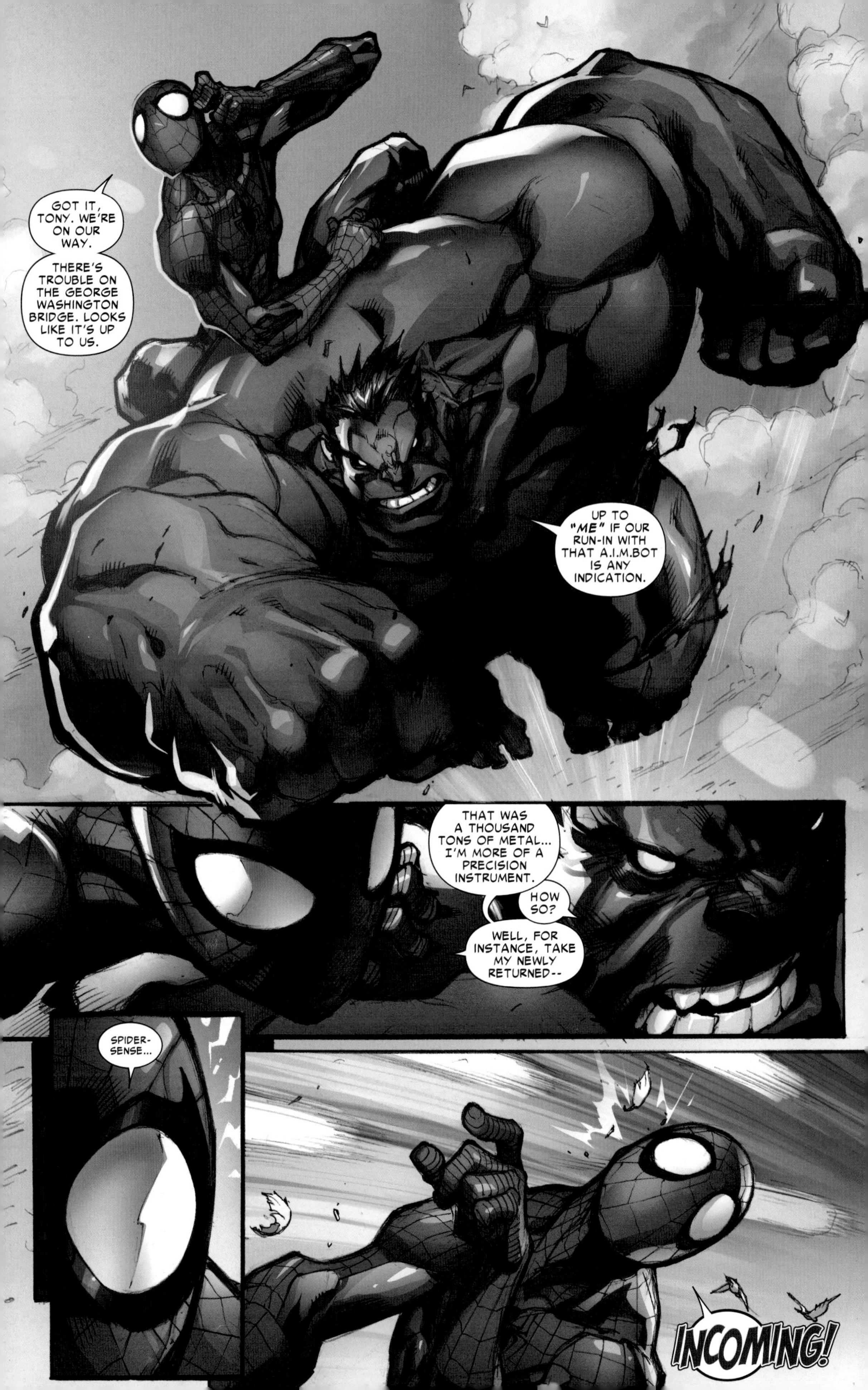
GOT IT, TONY. WE'RE ON OUR WAY.
THERE'S TROUBLE ON THE GEORGE WASHINGTON BRIDGE. LOOKS LIKE IT'S UP TO US.
UP TO "ME" IF OUR RUN-IN WITH THAT A.I.M.BOT IS ANY INDICATION.
THAT WAS A THOUSAND TONS OF METAL... I'M MORE OF A PRECISION INSTRUMENT.
HOW SO?
WELL, FOR INSTANCE, TAKE MY NEWLY RETURNED--
SPIDER-SENSE...
INCOMING!

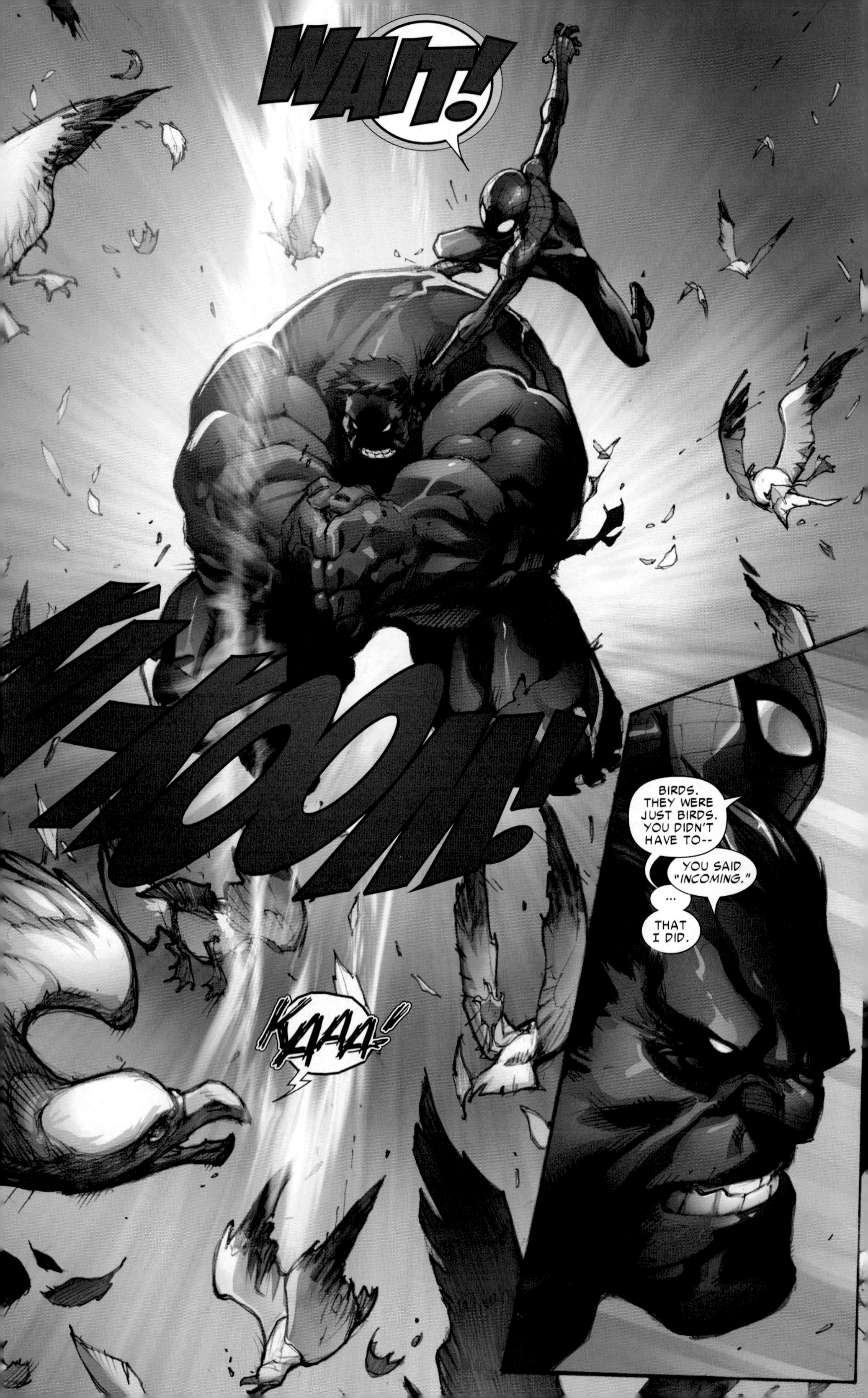
WAIT!
WHOOM!
KAAA!
BIRDS. THEY WERE JUST BIRDS. YOU DIDN'T HAVE TO--
YOU SAID "INCOMING."
...
THAT I DID.

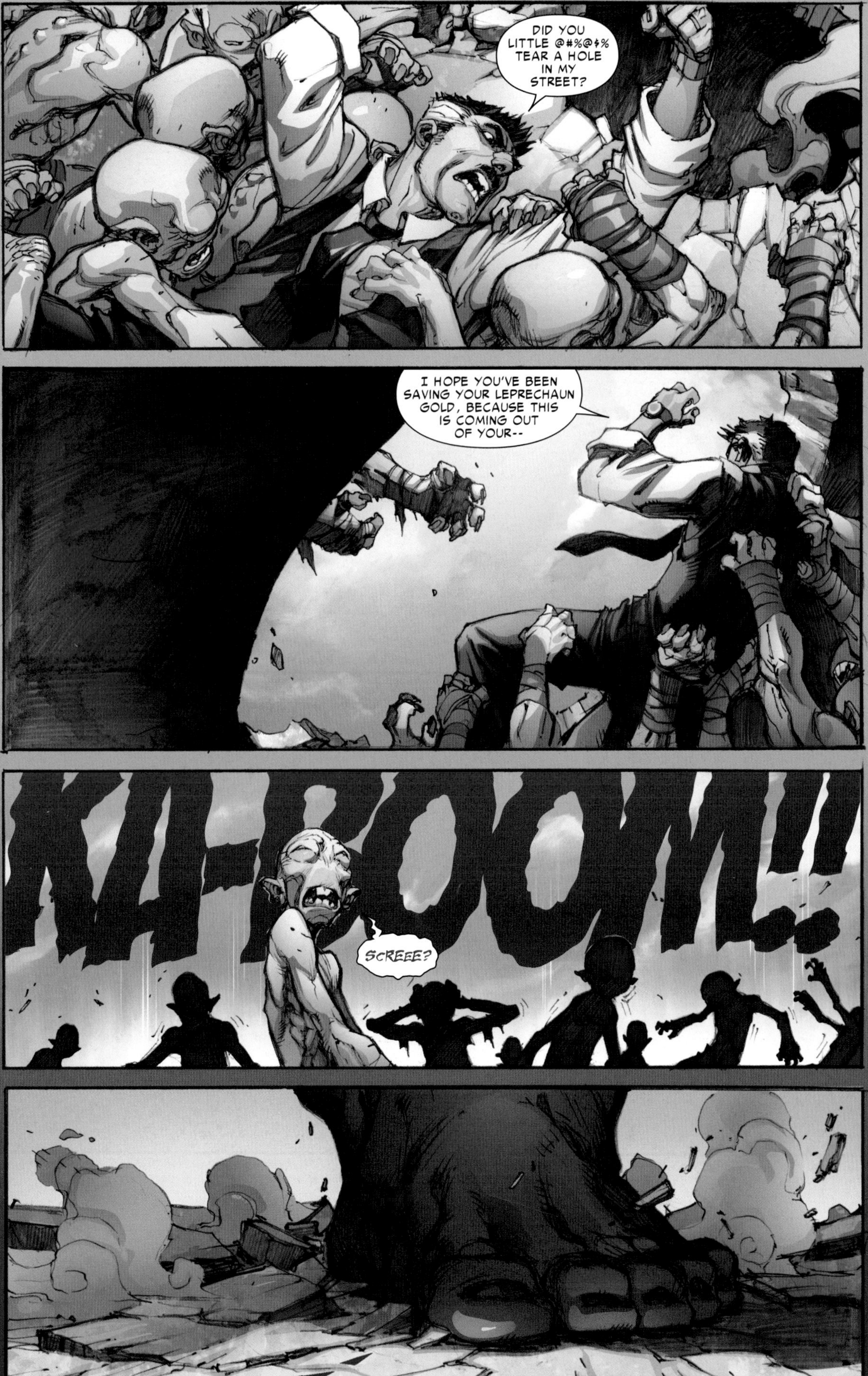
DID YOU LITTLE @#%@$% TEAR A HOLE IN MY STREET?
I HOPE YOU'VE BEEN SAVING YOUR LEPRECHAUN GOLD, BECAUSE THIS IS COMING OUT OF YOUR--
KA-BOOM!!
SCREEE?

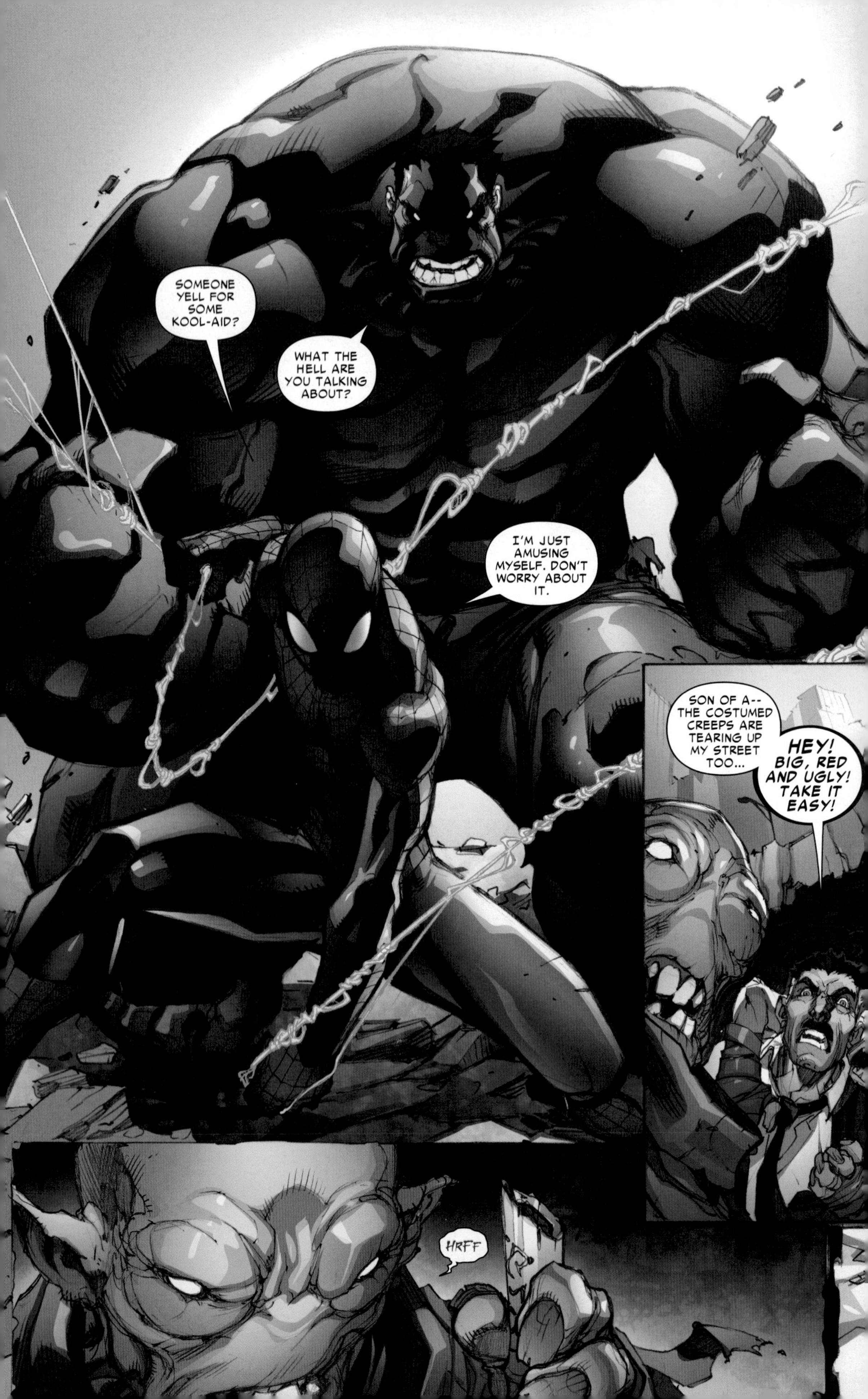
SOMEONE YELL FOR SOME KOOL-AID?
WHAT THE HELL ARE YOU TALKING ABOUT?
I'M JUST AMUSING MYSELF. DON'T WORRY ABOUT IT.
SON OF A-- THE COSTUMED CREEPS ARE TEARING UP MY STREET TOO...
HEY! BIG, RED AND UGLY! TAKE IT EASY!
HRFF

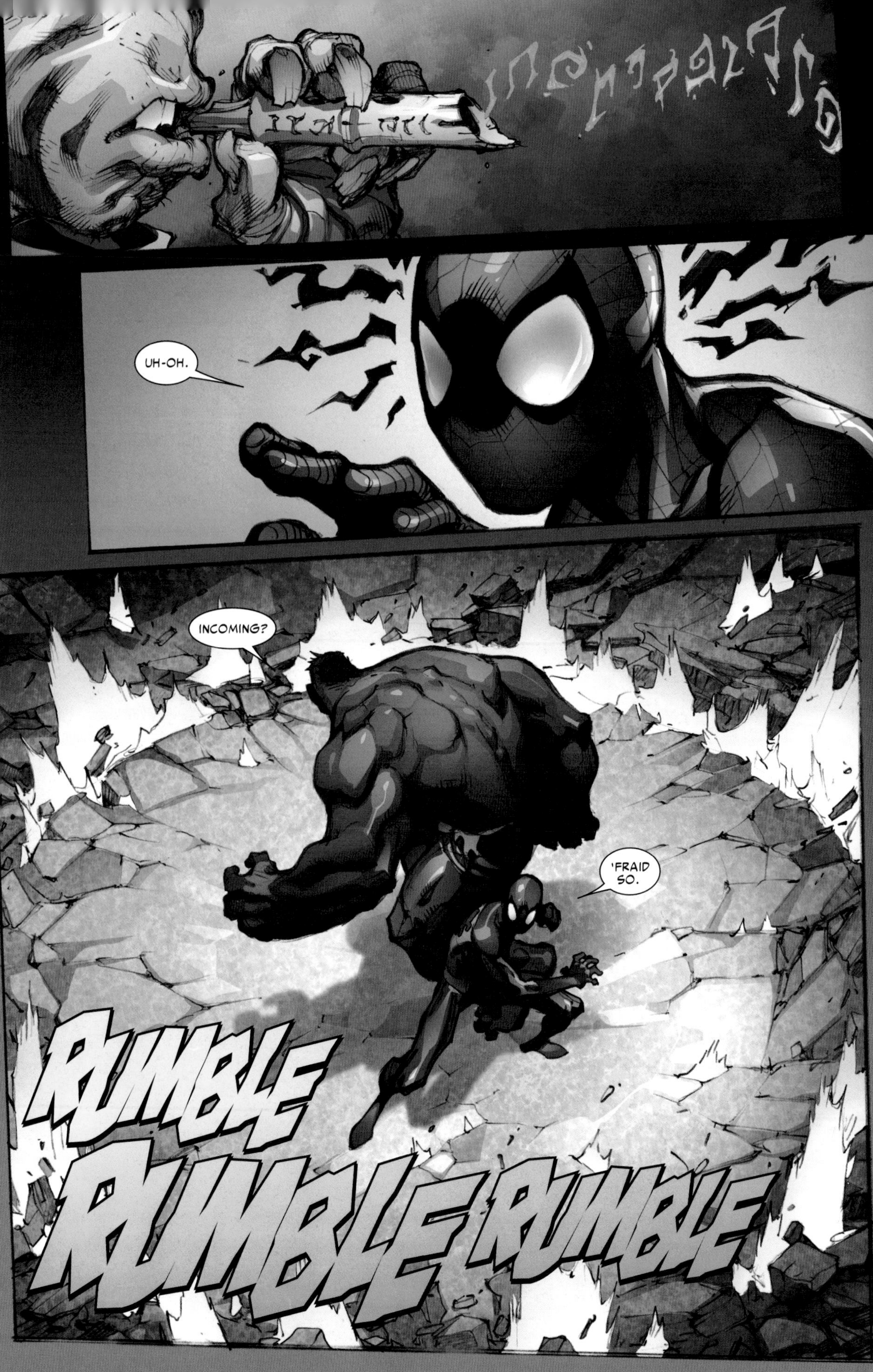
UH-OH.
INCOMING?
'FRAID SO.
RUMBLE
RUMBLE RUMBLE

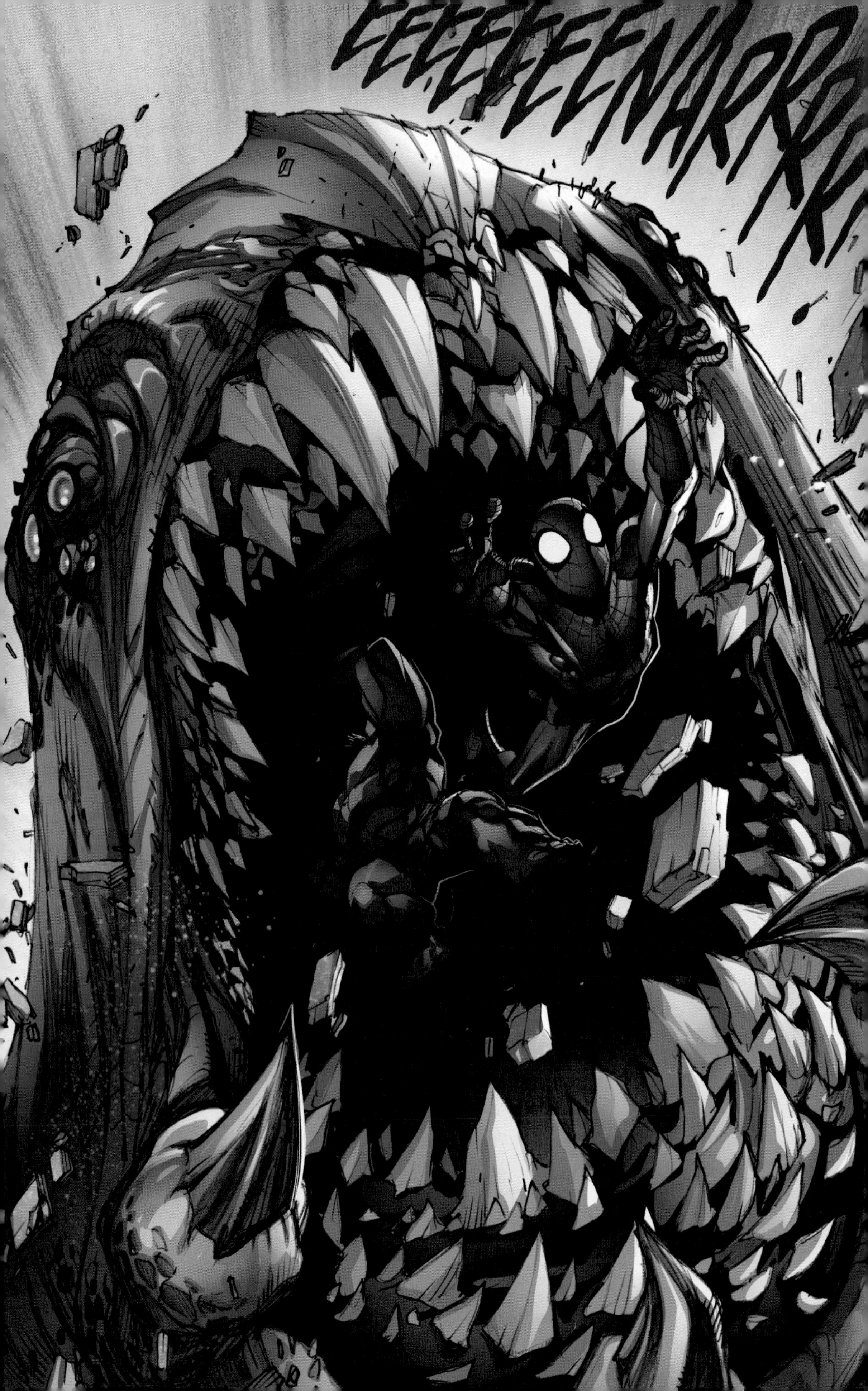
EEEEEENARRRR

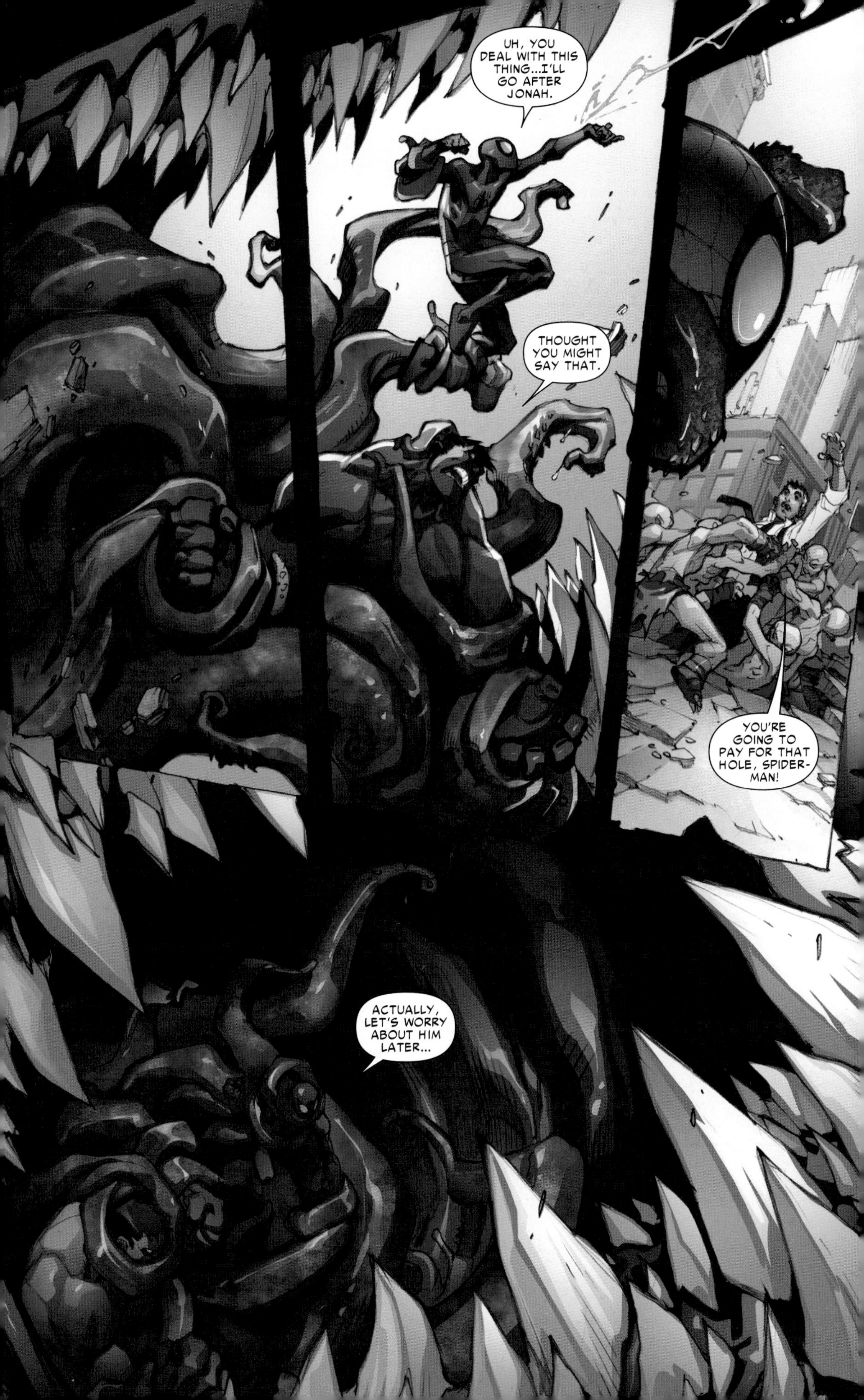
UH, YOU DEAL WITH THIS THING...I'LL GO AFTER JONAH.
THOUGHT YOU MIGHT SAY THAT.
YOU'RE GOING TO PAY FOR THAT HOLE, SPIDER-MAN!
ACTUALLY, LET'S WORRY ABOUT HIM LATER...

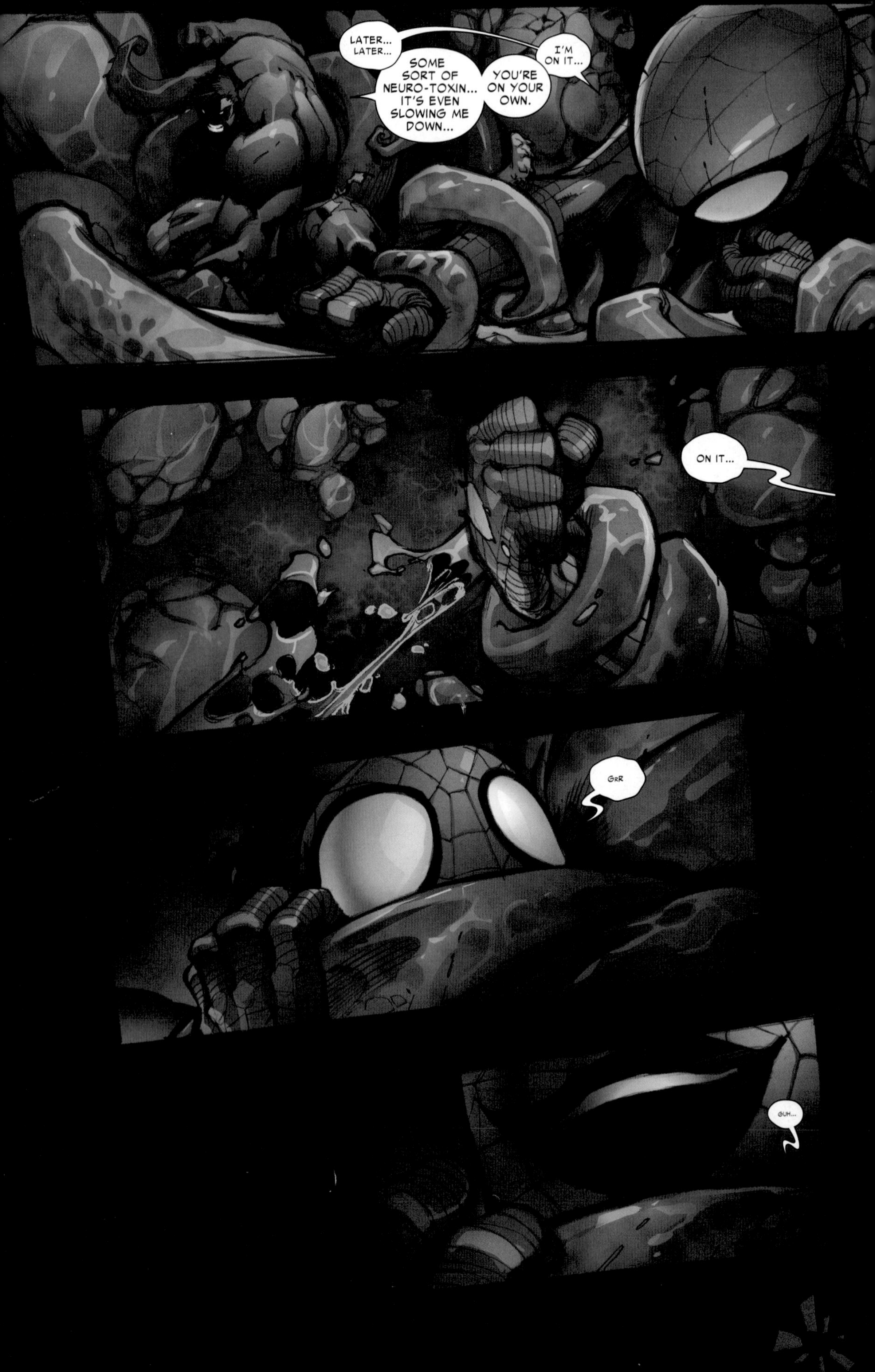
LATER... LATER...
I'M ON IT...
SOME SORT OF NEURO-TOXIN... IT'S EVEN SLOWING ME DOWN...
YOU'RE ON YOUR OWN.
ON IT...
GRR
GUH...

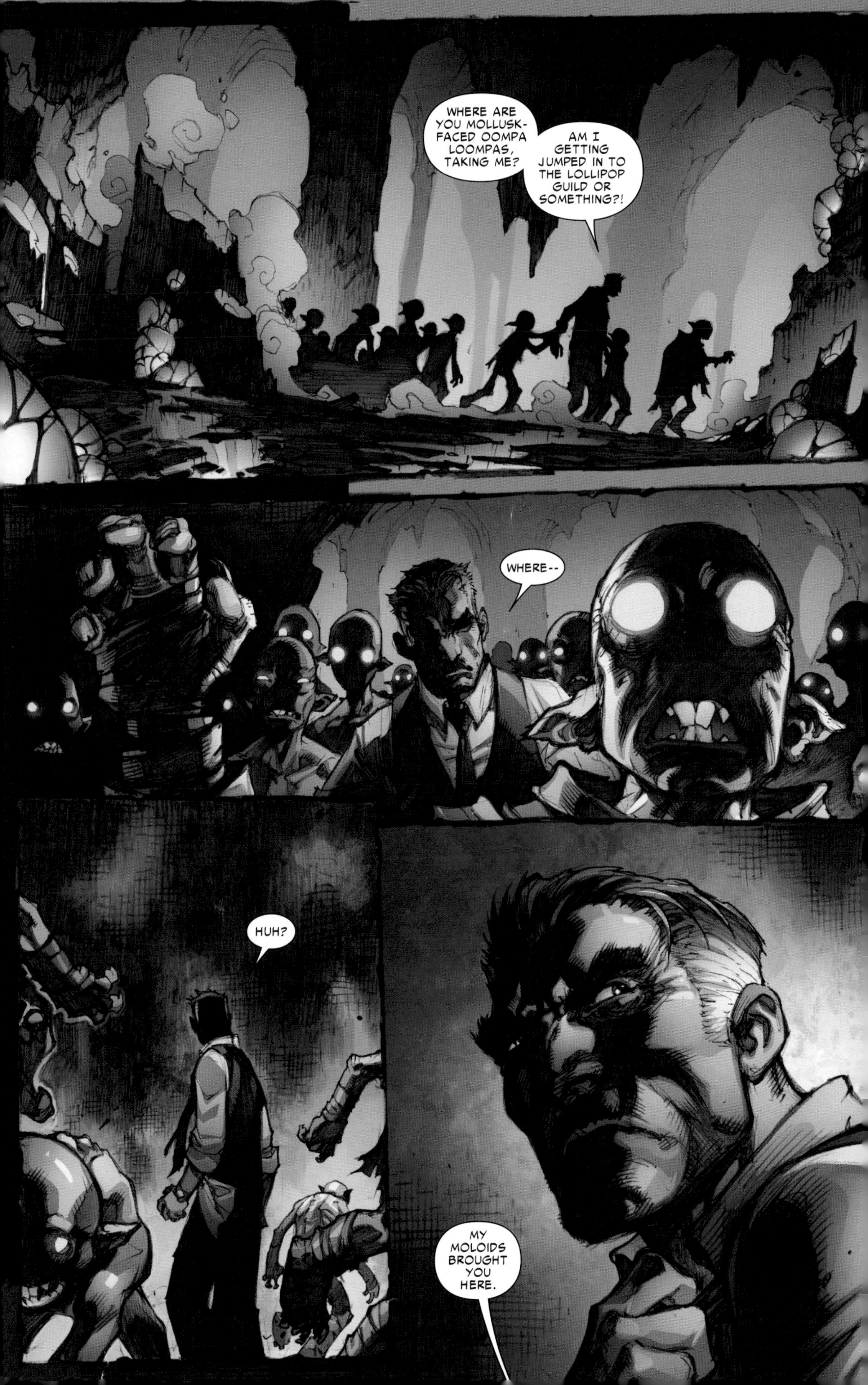
WHERE ARE YOU MOLLUSK-FACED OOMPA LOOMPAS, TAKING ME?
AM I GETTING JUMPED IN TO THE LOLLIPOP GUILD OR SOMETHING?!
WHERE--
HUH?
MY MOLOIDS BROUGHT YOU HERE.

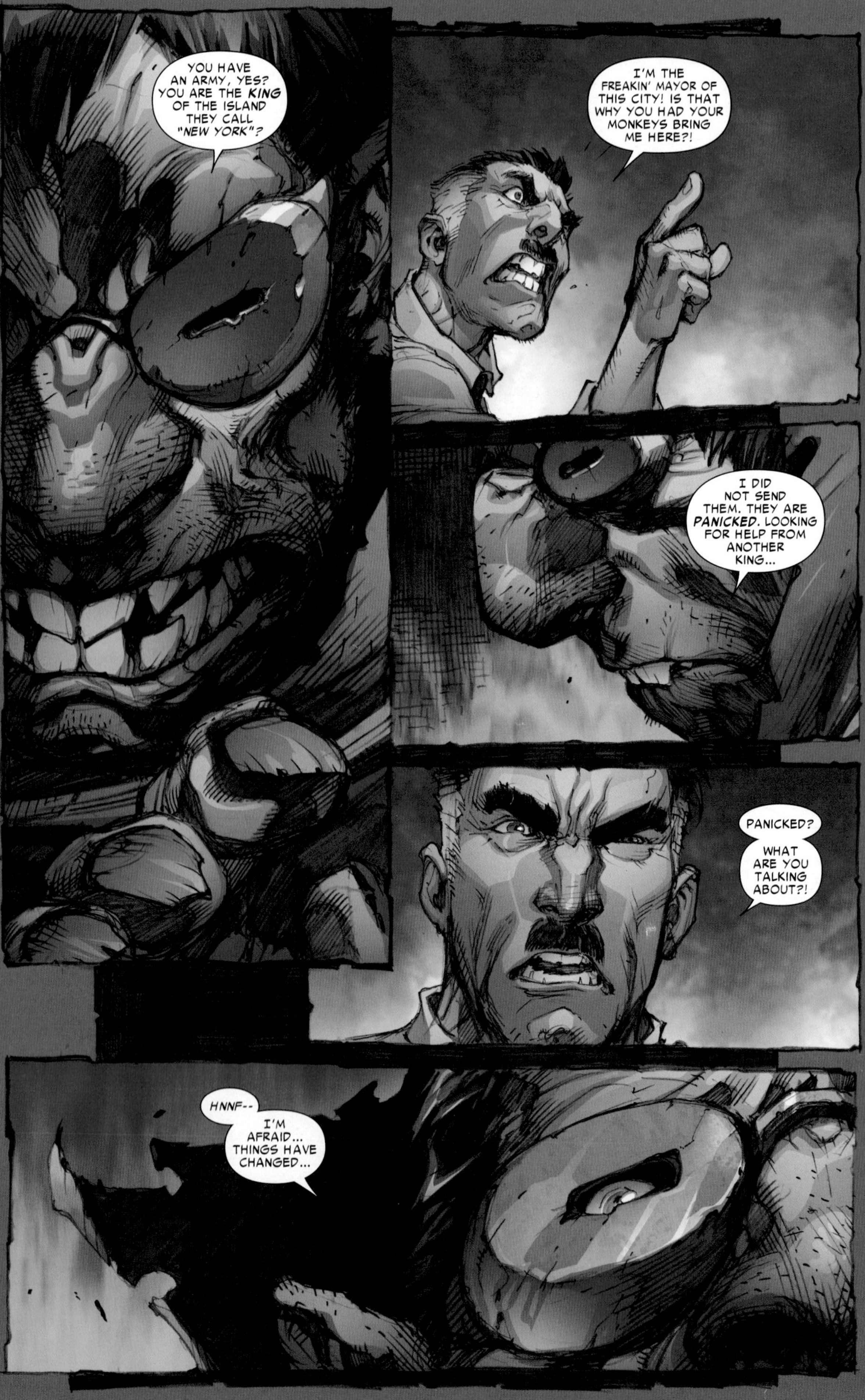
YOU HAVE AN ARMY, YES? YOU ARE THE KING OF THE ISLAND THEY CALL "NEW YORK"?
I'M THE FREAKIN' MAYOR OF THIS CITY! IS THAT WHY YOU HAD YOUR MONKEYS BRING ME HERE?!
I DID NOT SEND THEM. THEY ARE PANICKED. LOOKING FOR HELP FROM ANOTHER KING...
PANICKED?
WHAT ARE YOU TALKING ABOUT?!
HNNF--
I'M AFRAID... THINGS HAVE CHANGED...

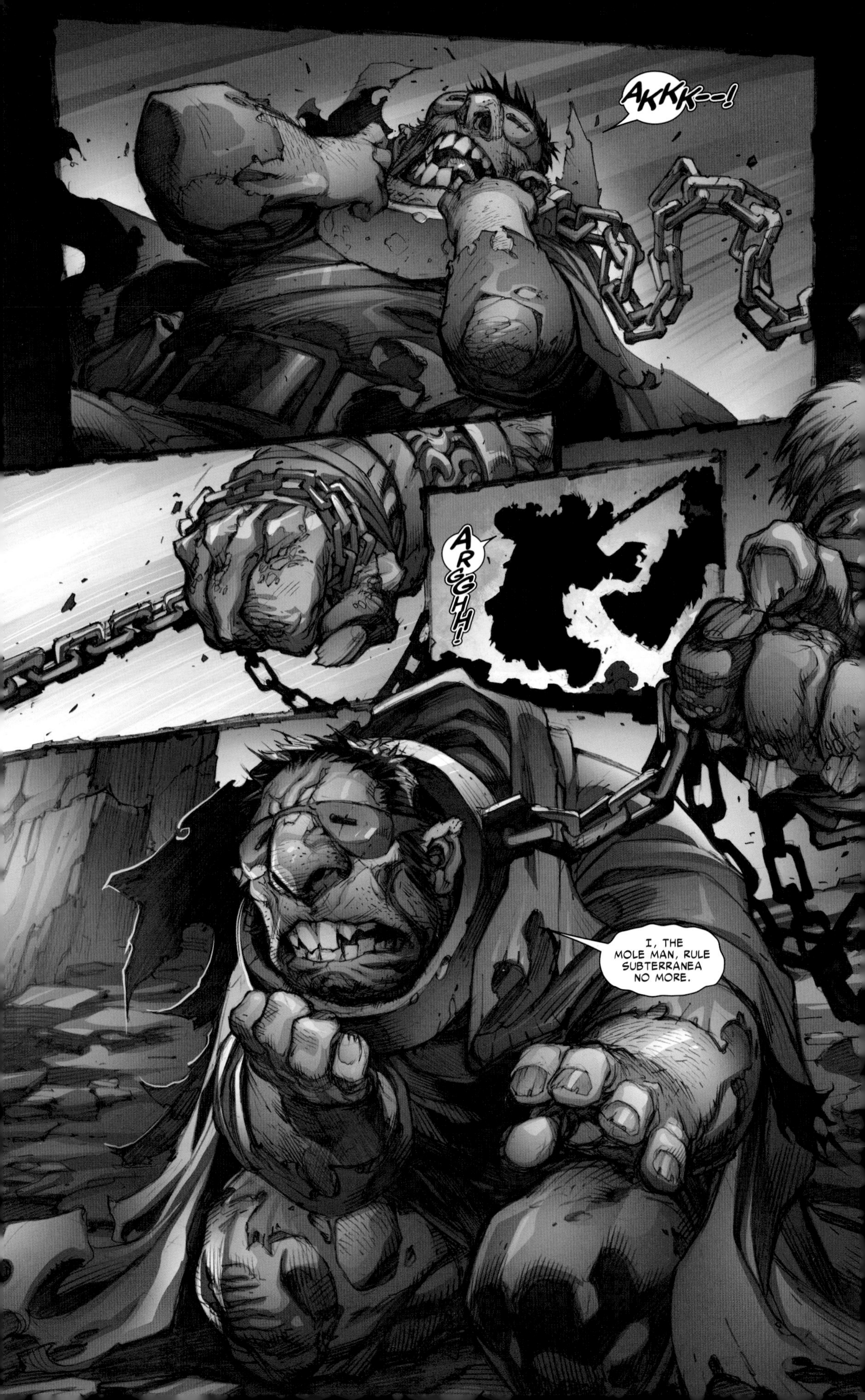
AKKK--!
ARGGHH!
I, THE MOLE MAN, RULE SUBTERRANEA NO MORE.

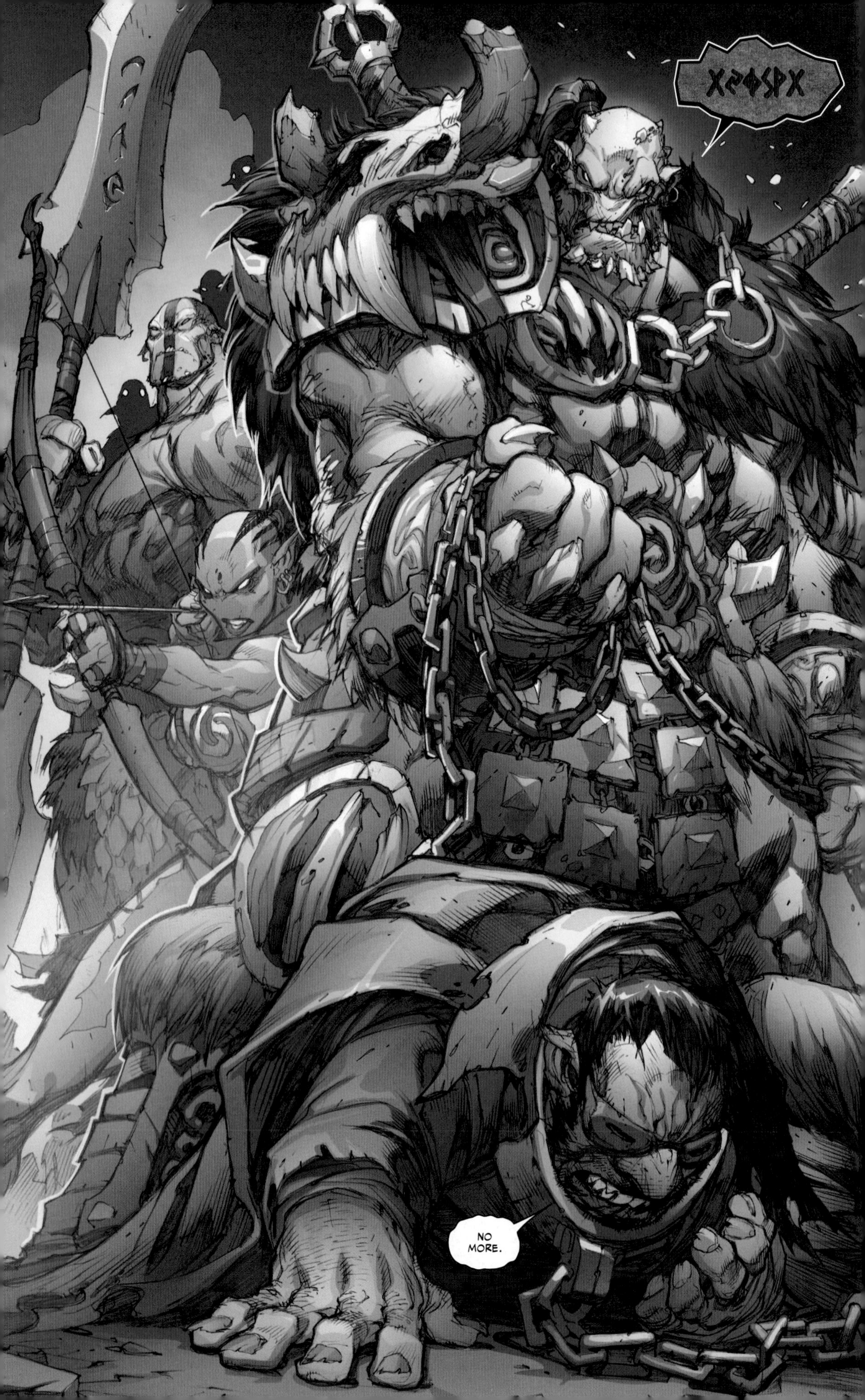
NO MORE.

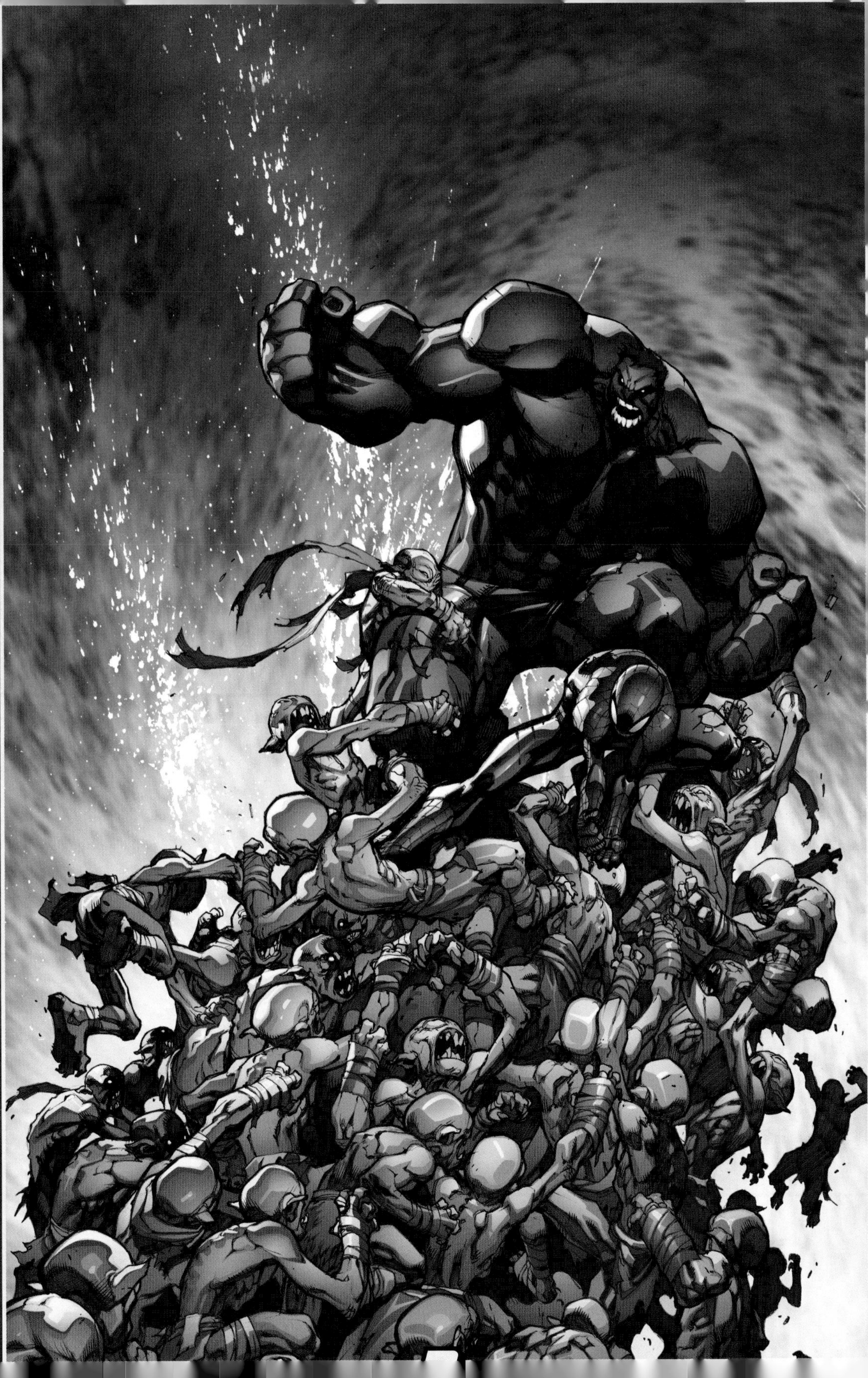

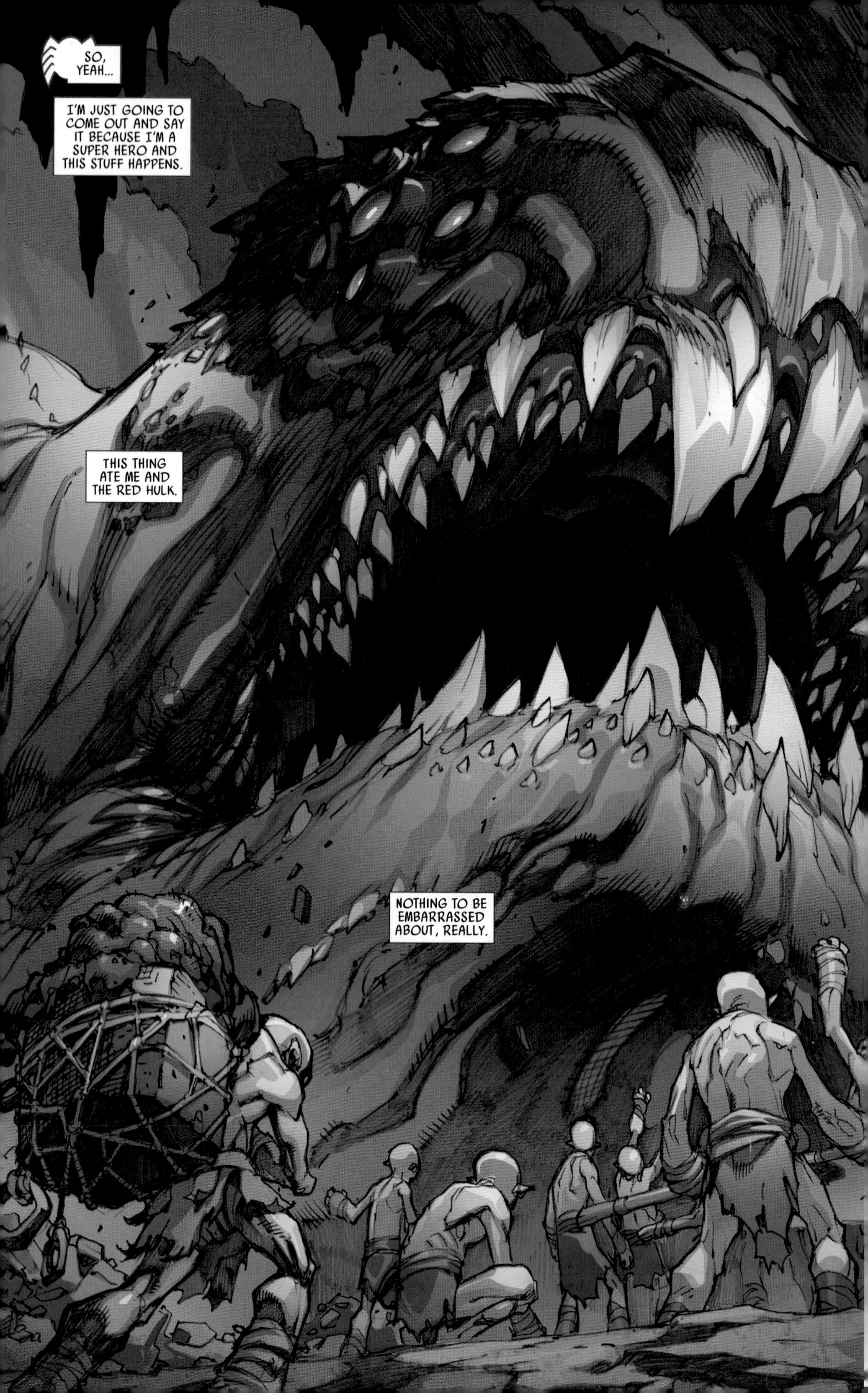
SO, YEAH...
I'M JUST GOING TO COME OUT AND SAY IT BECAUSE I'M A SUPER HERO AND THIS STUFF HAPPENS.
THIS THING ATE ME AND THE RED HULK.
NOTHING TO BE EMBARRASSED ABOUT, REALLY.

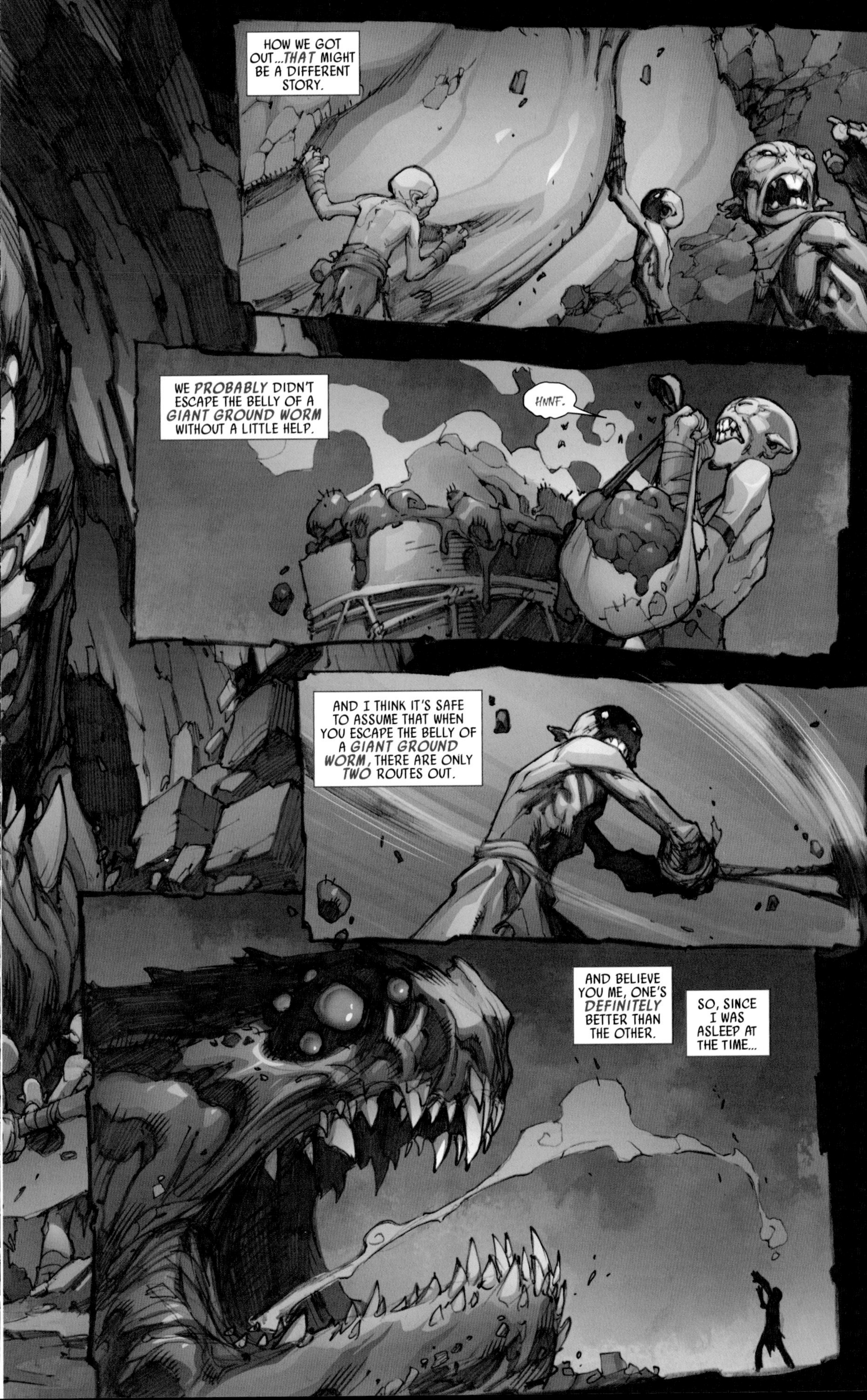
HOW WE GOT OUT...THAT MIGHT BE A DIFFERENT STORY.
WE PROBABLY DIDN'T ESCAPE THE BELLY OF A GIANT GROUND WORM WITHOUT A LITTLE HELP.
HNNF.
AND I THINK IT'S SAFE TO ASSUME THAT WHEN YOU ESCAPE THE BELLY OF A GIANT GROUND WORM, THERE ARE ONLY TWO ROUTES OUT.
AND BELIEVE YOU ME, ONE'S DEFINITELY BETTER THAN THE OTHER.
SO, SINCE I WAS ASLEEP AT THE TIME...

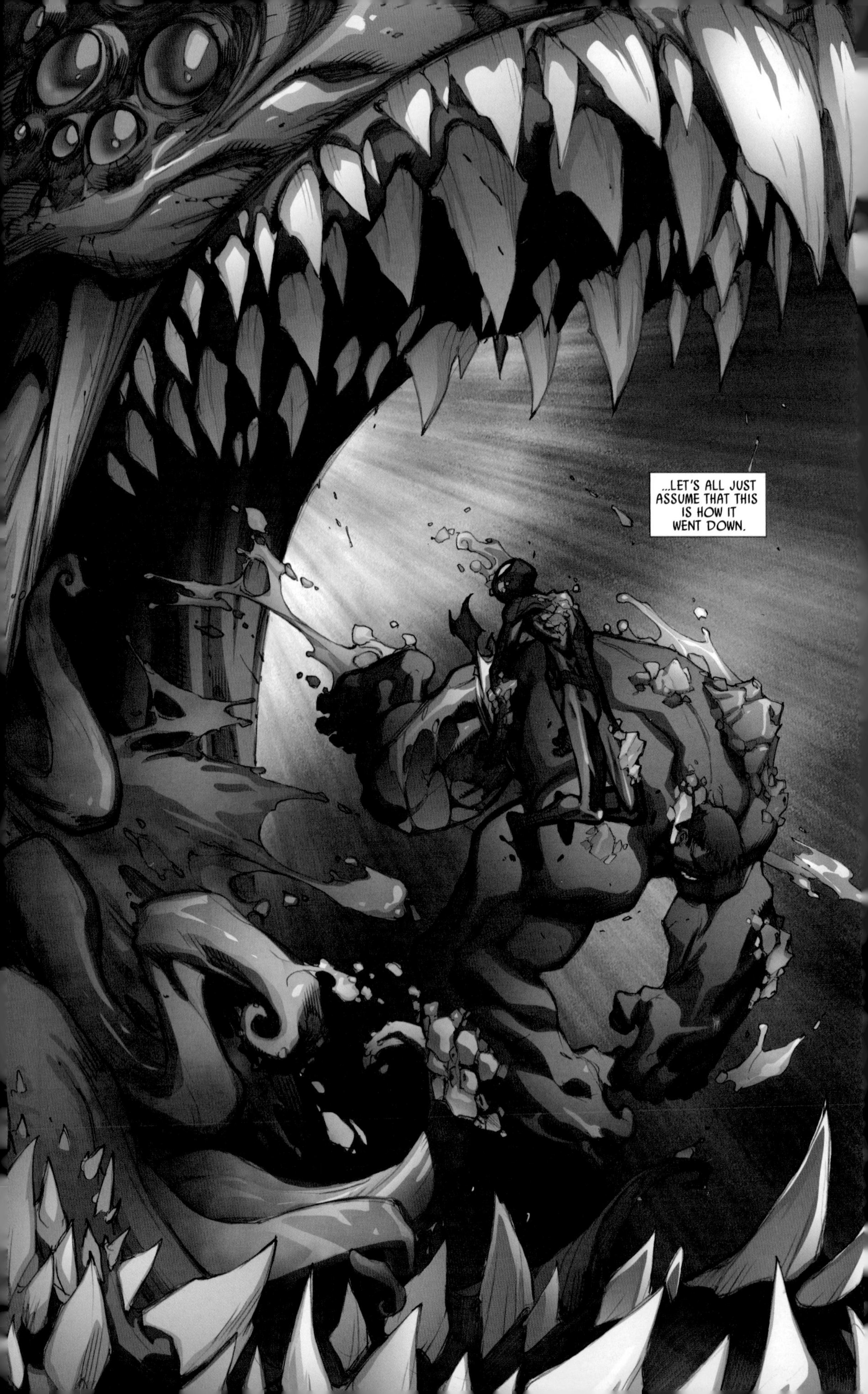
...LET'S ALL JUST ASSUME THAT THIS IS HOW IT WENT DOWN.

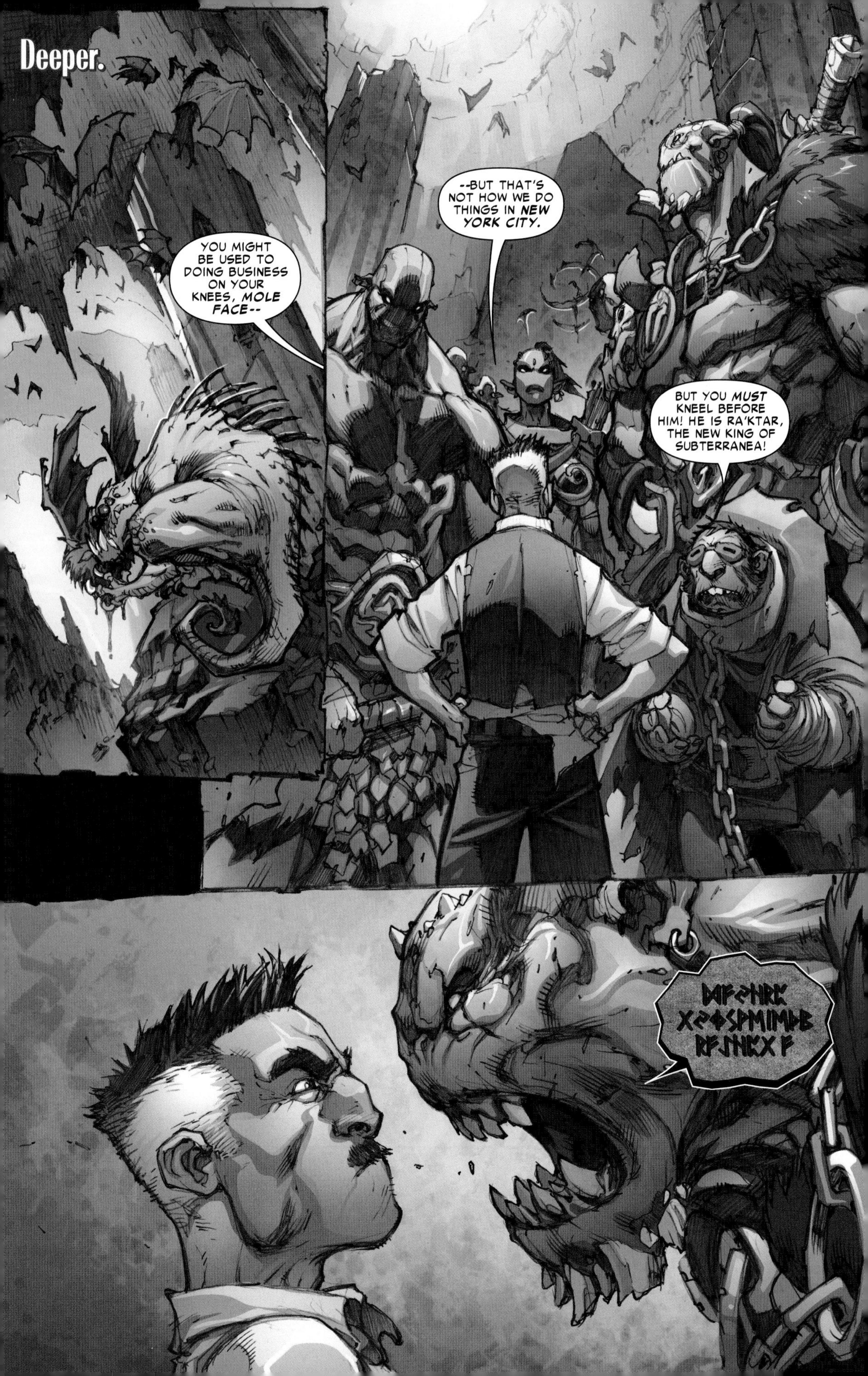
Deeper.
YOU MIGHT BE USED TO DOING BUSINESS ON YOUR KNEES, MOLE FACE--
--BUT THAT'S NOT HOW WE DO THINGS IN NEW YORK CITY.
BUT YOU MUST KNEEL BEFORE HIM! HE IS RA'KTAR, THE NEW KING OF SUBTERRANEA!

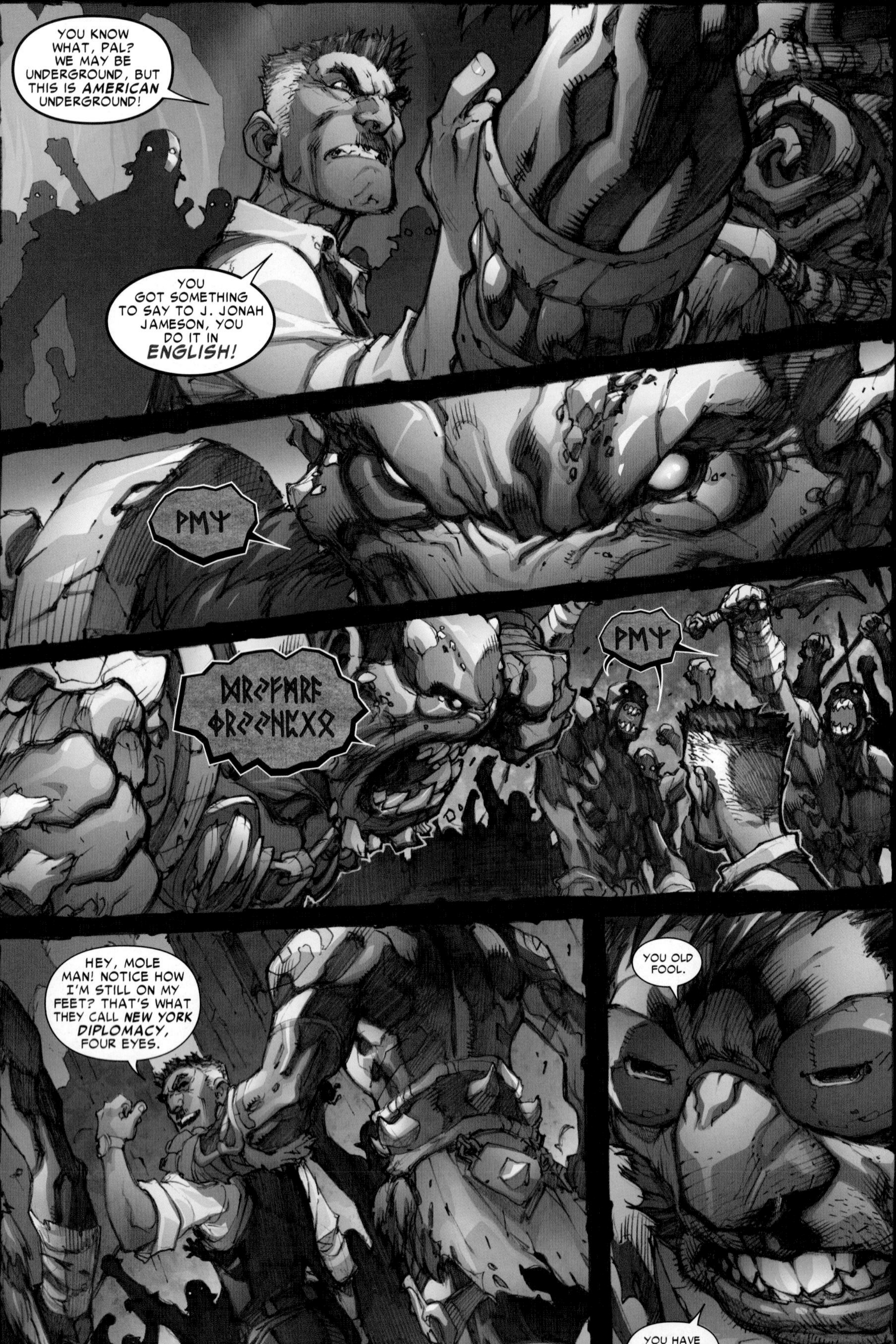
YOU KNOW WHAT, PAL? WE MAY BE UNDERGROUND, BUT THIS IS AMERICAN UNDERGROUND!
YOU GOT SOMETHING TO SAY TO J. JONAH JAMESON, YOU DO IT IN ENGLISH!
HEY, MOLE MAN! NOTICE HOW I'M STILL ON MY FEET? THAT'S WHAT THEY CALL NEW YORK DIPLOMACY, FOUR EYES.
YOU OLD FOOL.
YOU HAVE NO IDEA WHAT YOU'VE DONE.

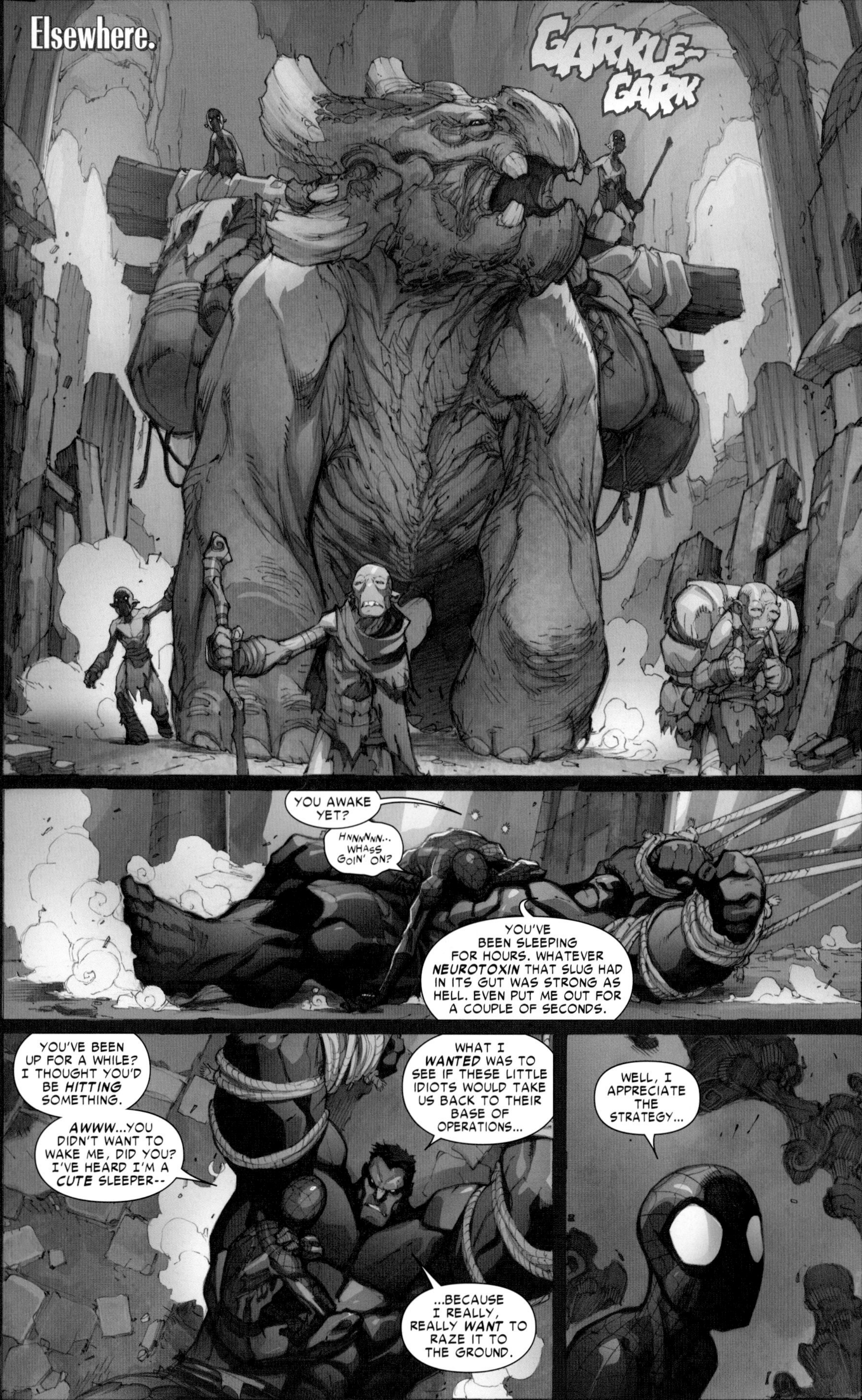
Elsewhere.
GARKLE-GARK
YOU AWAKE YET?
HNNNNNN... WHASS GOIN' ON?
YOU'VE BEEN SLEEPING FOR HOURS. WHATEVER NEUROTOXIN THAT SLUG HAD IN ITS GUT WAS STRONG AS HELL. EVEN PUT ME OUT FOR A COUPLE OF SECONDS.
YOU'VE BEEN UP FOR A WHILE? I THOUGHT YOU'D BE HITTING SOMETHING.
AWWW...YOU DIDN'T WANT TO WAKE ME, DID YOU? I'VE HEARD I'M A CUTE SLEEPER--
WHAT I WANTED WAS TO SEE IF THESE LITTLE IDIOTS WOULD TAKE US BACK TO THEIR BASE OF OPERATIONS...
...BECAUSE I REALLY, REALLY WANT TO RAZE IT TO THE GROUND.
WELL, I APPRECIATE THE STRATEGY...

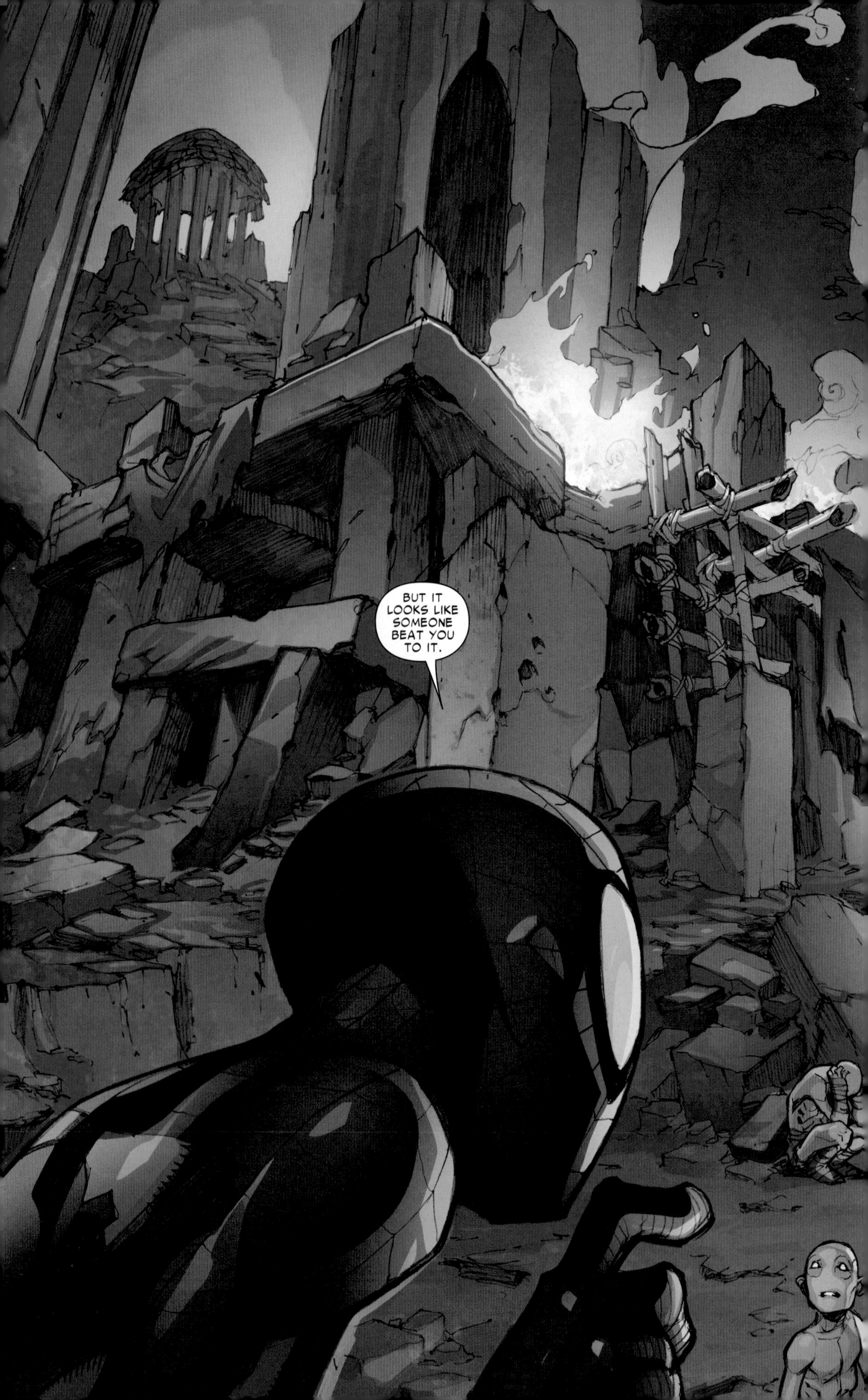
BUT IT LOOKS LIKE SOMEONE BEAT YOU TO IT.

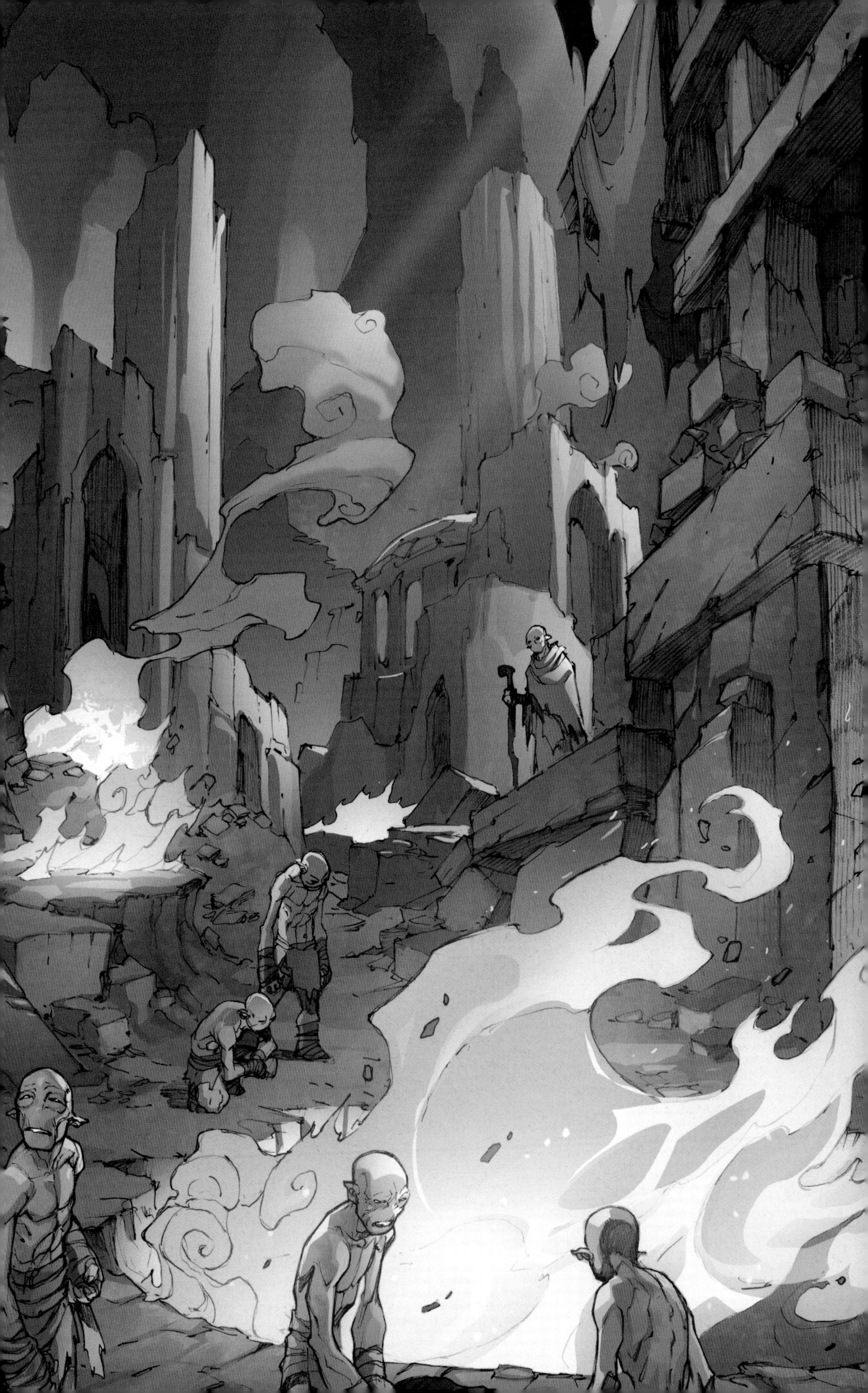

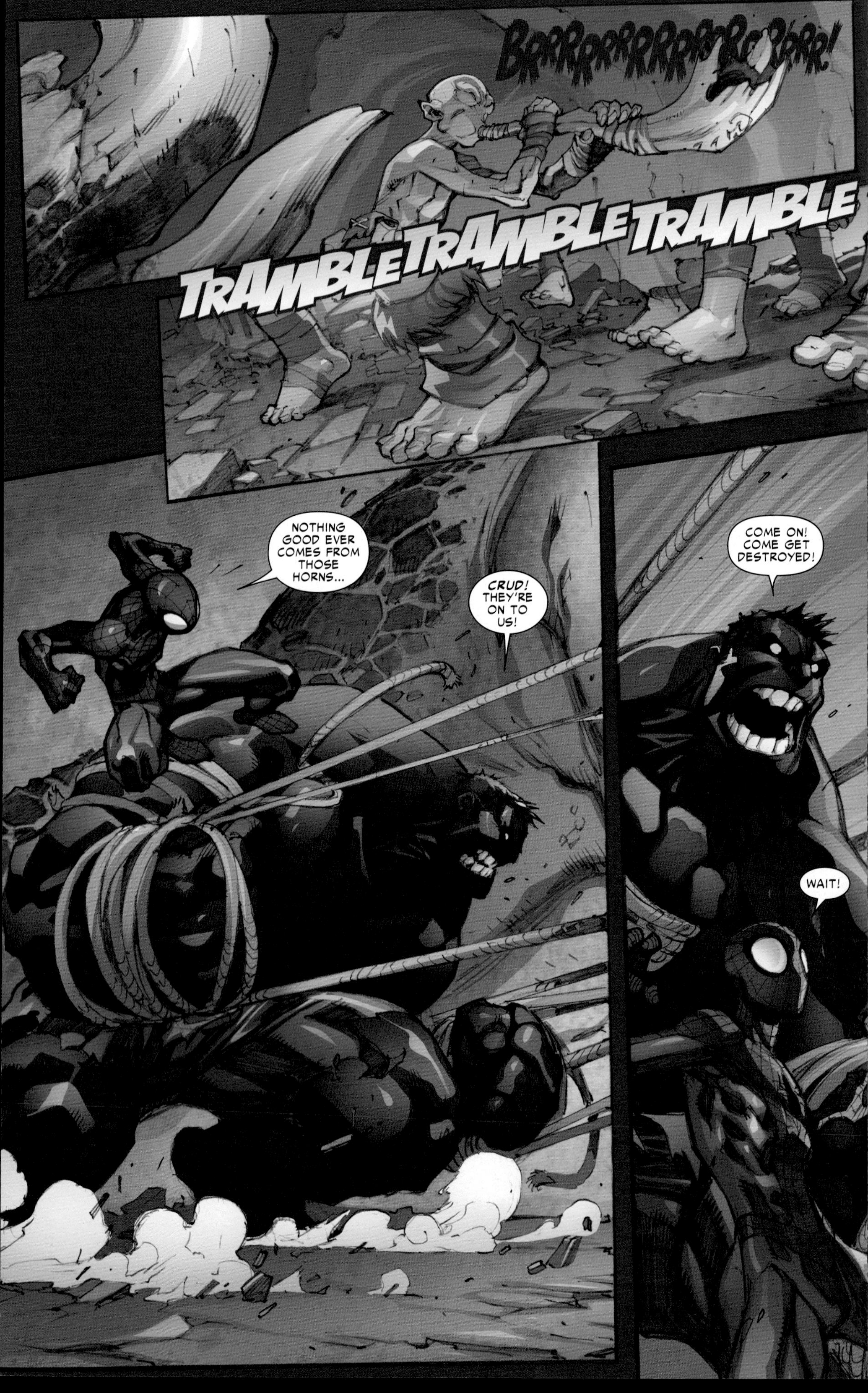
BRRRRRRRRRRRRRRRRR!
TRAMBLE TRAMBLE TRAMBLE
NOTHING GOOD EVER COMES FROM THOSE HORNS...
CRUD! THEY'RE ON TO US!
COME ON! COME GET DESTROYED!
WAIT!

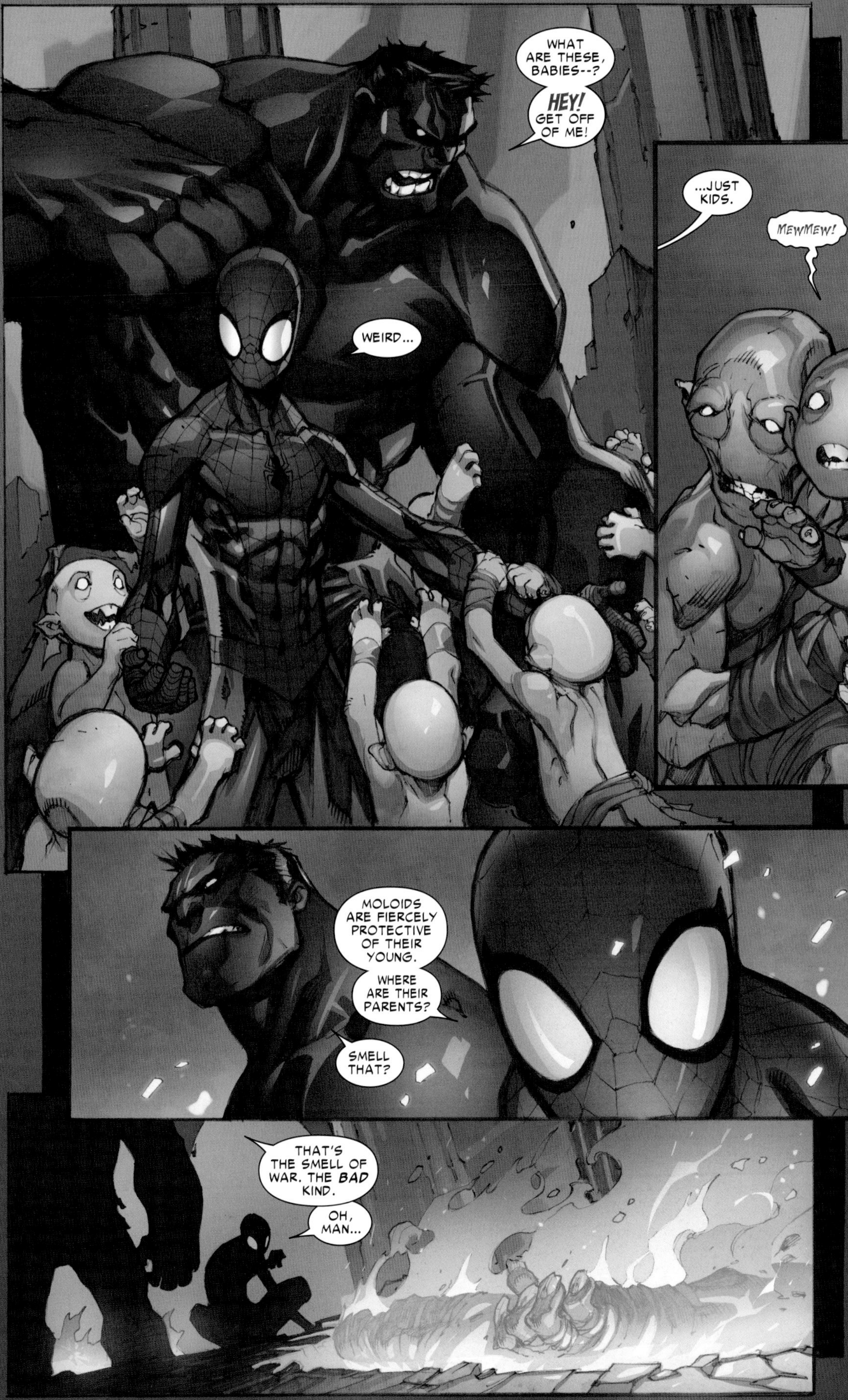
WHAT ARE THESE, BABIES--?
HEY! GET OFF OF ME!
WEIRD...
...JUST KIDS.
MEWMEW!
MOLOIDS ARE FIERCELY PROTECTIVE OF THEIR YOUNG.
WHERE ARE THEIR PARENTS?
SMELL THAT?
THAT'S THE SMELL OF WAR. THE BAD KIND.
OH, MAN...

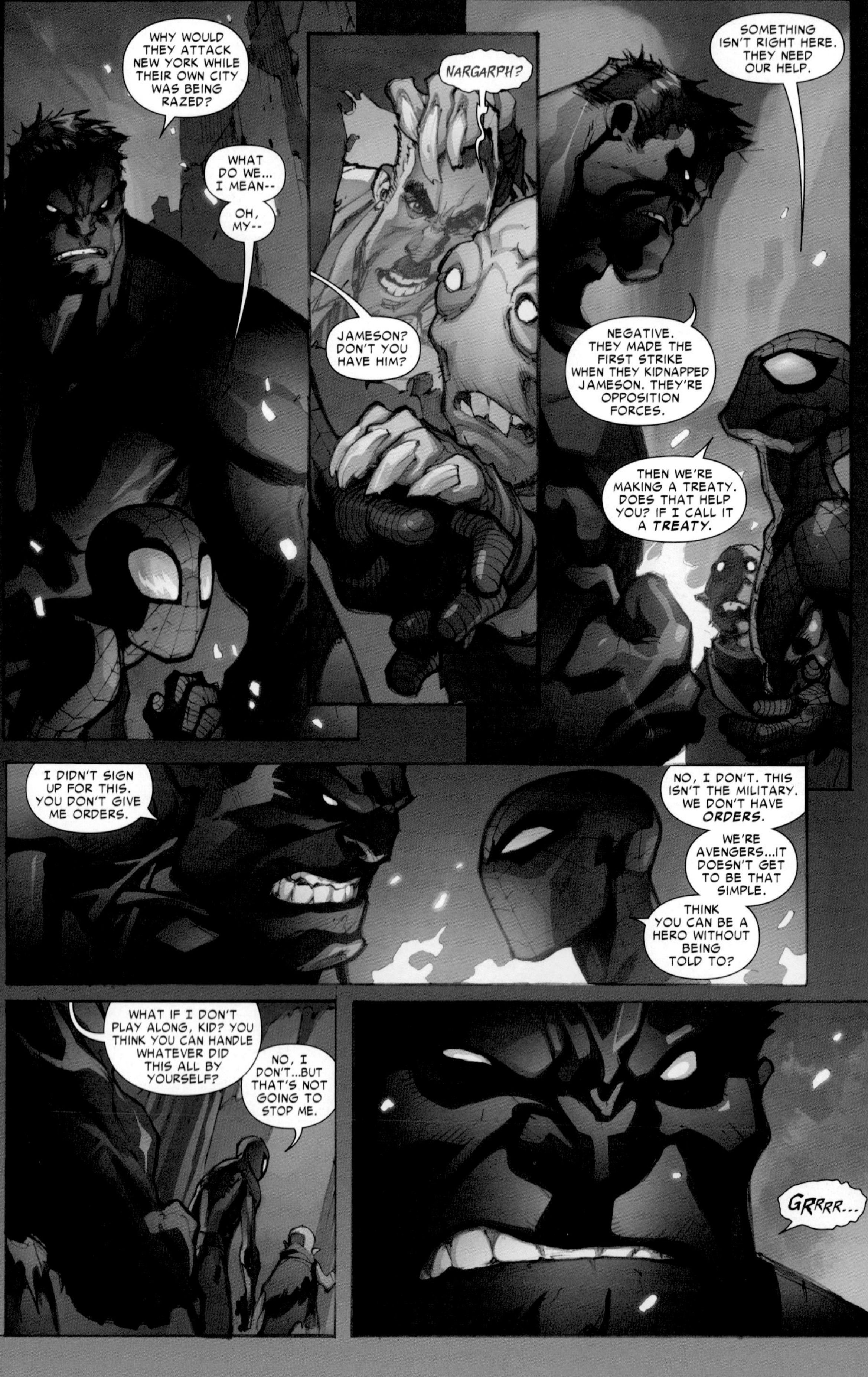
WHY WOULD THEY ATTACK NEW YORK WHILE THEIR OWN CITY WAS BEING RAZED?
WHAT DO WE... I MEAN--
OH, MY--
NARGARPH?
JAMESON? DON'T YOU HAVE HIM?
SOMETHING ISN'T RIGHT HERE. THEY NEED OUR HELP.
NEGATIVE. THEY MADE THE FIRST STRIKE WHEN THEY KIDNAPPED JAMESON. THEY'RE OPPOSITION FORCES.
THEN WE'RE MAKING A TREATY. DOES THAT HELP YOU? IF I CALL IT A TREATY.
I DIDN'T SIGN UP FOR THIS. YOU DON'T GIVE ME ORDERS.
NO, I DON'T. THIS ISN'T THE MILITARY. WE DON'T HAVE ORDERS.
WE'RE AVENGERS...IT DOESN'T GET TO BE THAT SIMPLE.
THINK YOU CAN BE A HERO WITHOUT BEING TOLD TO?
WHAT IF I DON'T PLAY ALONG, KID? YOU THINK YOU CAN HANDLE WHATEVER DID THIS ALL BY YOURSELF?
NO, I DON'T...BUT THAT'S NOT GOING TO STOP ME.
GRRRR...

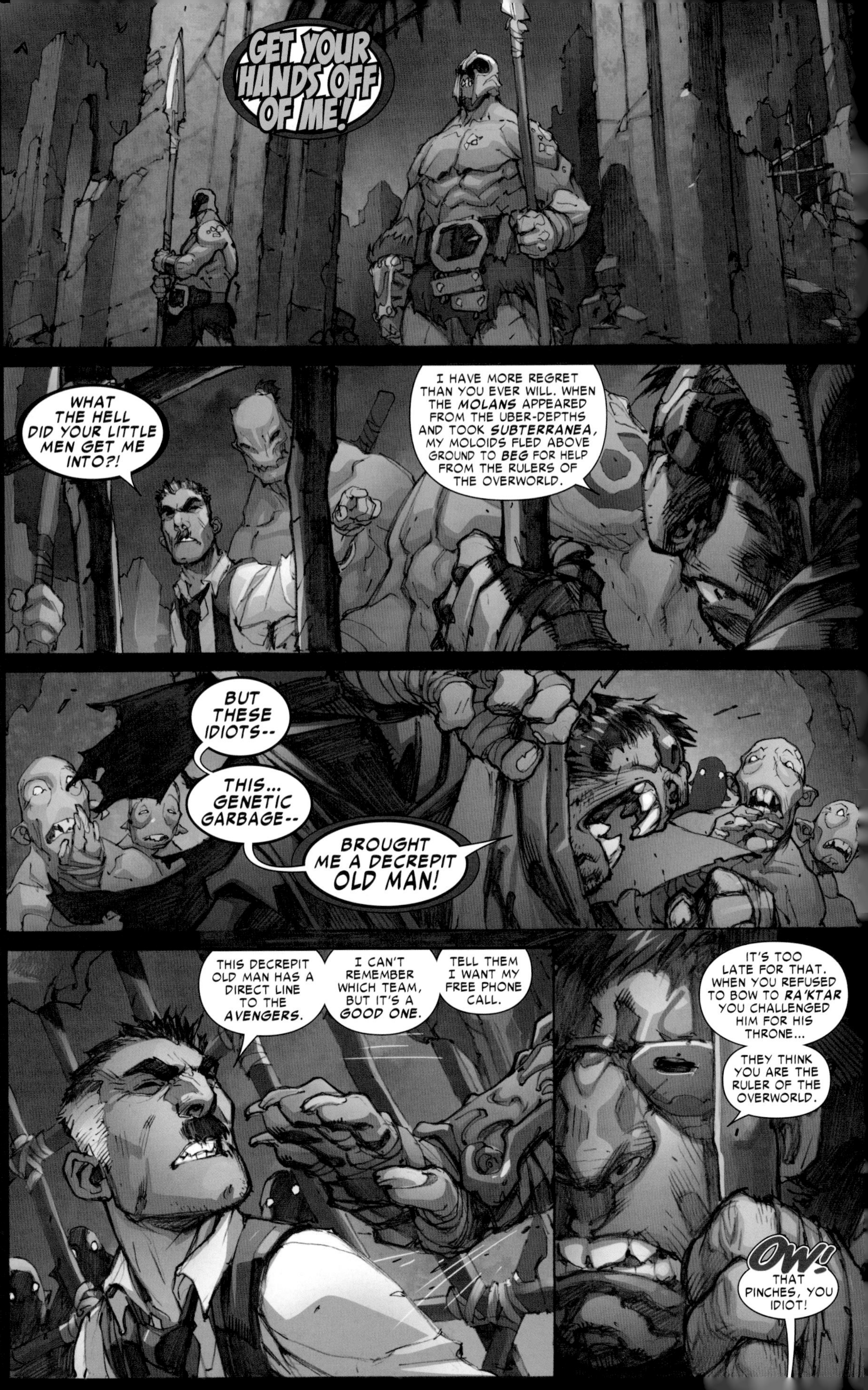

GET YOUR HANDS OFF OF ME!
WHAT THE HELL DID YOUR LITTLE MEN GET ME INTO?!
I HAVE MORE REGRET THAN YOU EVER WILL. WHEN THE MOLANS APPEARED FROM THE UBER-DEPTHS AND TOOK SUBTERRANEA, MY MOLOIDS FLED ABOVE GROUND TO BEG FOR HELP FROM THE RULERS OF THE OVERWORLD.
BUT THESE IDIOTS--
THIS... GENETIC GARBAGE--
BROUGHT ME A DECREPIT OLD MAN!
THIS DECREPIT OLD MAN HAS A DIRECT LINE TO THE AVENGERS.
I CAN'T REMEMBER WHICH TEAM, BUT IT'S A GOOD ONE.
TELL THEM I WANT MY FREE PHONE CALL.
IT'S TOO LATE FOR THAT. WHEN YOU REFUSED TO BOW TO RA'KTAR YOU CHALLENGED HIM FOR HIS THRONE...
THEY THINK YOU ARE THE RULER OF THE OVERWORLD.
OW! THAT PINCHES, YOU IDIOT!

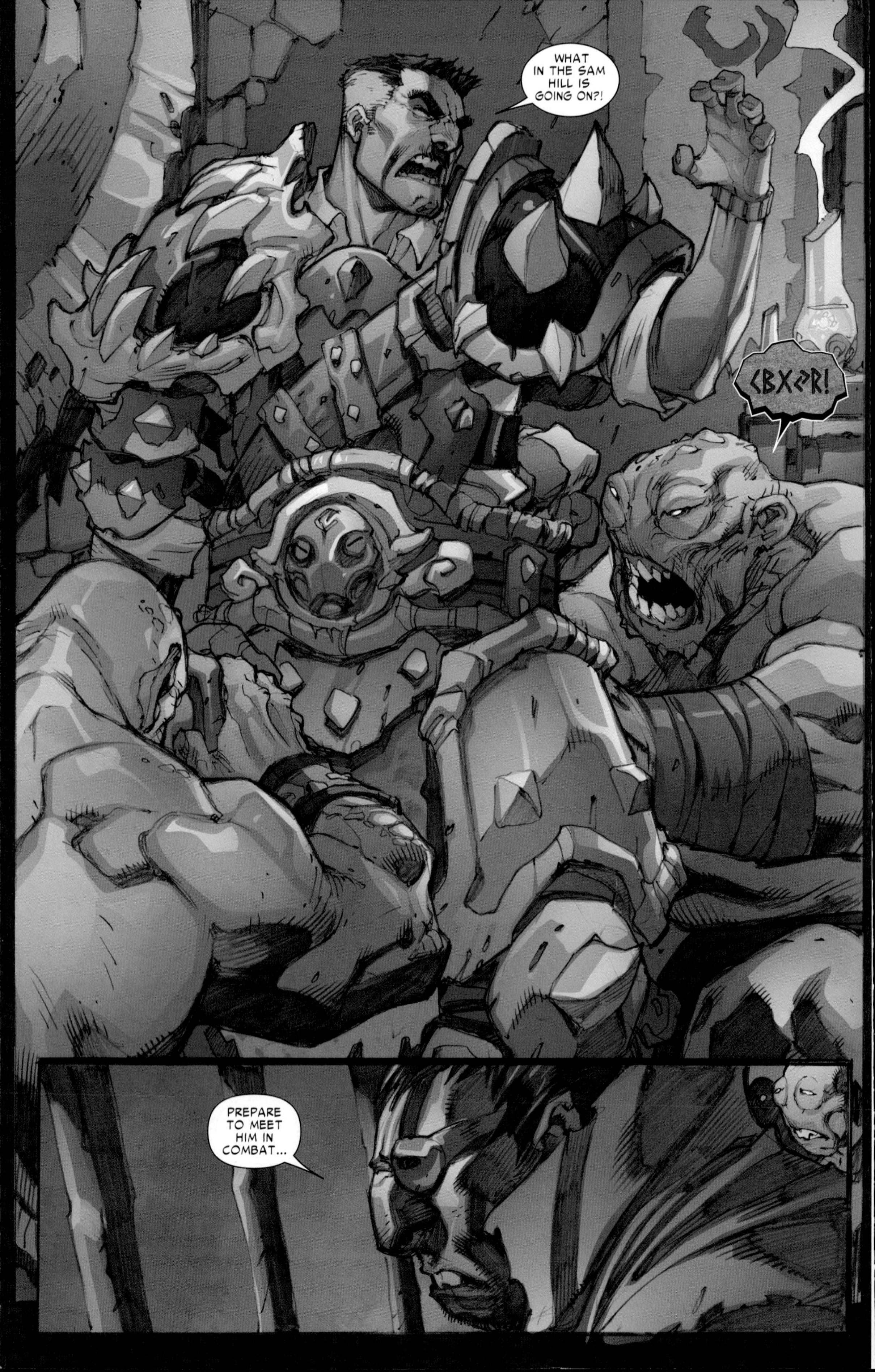
WHAT IN THE SAM HILL IS GOING ON?!
PREPARE TO MEET HIM IN COMBAT...

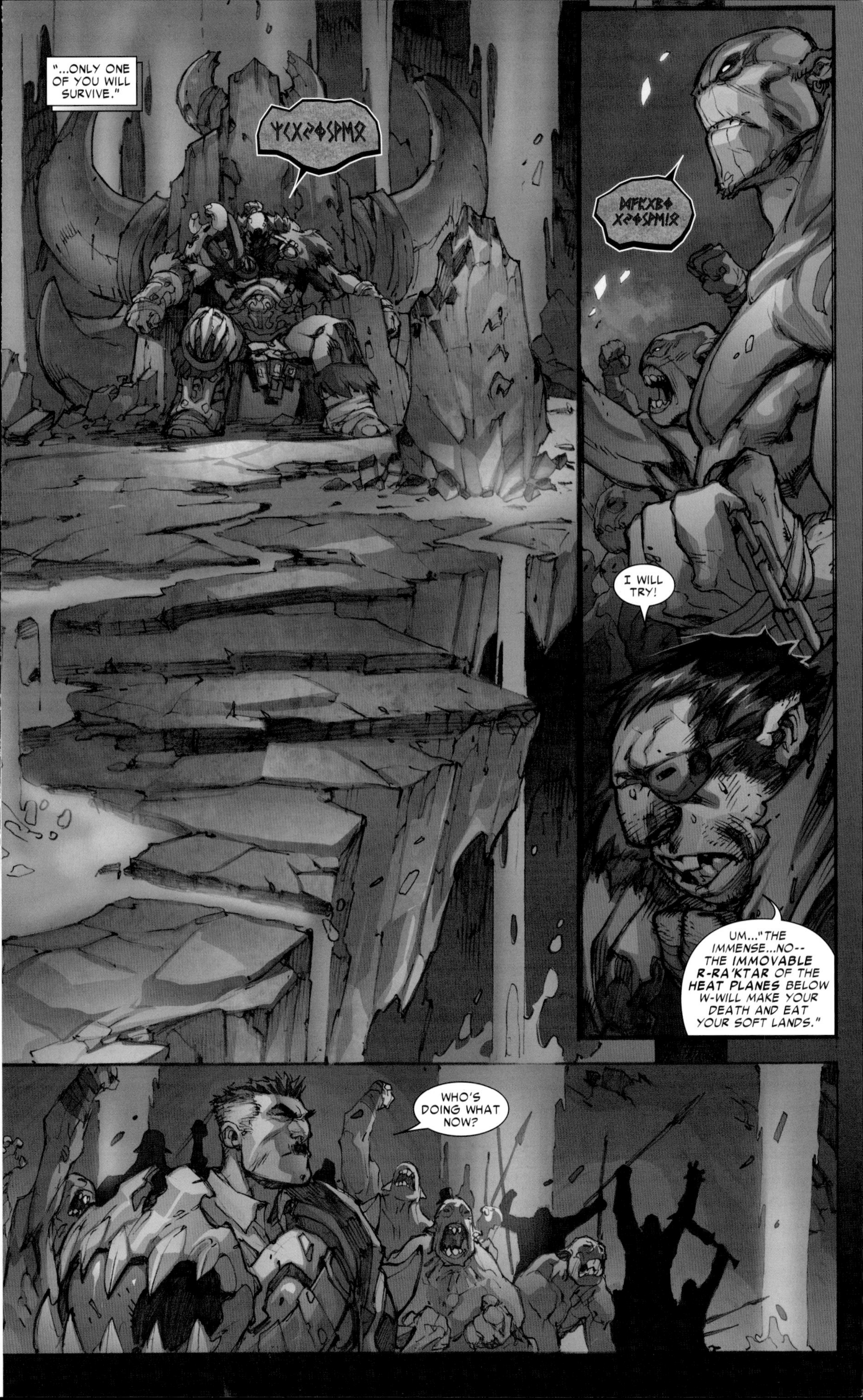
"...ONLY ONE OF YOU WILL SURVIVE."
I WILL TRY!
UM..."THE IMMENSE...NO-- THE IMMOVABLE R-RA'KTAR OF THE HEAT PLANES BELOW W-WILL MAKE YOUR DEATH AND EAT YOUR SOFT LANDS."
WHO'S DOING WHAT NOW?

�759ᛟᛗᛟ

FᚷF ᛋᛏᛒᚱ

"FROM RA'KTAR'S LANDS COMES THE HARD STONE."

"THE HARD STONE MAKES THE GOD EDGE."

FᚷF FᚷF

RORᚷ ᛋᛏᛒᚱ

"THE GOD EDGE MAKES THE KING BLADE."

"AGAINST THE KING BLADE, ALL THINGS BECOME TWO."

"KING BLADE," HUH?

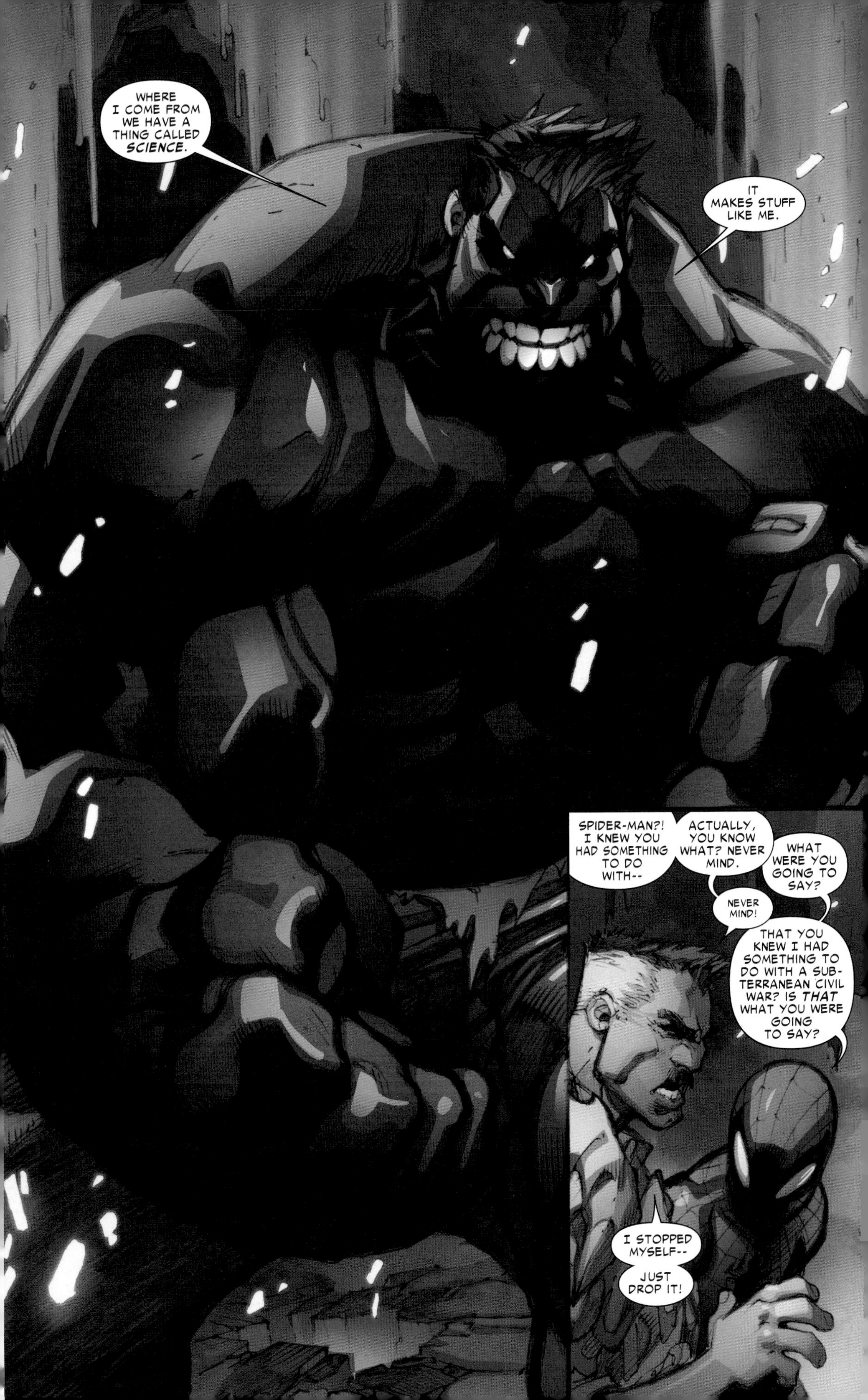
WHERE I COME FROM WE HAVE A THING CALLED *SCIENCE*.
IT MAKES STUFF LIKE ME.
SPIDER-MAN?! I KNEW YOU HAD SOMETHING TO DO WITH--
ACTUALLY, YOU KNOW WHAT? NEVER MIND.
WHAT WERE YOU GOING TO SAY?
NEVER MIND!
THAT YOU KNEW I HAD SOMETHING TO DO WITH A SUB-TERRANEAN CIVIL WAR? IS *THAT* WHAT YOU WERE GOING TO SAY?
I STOPPED MYSELF--
JUST DROP IT!

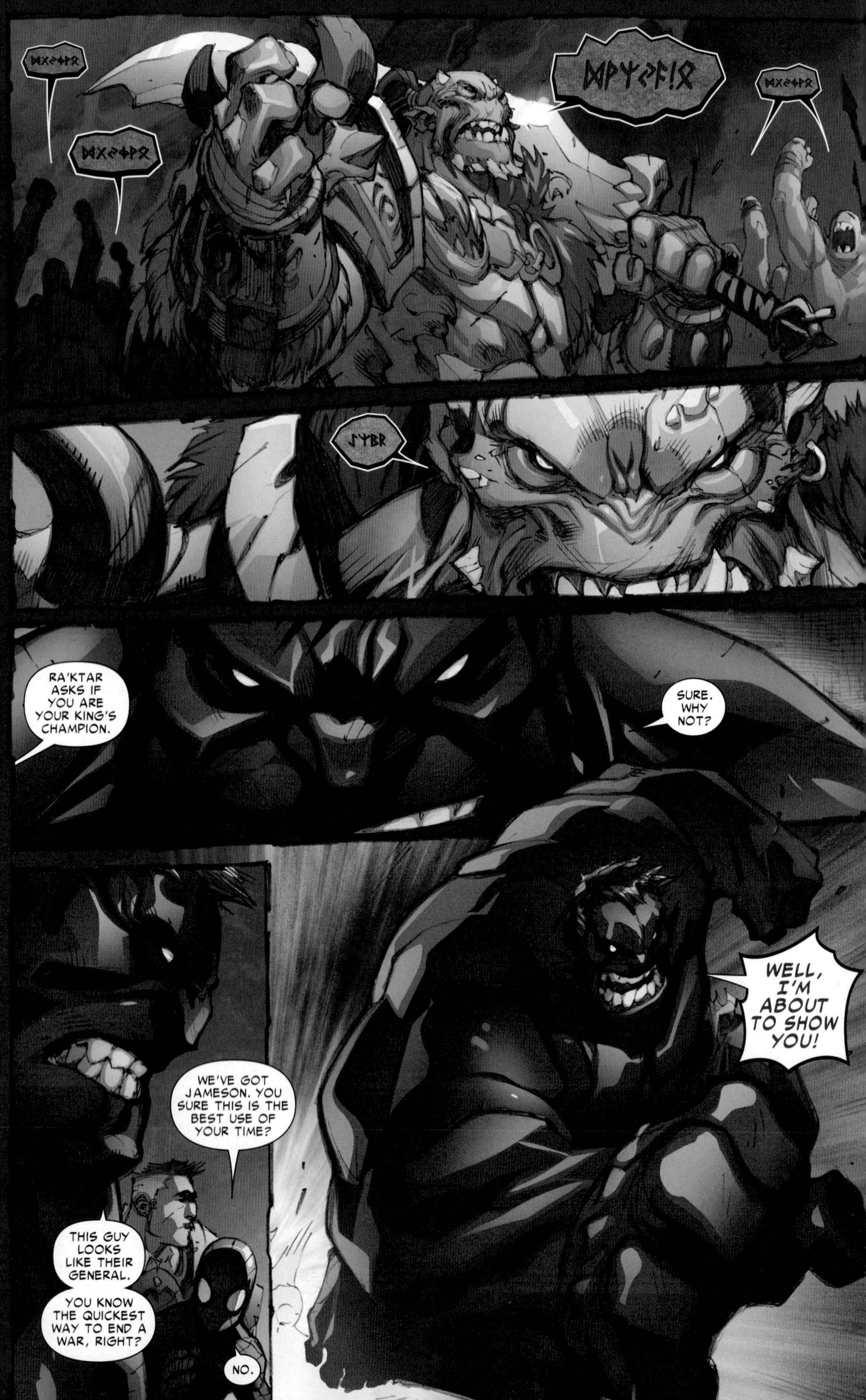

RA'KTAR ASKS IF YOU ARE YOUR KING'S CHAMPION.
SURE. WHY NOT?
THIS GUY LOOKS LIKE THEIR GENERAL.
YOU KNOW THE QUICKEST WAY TO END A WAR, RIGHT?
NO.
WE'VE GOT JAMESON. YOU SURE THIS IS THE BEST USE OF YOUR TIME?
WELL, I'M ABOUT TO SHOW YOU!

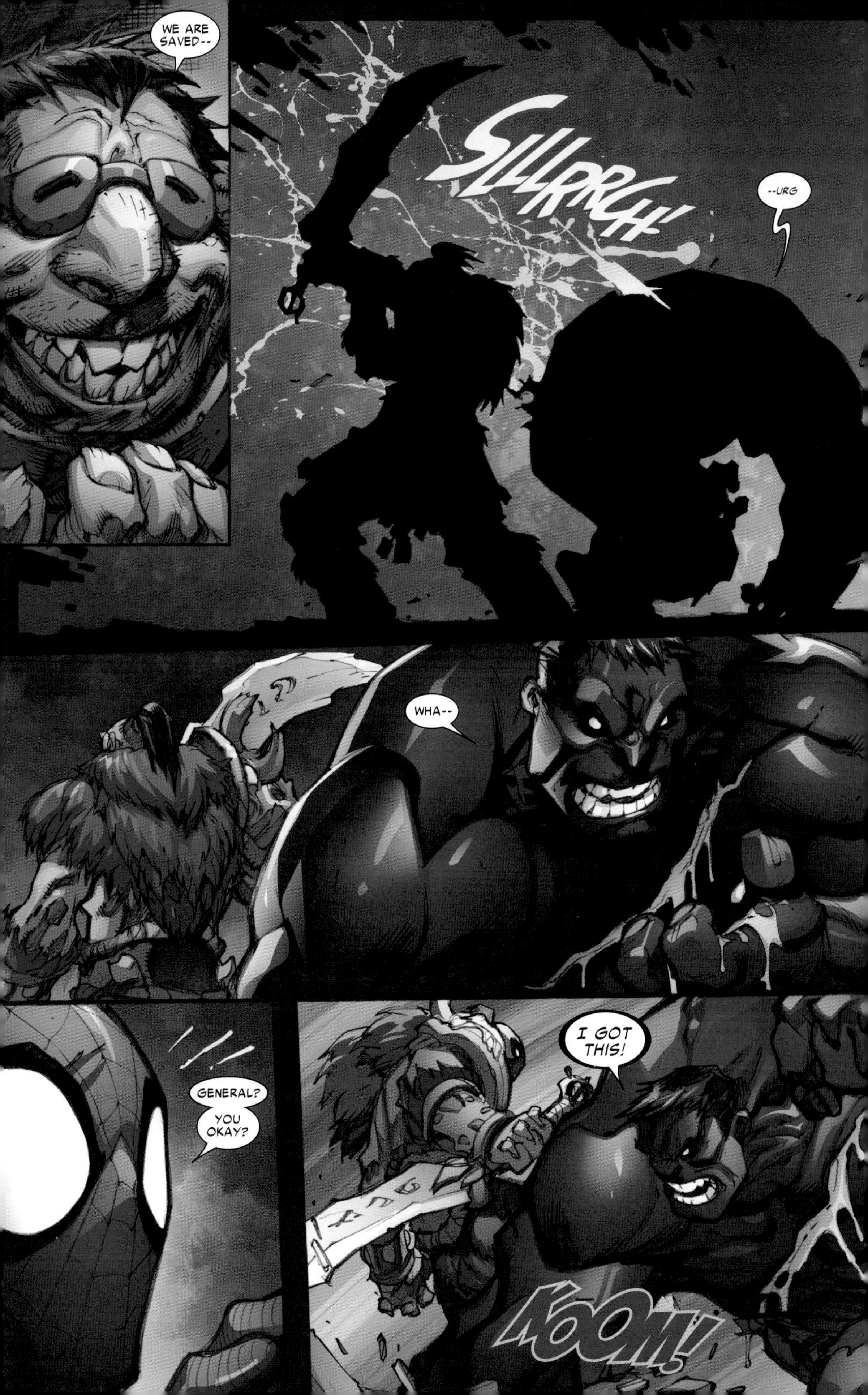
WE ARE SAVED--
SHLRRCH!
--URG
WHA--
!!!
GENERAL?
YOU OKAY?
I GOT THIS!
KOOM!

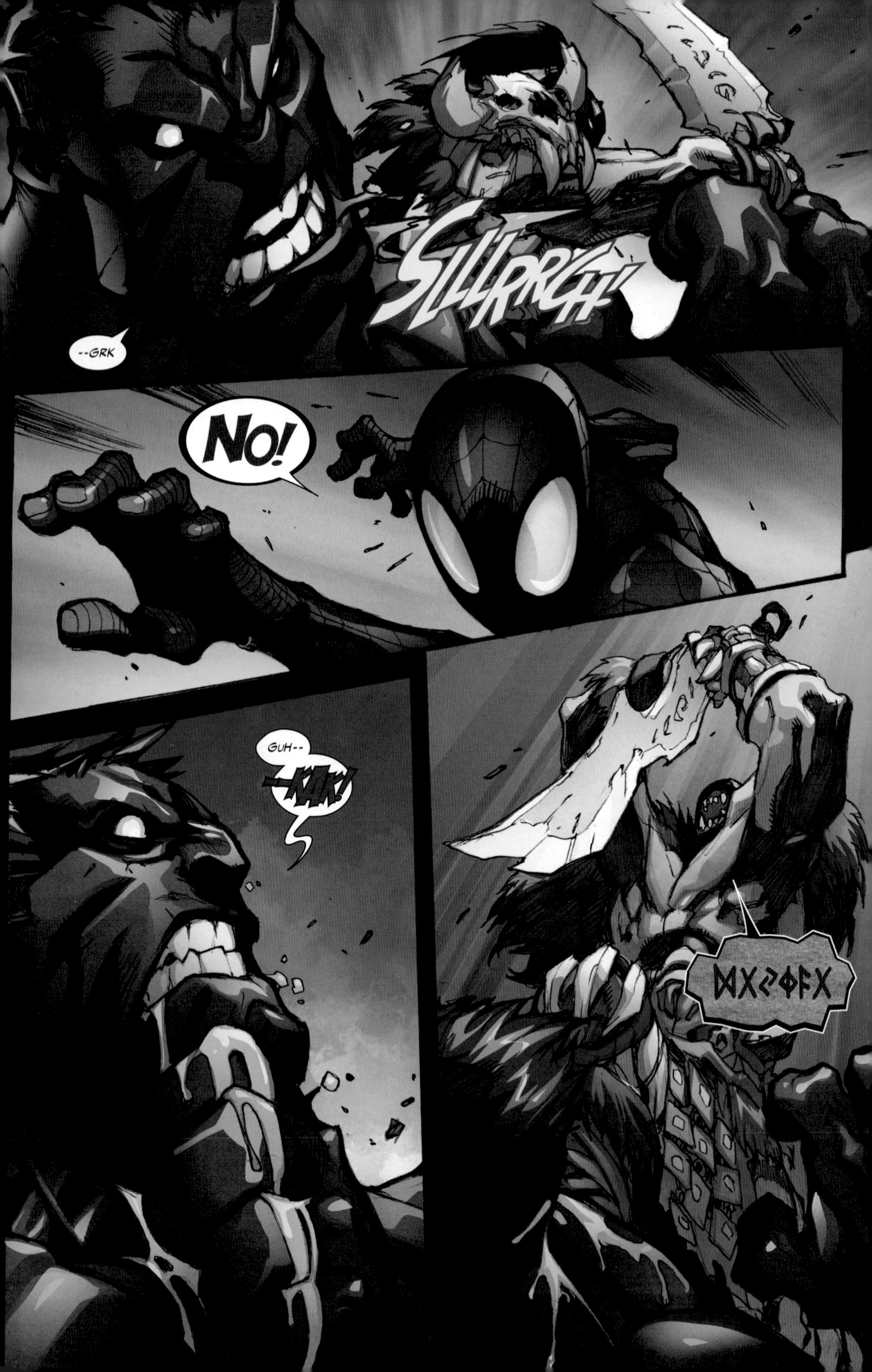
SLLLRRCH!
--GRK
NO!
GUH--
--KAK!

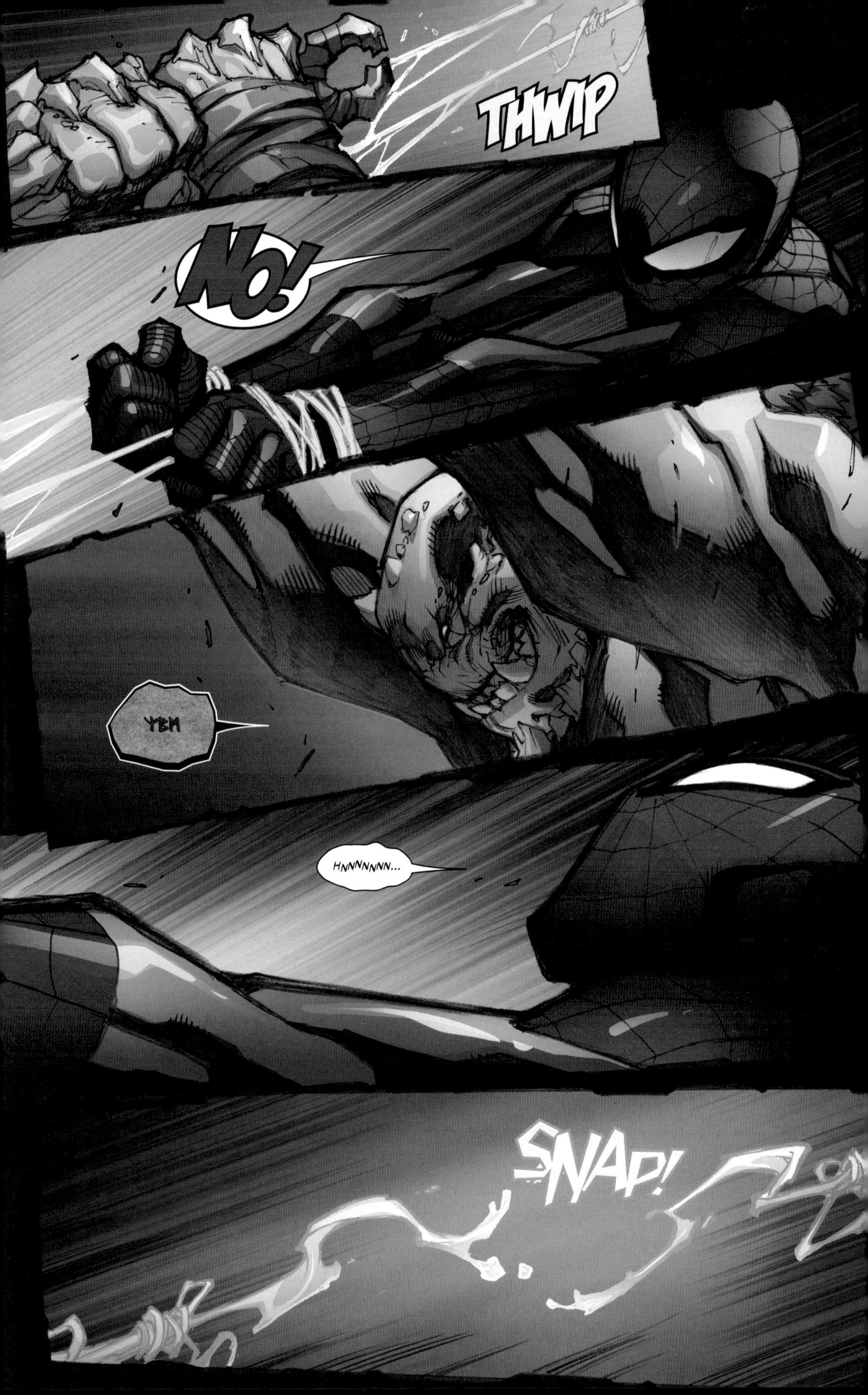
THWIP
NO!
YBM
HNNNNNNN...
SNAP!

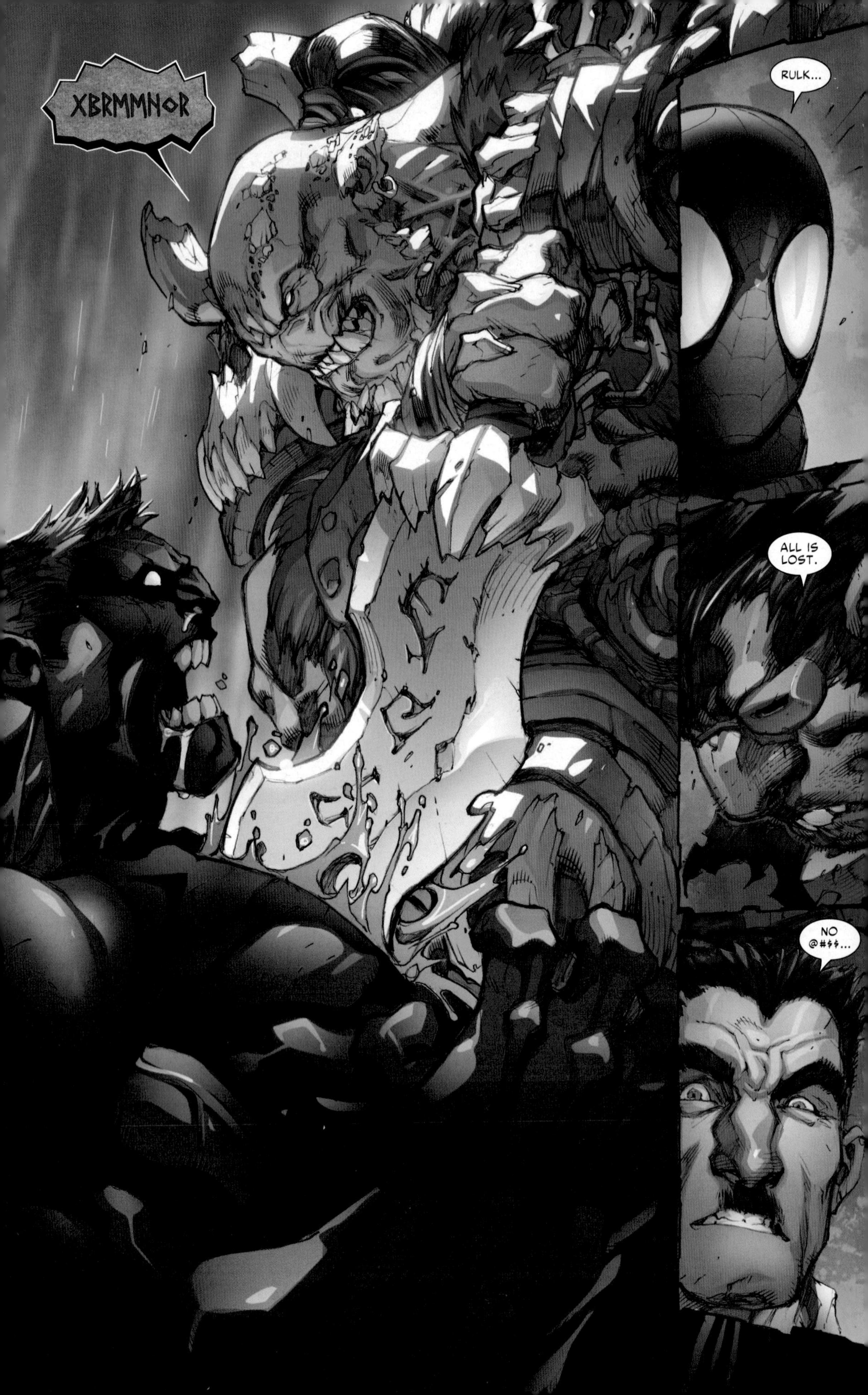
XBRMMNOR
RULK...
ALL IS LOST.
NO @#$$...

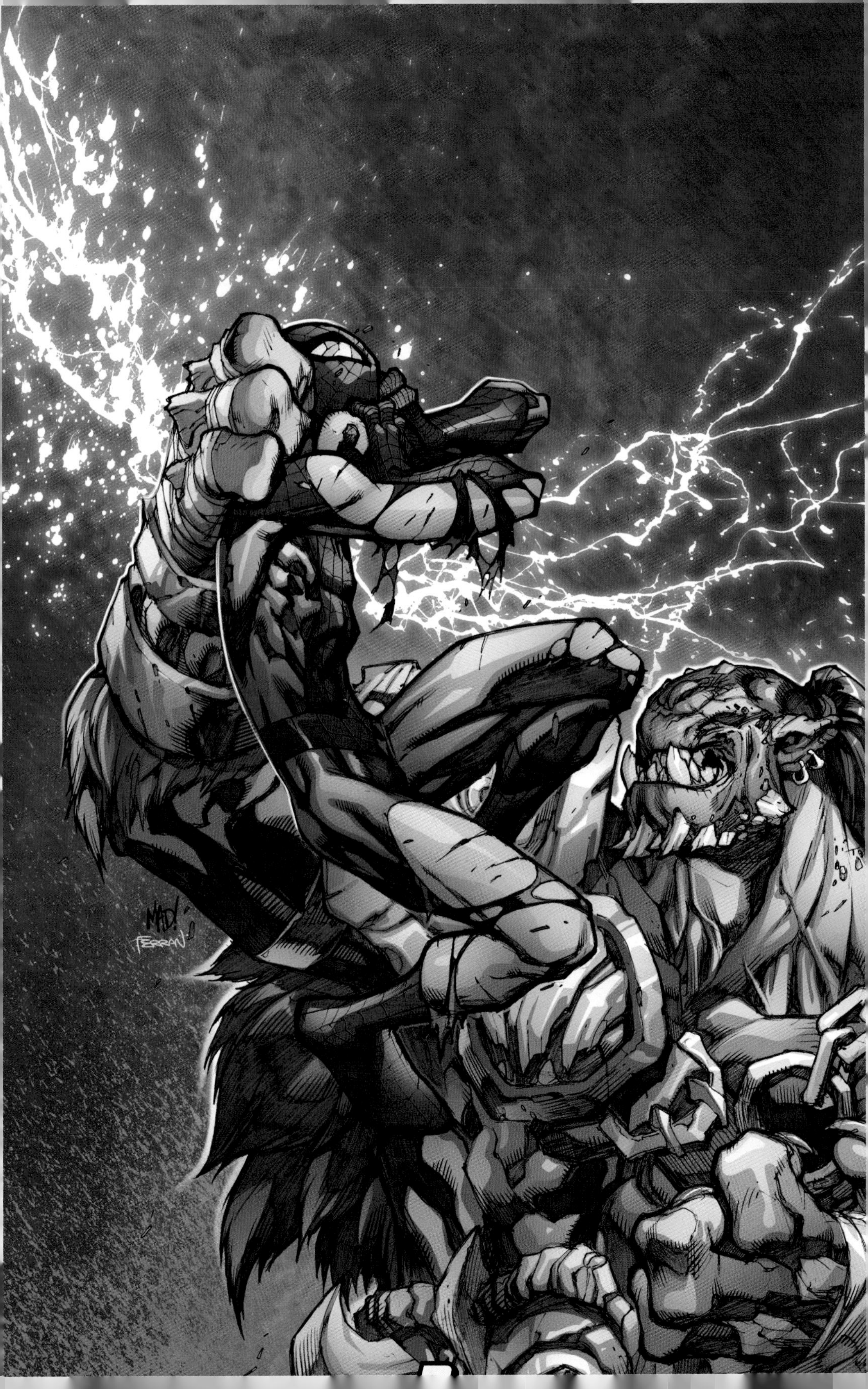
MAD!
FERRAN

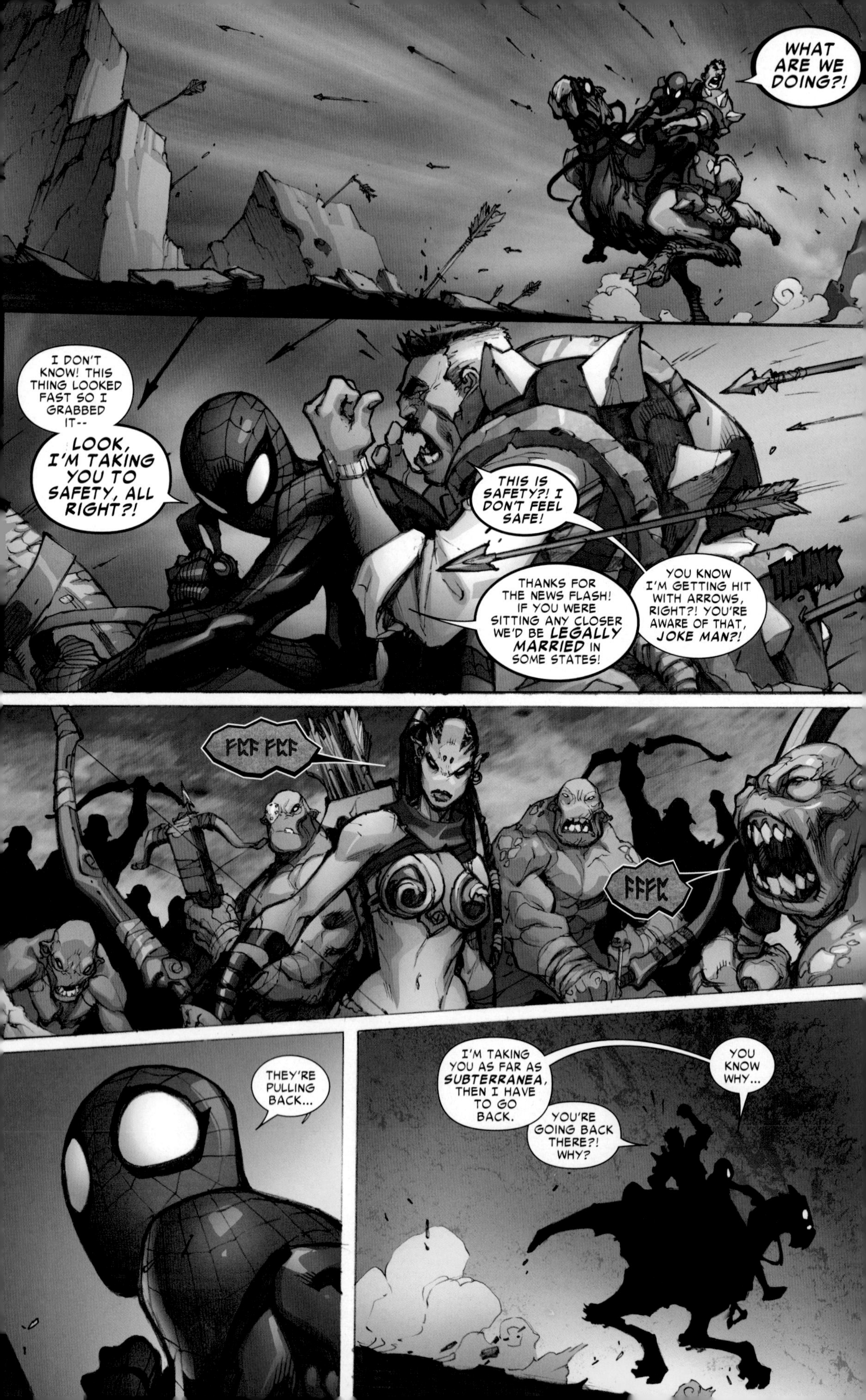
WHAT ARE WE DOING?!
I DON'T KNOW! THIS THING LOOKED FAST SO I GRABBED IT--
LOOK, I'M TAKING YOU TO SAFETY, ALL RIGHT?!
THIS IS SAFETY?! I DON'T FEEL SAFE!
YOU KNOW I'M GETTING HIT WITH ARROWS, RIGHT?! YOU'RE AWARE OF THAT, JOKE MAN?!
THANKS FOR THE NEWS FLASH! IF YOU WERE SITTING ANY CLOSER WE'D BE LEGALLY MARRIED IN SOME STATES!
THUNK
THEY'RE PULLING BACK...
I'M TAKING YOU AS FAR AS SUBTERRANEA, THEN I HAVE TO GO BACK.
YOU'RE GOING BACK THERE?! WHY?
YOU KNOW WHY...

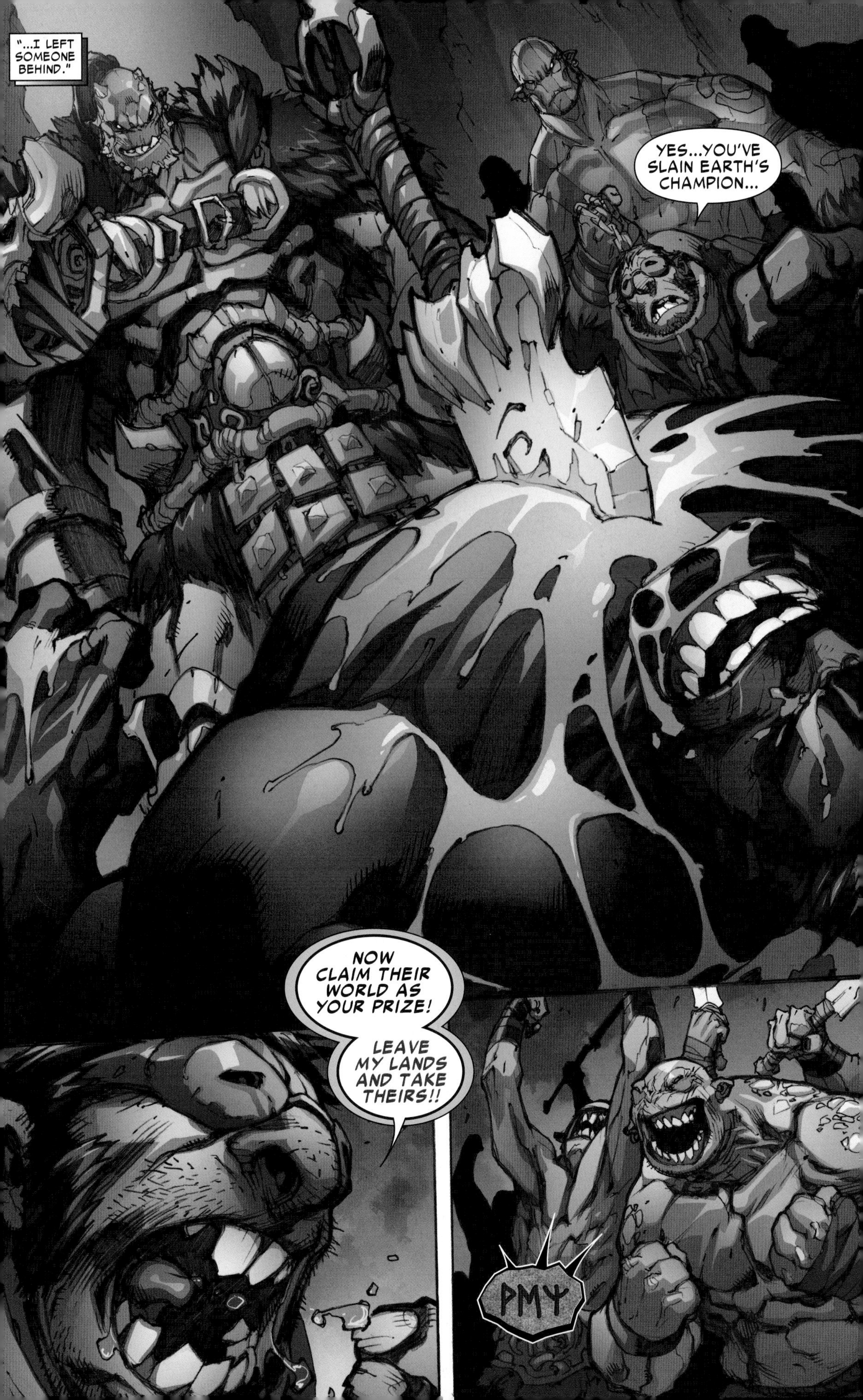
"...I LEFT SOMEONE BEHIND."
YES...YOU'VE SLAIN EARTH'S CHAMPION...
NOW CLAIM THEIR WORLD AS YOUR PRIZE!
LEAVE MY LANDS AND TAKE THEIRS!!
ᚹᛗᛉ

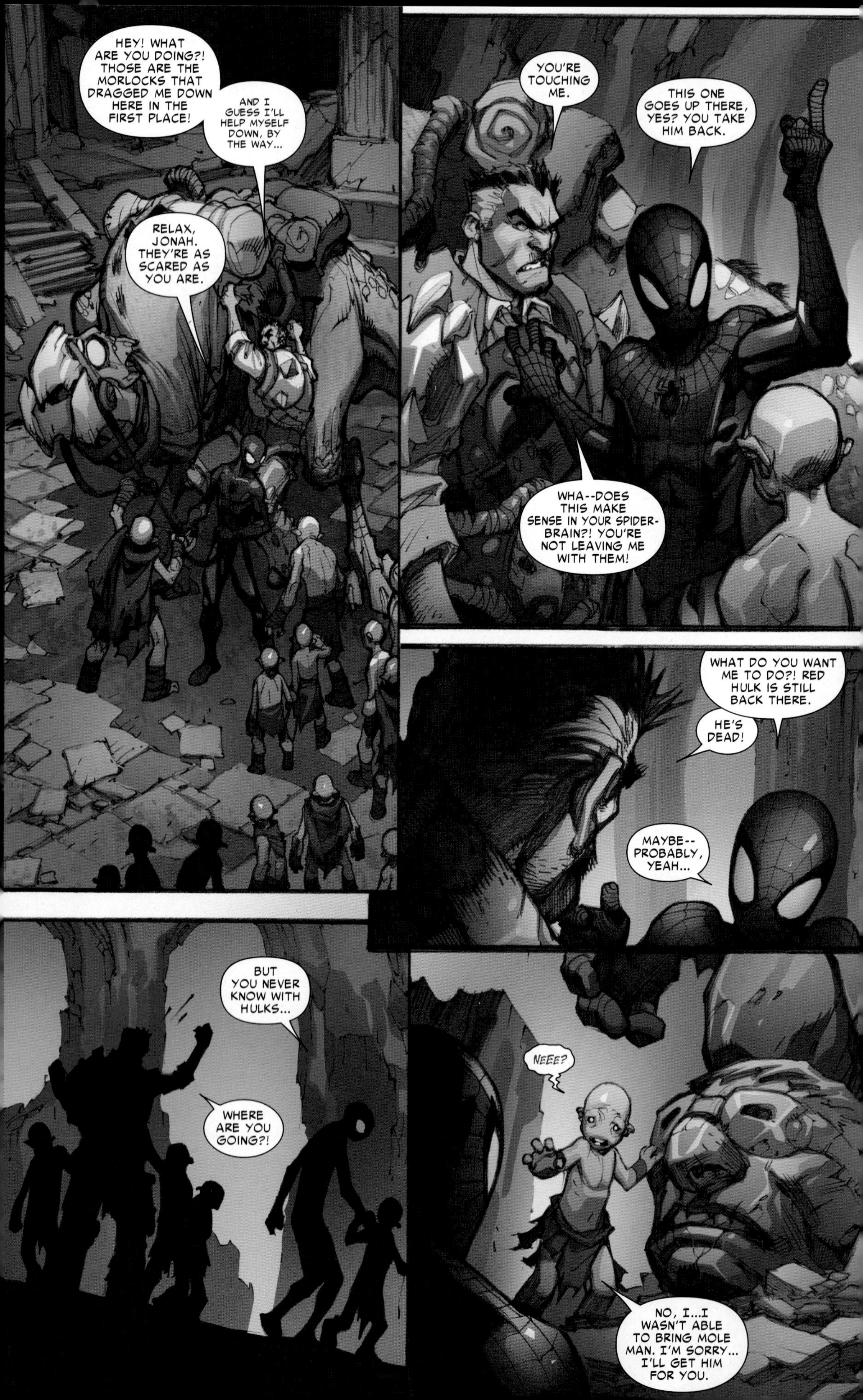
HEY! WHAT ARE YOU DOING?! THOSE ARE THE MORLOCKS THAT DRAGGED ME DOWN HERE IN THE FIRST PLACE!
AND I GUESS I'LL HELP MYSELF DOWN, BY THE WAY...
RELAX, JONAH. THEY'RE AS SCARED AS YOU ARE.
YOU'RE TOUCHING ME.
THIS ONE GOES UP THERE, YES? YOU TAKE HIM BACK.
WHA--DOES THIS MAKE SENSE IN YOUR SPIDER-BRAIN?! YOU'RE NOT LEAVING ME WITH THEM!
WHAT DO YOU WANT ME TO DO?! RED HULK IS STILL BACK THERE.
HE'S DEAD!
MAYBE--PROBABLY, YEAH...
BUT YOU NEVER KNOW WITH HULKS...
WHERE ARE YOU GOING?!
NEEE?
NO, I...I WASN'T ABLE TO BRING MOLE MAN. I'M SORRY... I'LL GET HIM FOR YOU.

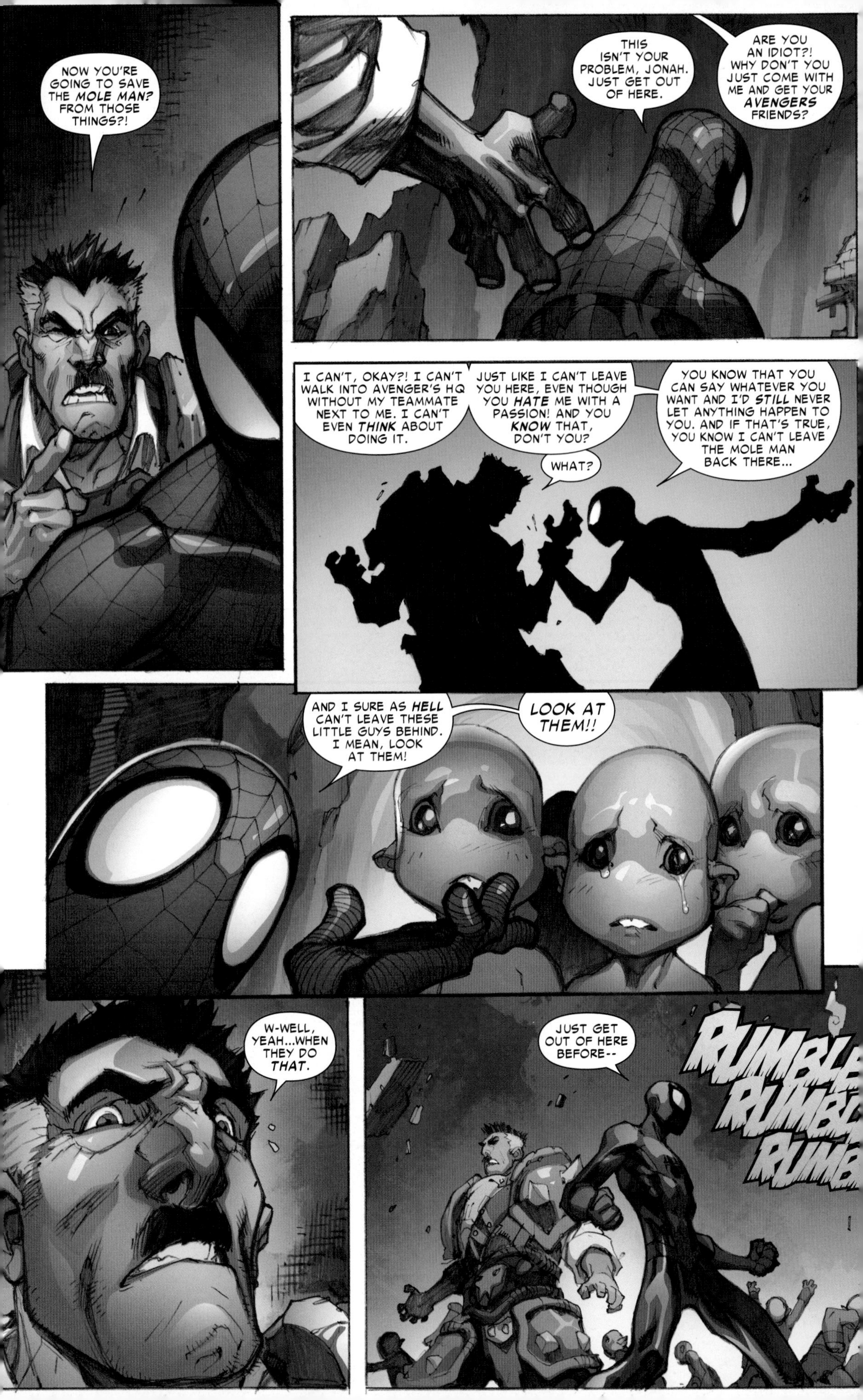
NOW YOU'RE GOING TO SAVE THE *MOLE MAN?* FROM THOSE THINGS?!
THIS ISN'T YOUR PROBLEM, JONAH. JUST GET OUT OF HERE.
ARE YOU AN IDIOT?! WHY DON'T YOU JUST COME WITH ME AND GET YOUR *AVENGERS* FRIENDS?
I CAN'T, OKAY?! I CAN'T WALK INTO AVENGER'S HQ WITHOUT MY TEAMMATE NEXT TO ME. I CAN'T EVEN *THINK* ABOUT DOING IT.
JUST LIKE I CAN'T LEAVE YOU HERE, EVEN THOUGH YOU *HATE* ME WITH A PASSION! AND YOU *KNOW* THAT, DON'T YOU?
WHAT?
YOU KNOW THAT YOU CAN SAY WHATEVER YOU WANT AND I'D *STILL* NEVER LET ANYTHING HAPPEN TO YOU. AND IF THAT'S TRUE, YOU KNOW I CAN'T LEAVE THE MOLE MAN BACK THERE...
AND I SURE AS *HELL* CAN'T LEAVE THESE LITTLE GUYS BEHIND. I MEAN, LOOK AT THEM!
LOOK AT THEM!!
W-WELL, YEAH...WHEN THEY DO *THAT*.
JUST GET OUT OF HERE BEFORE--

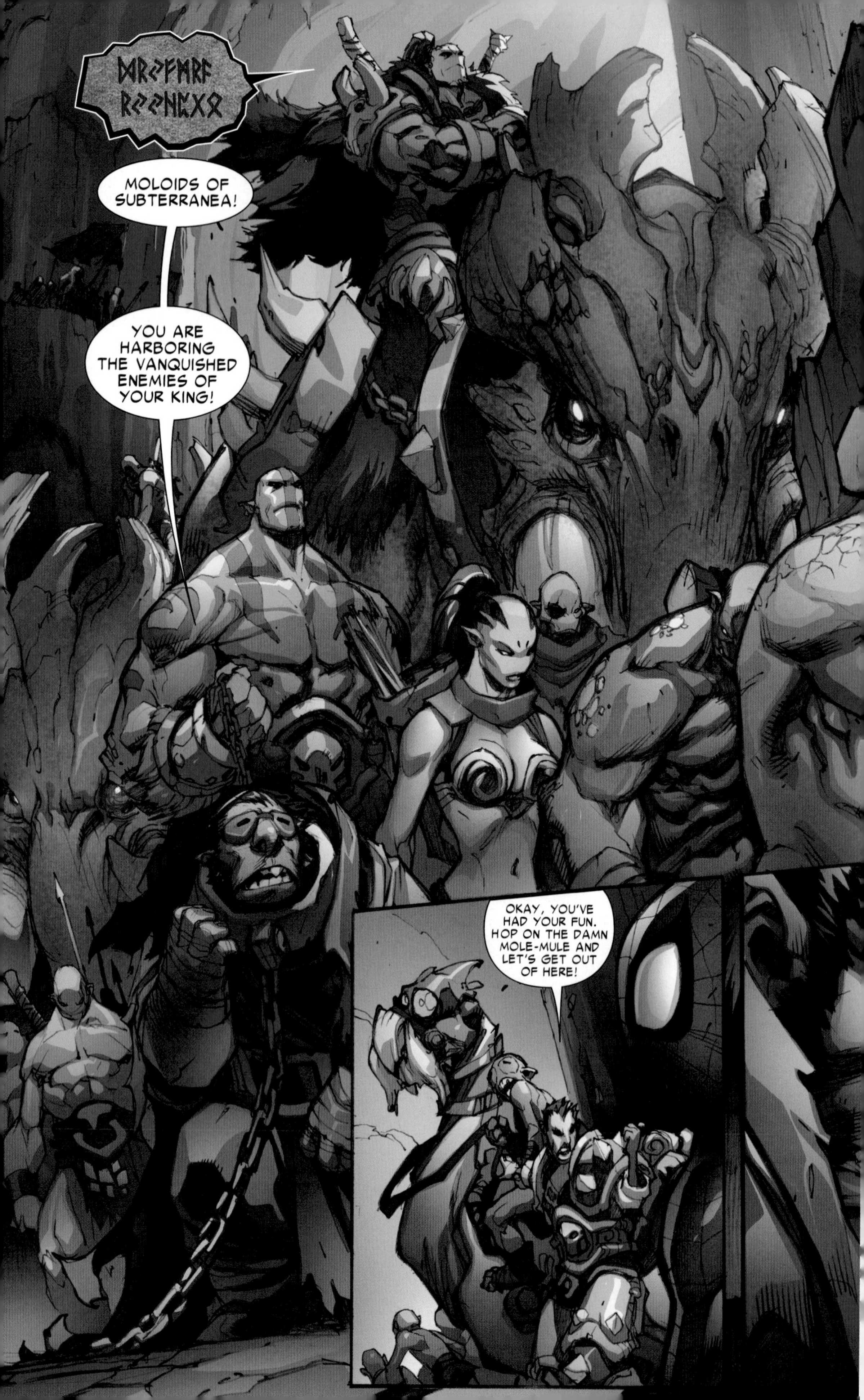
MOLOIDS OF SUBTERRANEA!
YOU ARE HARBORING THE VANQUISHED ENEMIES OF YOUR KING!
OKAY, YOU'VE HAD YOUR FUN. HOP ON THE DAMN MOLE-MULE AND LET'S GET OUT OF HERE!

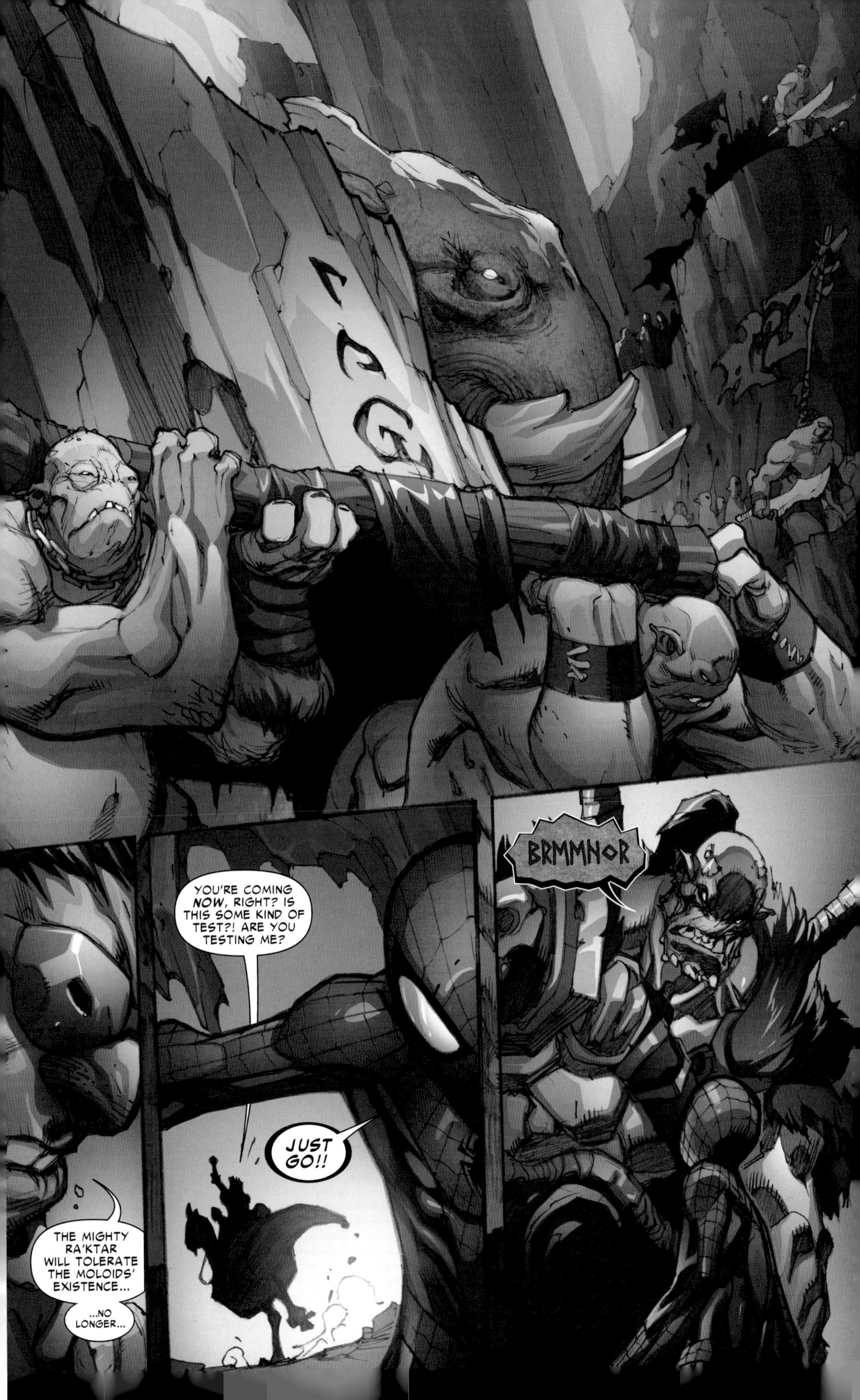
THE MIGHTY RA'KTAR WILL TOLERATE THE MOLOIDS' EXISTENCE...
...NO LONGER...
YOU'RE COMING NOW, RIGHT? IS THIS SOME KIND OF TEST?! ARE YOU TESTING ME?
JUST GO!!
BRMMNOR

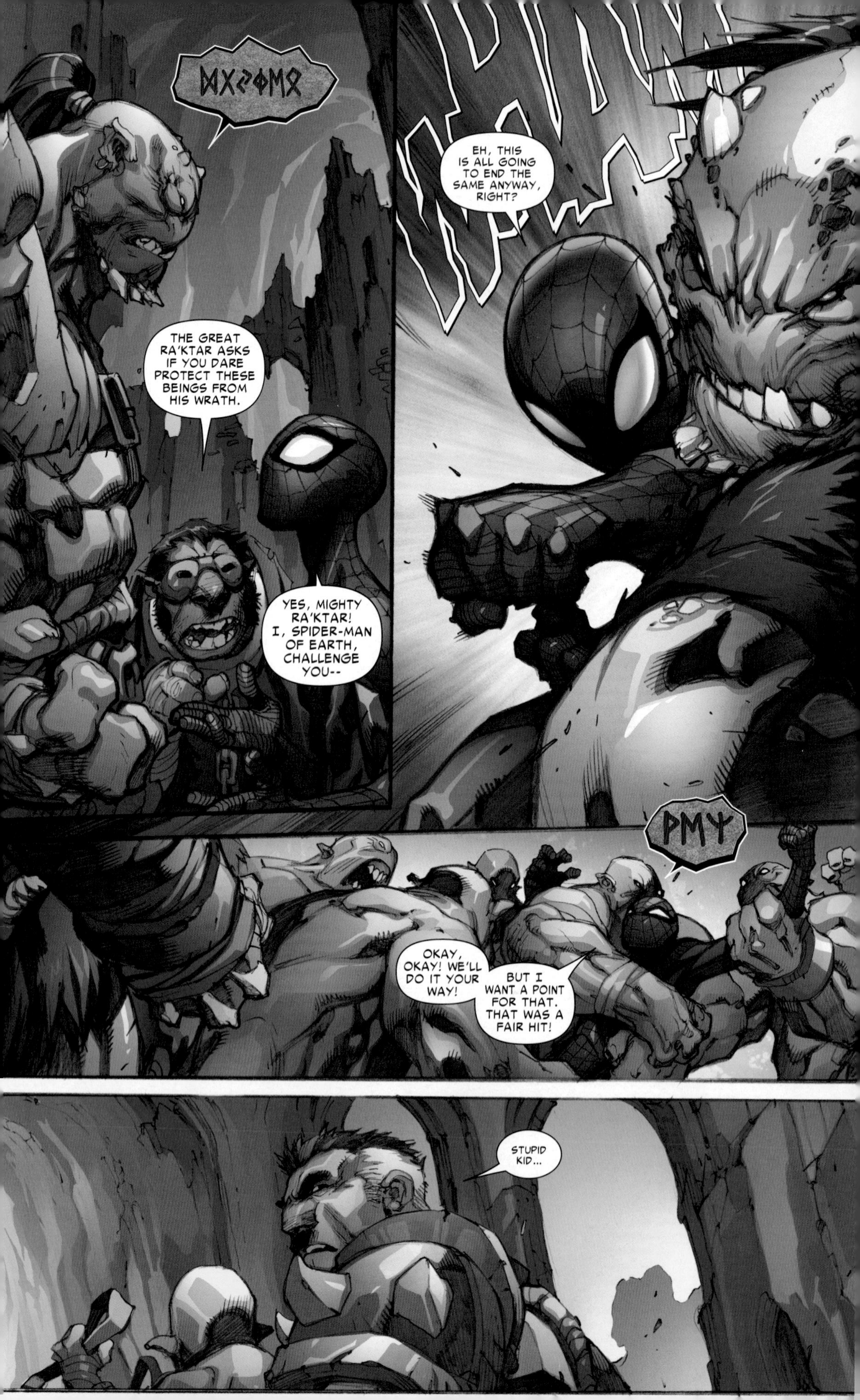
THE GREAT RA'KTAR ASKS IF YOU DARE PROTECT THESE BEINGS FROM HIS WRATH.
YES, MIGHTY RA'KTAR! I, SPIDER-MAN OF EARTH, CHALLENGE YOU--
EH, THIS IS ALL GOING TO END THE SAME ANYWAY, RIGHT?
OKAY, OKAY! WE'LL DO IT YOUR WAY!
BUT I WANT A POINT FOR THAT. THAT WAS A FAIR HIT!
STUPID KID...

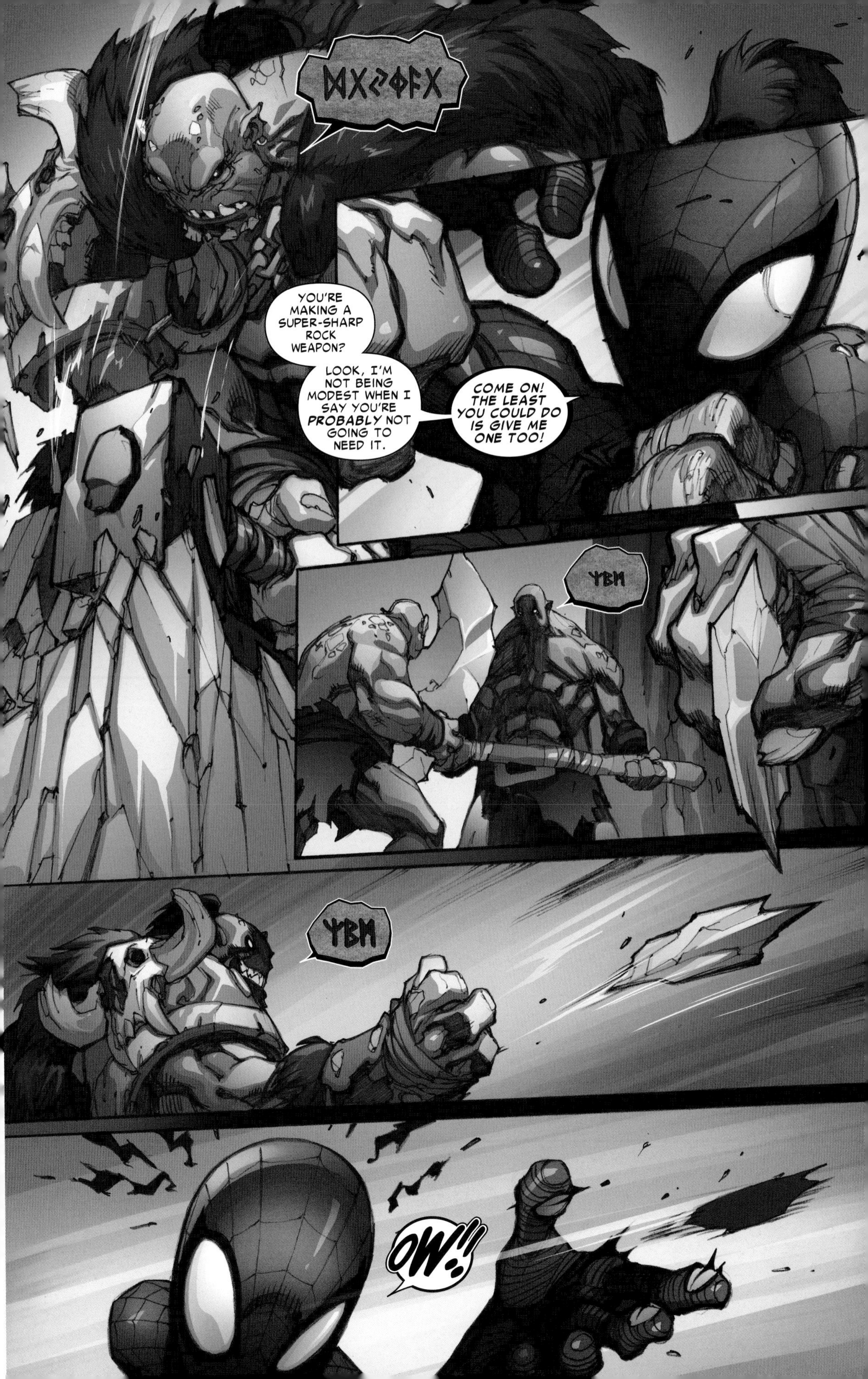
YOU'RE MAKING A SUPER-SHARP ROCK WEAPON?
LOOK, I'M NOT BEING MODEST WHEN I SAY YOU'RE PROBABLY NOT GOING TO NEED IT.
COME ON! THE LEAST YOU COULD DO IS GIVE ME ONE TOO!
OW!!

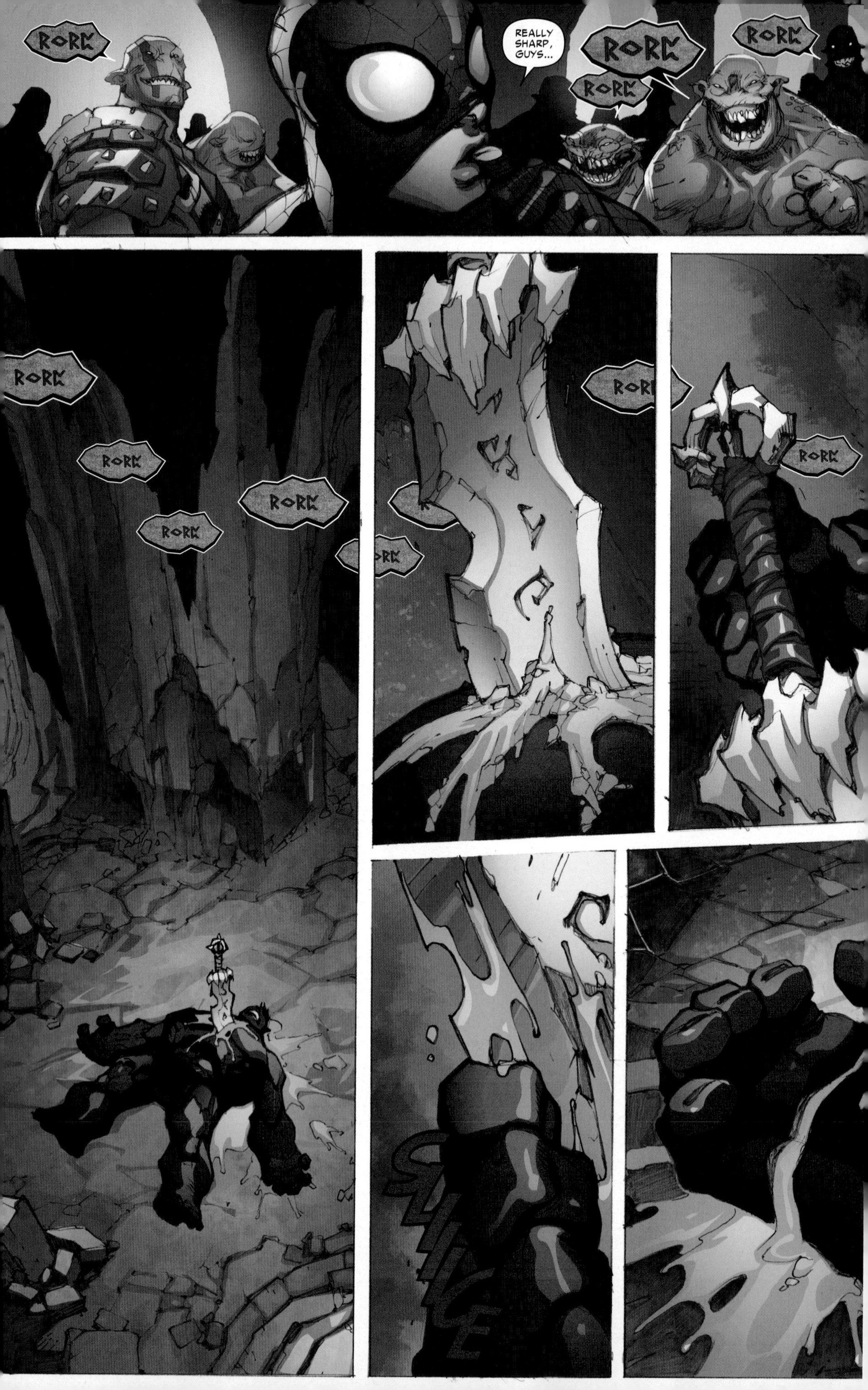
RORK
REALLY SHARP, GUYS...
RORK
RORK
RORK
RORK
RORK
RORK
RORK
RORK

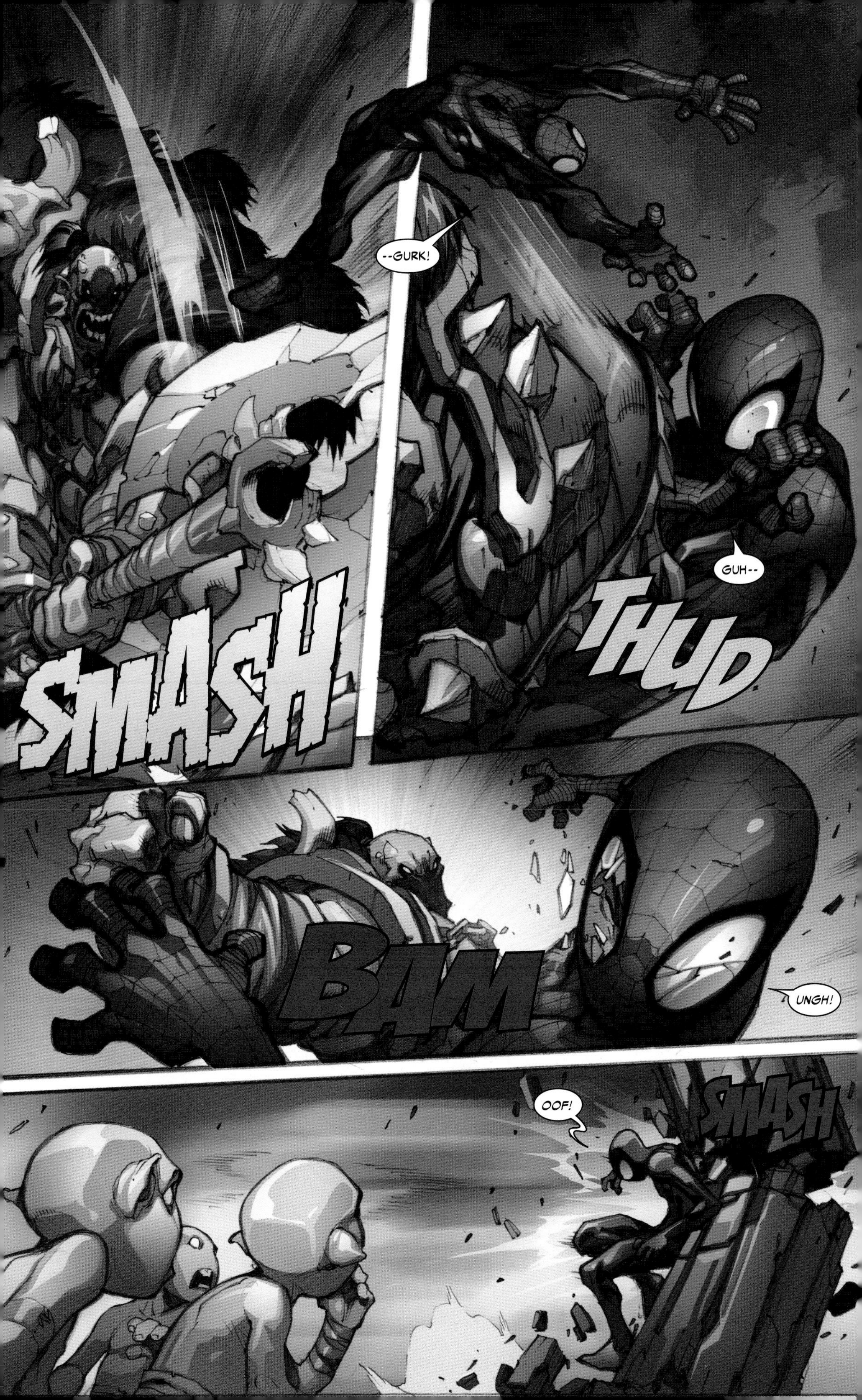
--GURK!
SMASH
GUH--
THUD
BAM
UNGH!
OOF!
SMASH

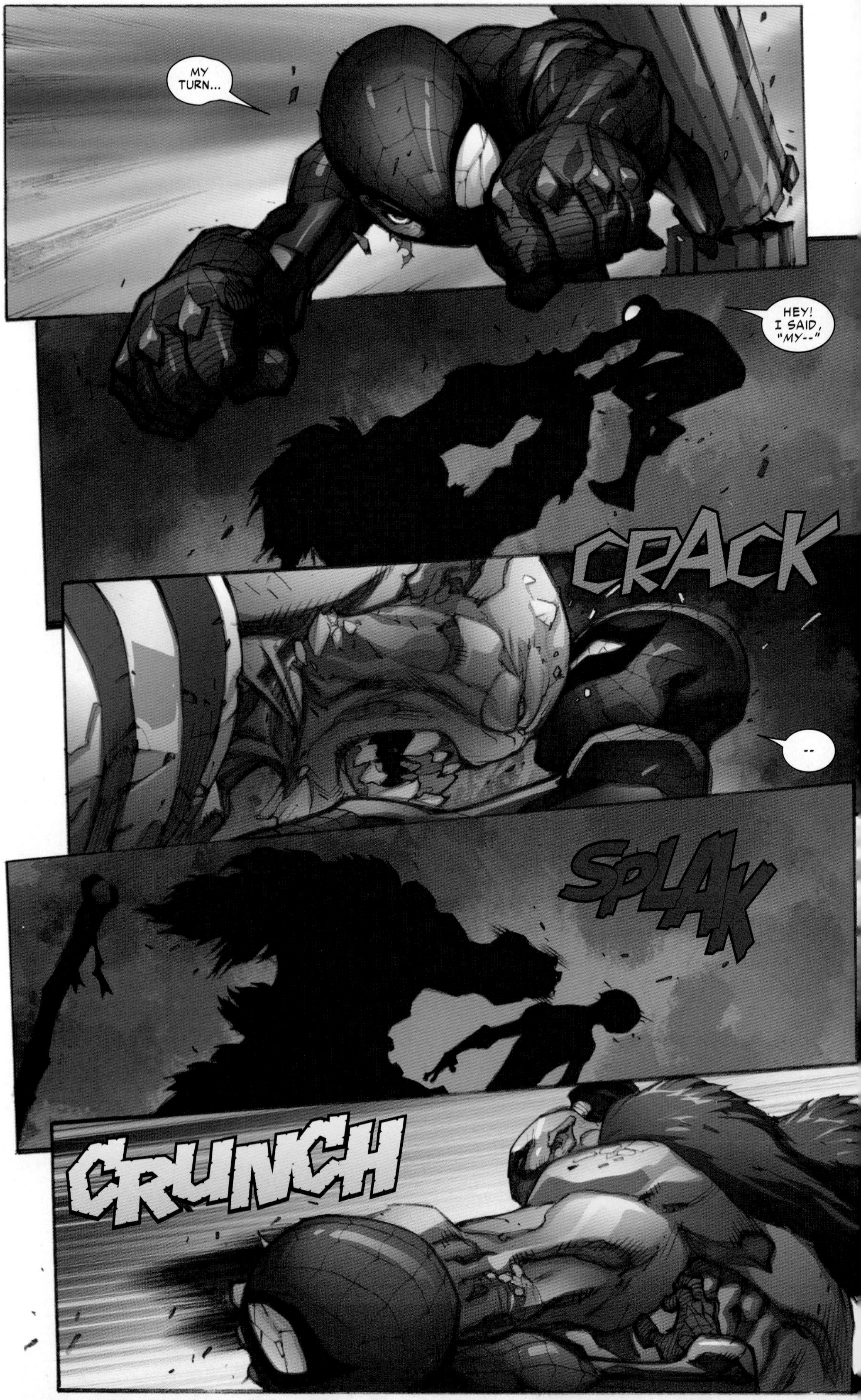
MY TURN...
HEY! I SAID, "MY--"
CRACK
--
SPLAK
CRUNCH

THE...*KAFF!* THE AVENGERS ARE...

...ARE GONNA BE REALLY... *HNN...*

...REALLY MAD IF YOU KILL ME.

I'M KIND OF THEIR MASCOT.

ᚹᚱᚠᛖᚠᛗᚱᚠ ᚱᚱᛖᛋᛖᚾᛖᚷᛋ

RA'KTAR REMINDS YOU THAT YOU HAVE NO STAKE TO THESE LANDS. WALK AWAY AND LEAVE HIM TO HIS SLAUGHTER.

PASS.

ᚠᛖᚠ ᚠᛖᚠ

THE GREAT RA'KTAR ASKS IF YOU ARE READY TO DIE...

N-NOT YET... I MEAN...YEAH, IT LOOKS LIKE THAT'S HOW IT'S GOING TO SHAKE OUT, BUT, HEH HEH...

I'VE GOT A FOURTH QUARTER ADDITION TO THE BUCKET LIST.

THWIP!

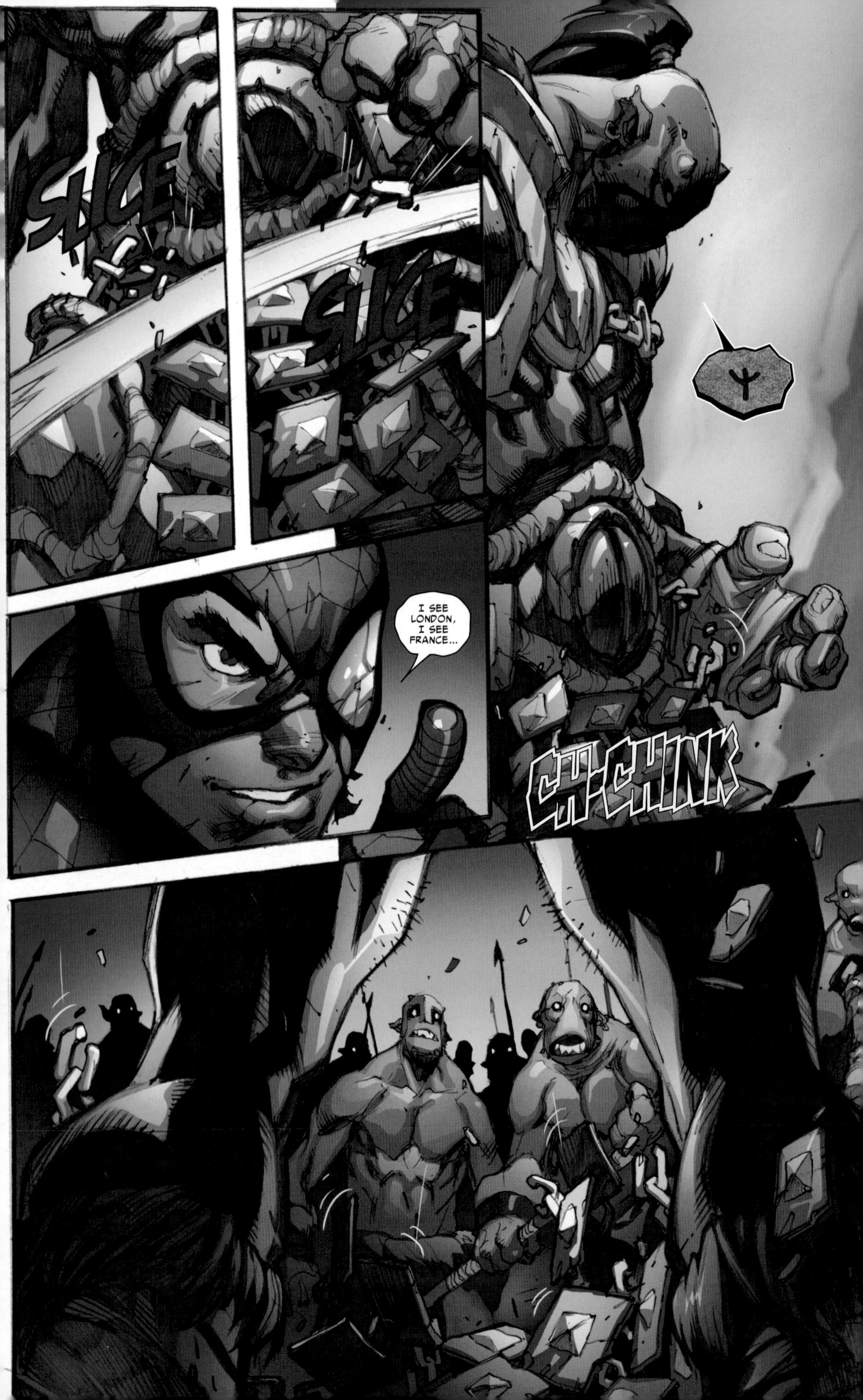
SLICE
SLICE
I SEE LONDON, I SEE FRANCE...
CH-CHINK

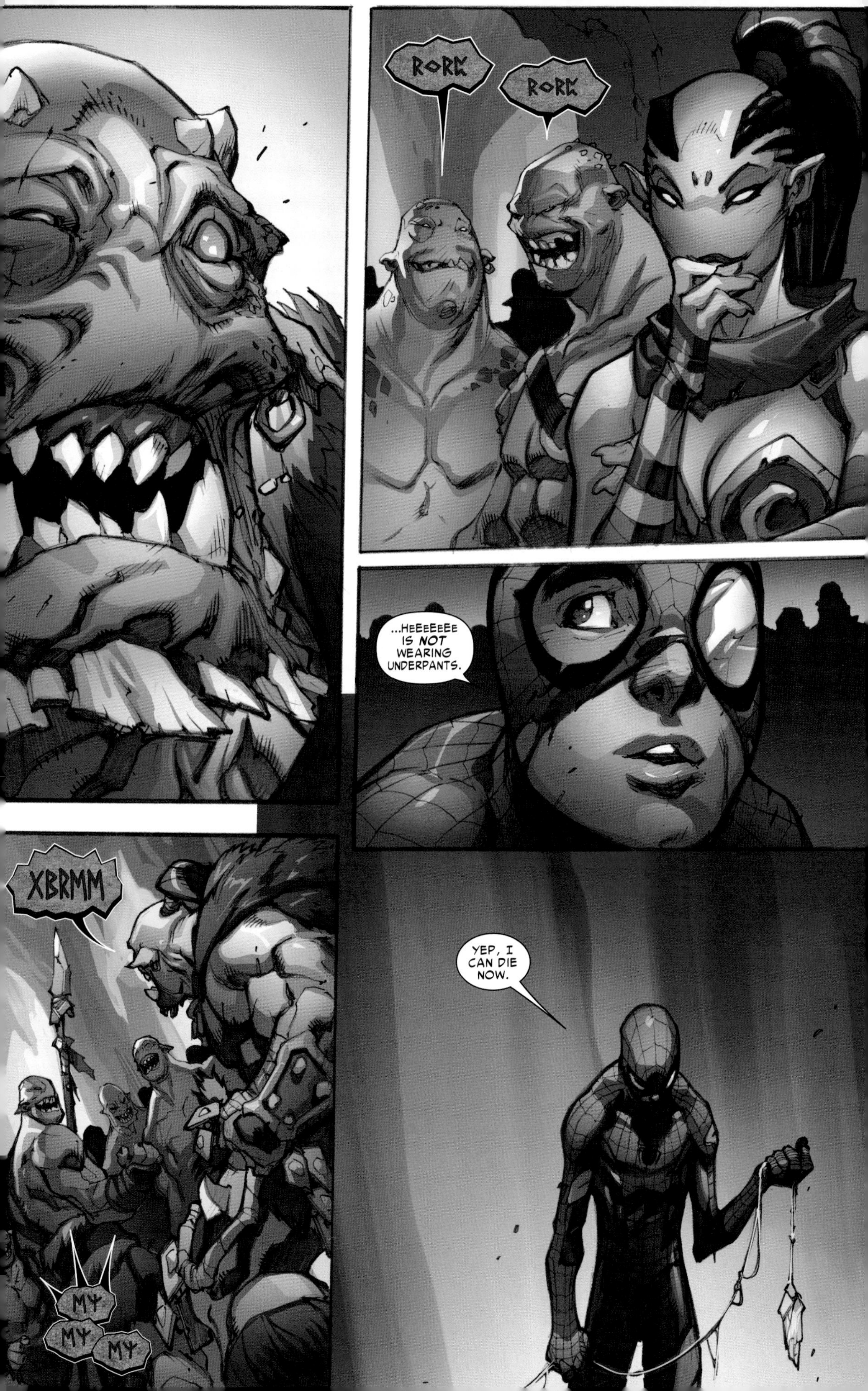
RORK
RORK
...HEEEEEEE IS *NOT* WEARING UNDERPANTS.
XBRMM
MY
MY
MY
YEP, I CAN DIE NOW.

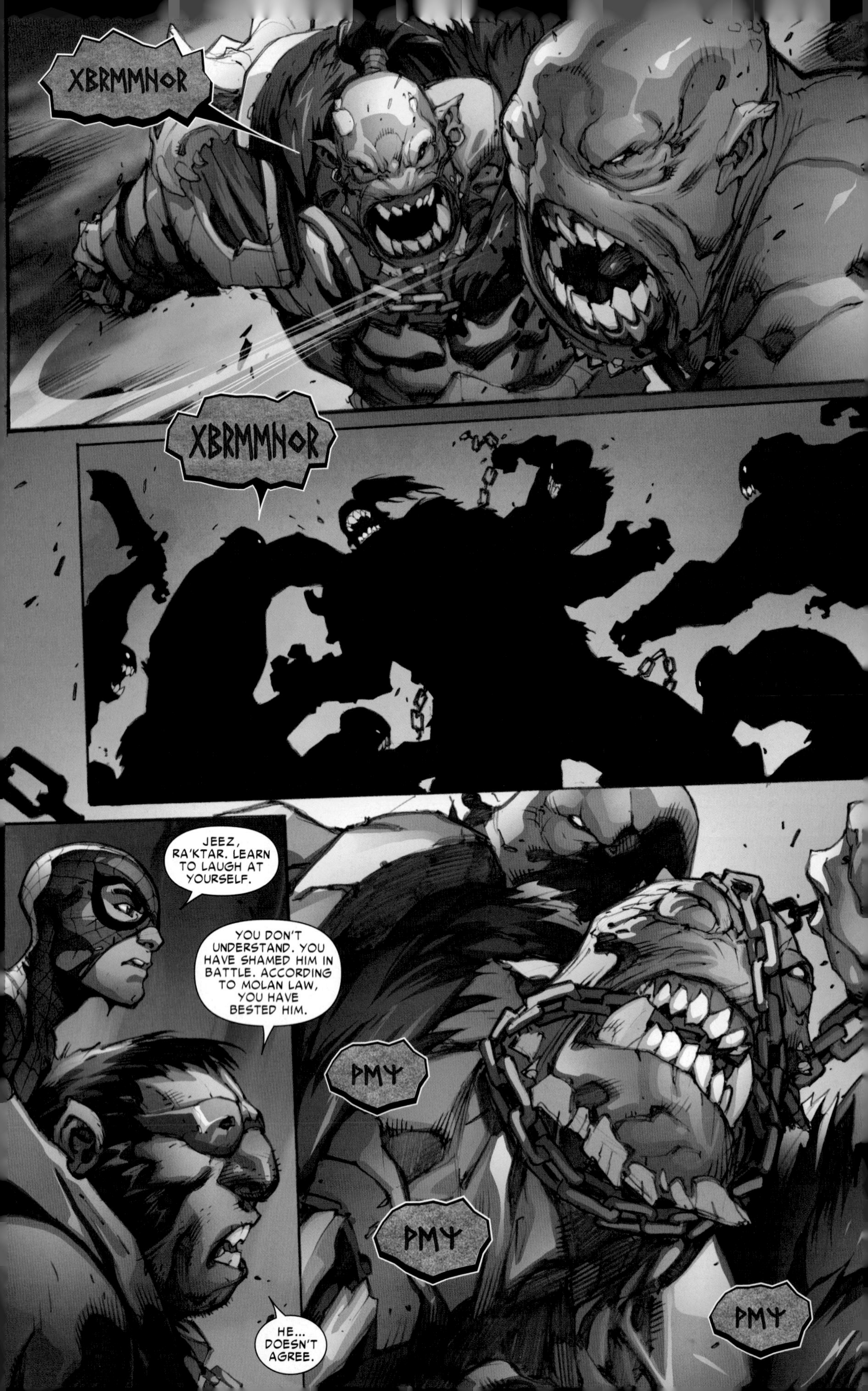
XBRMMNOR
XBRMMNOR
JEEZ, RA'KTAR. LEARN TO LAUGH AT YOURSELF.
YOU DON'T UNDERSTAND. YOU HAVE SHAMED HIM IN BATTLE. ACCORDING TO MOLAN LAW, YOU HAVE BESTED HIM.
PMY
PMY
HE... DOESN'T AGREE.
PMY

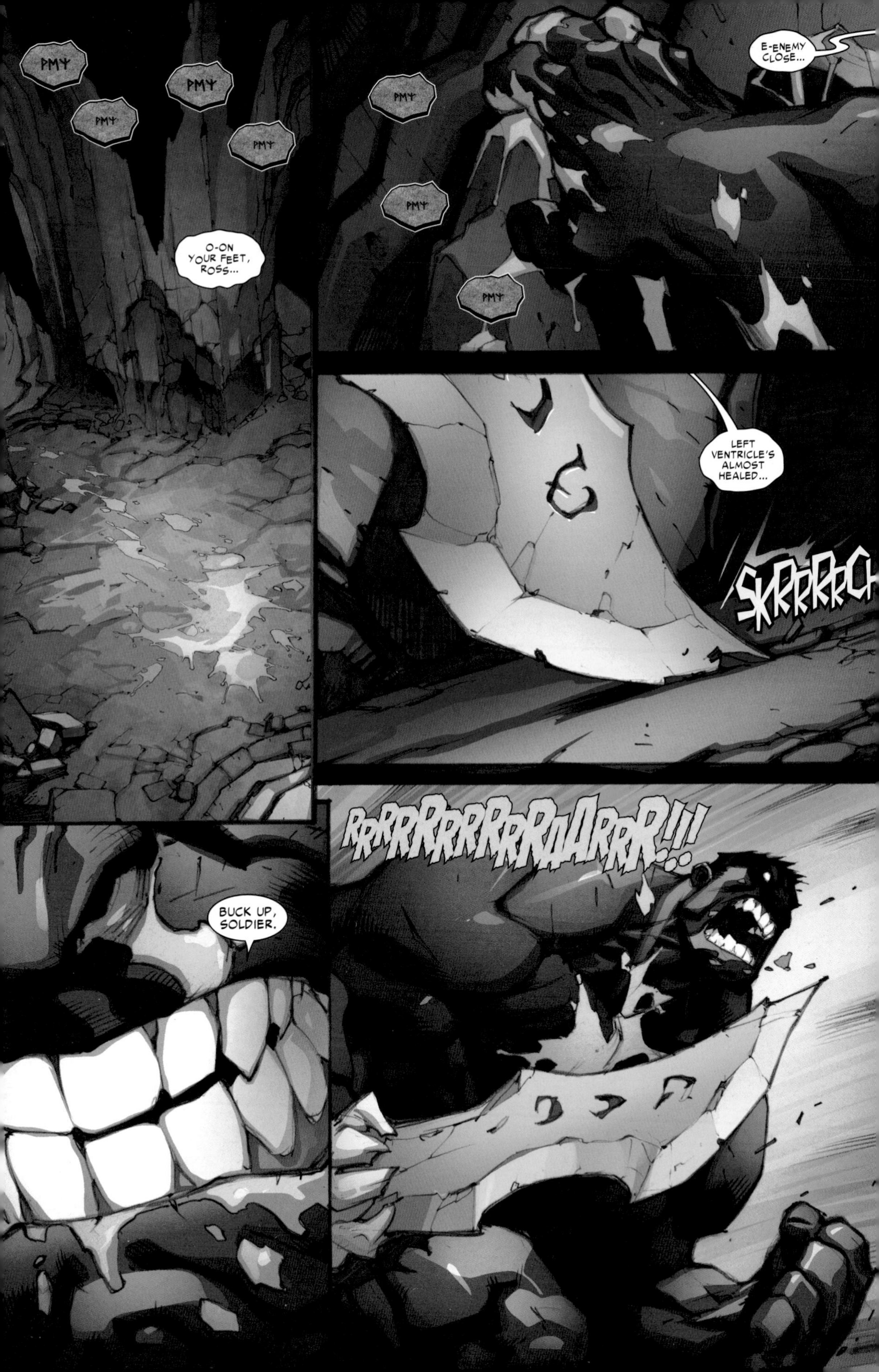
PMY
PMY
PMY
PMY
O-ON YOUR FEET, ROSS...
PMY
PMY
PMY
E-ENEMY CLOSE...
LEFT VENTRICLE'S ALMOST HEALED...
SKRRRRCH
BUCK UP, SOLDIER.
RRRRRRRRRRRRAARRR!!!

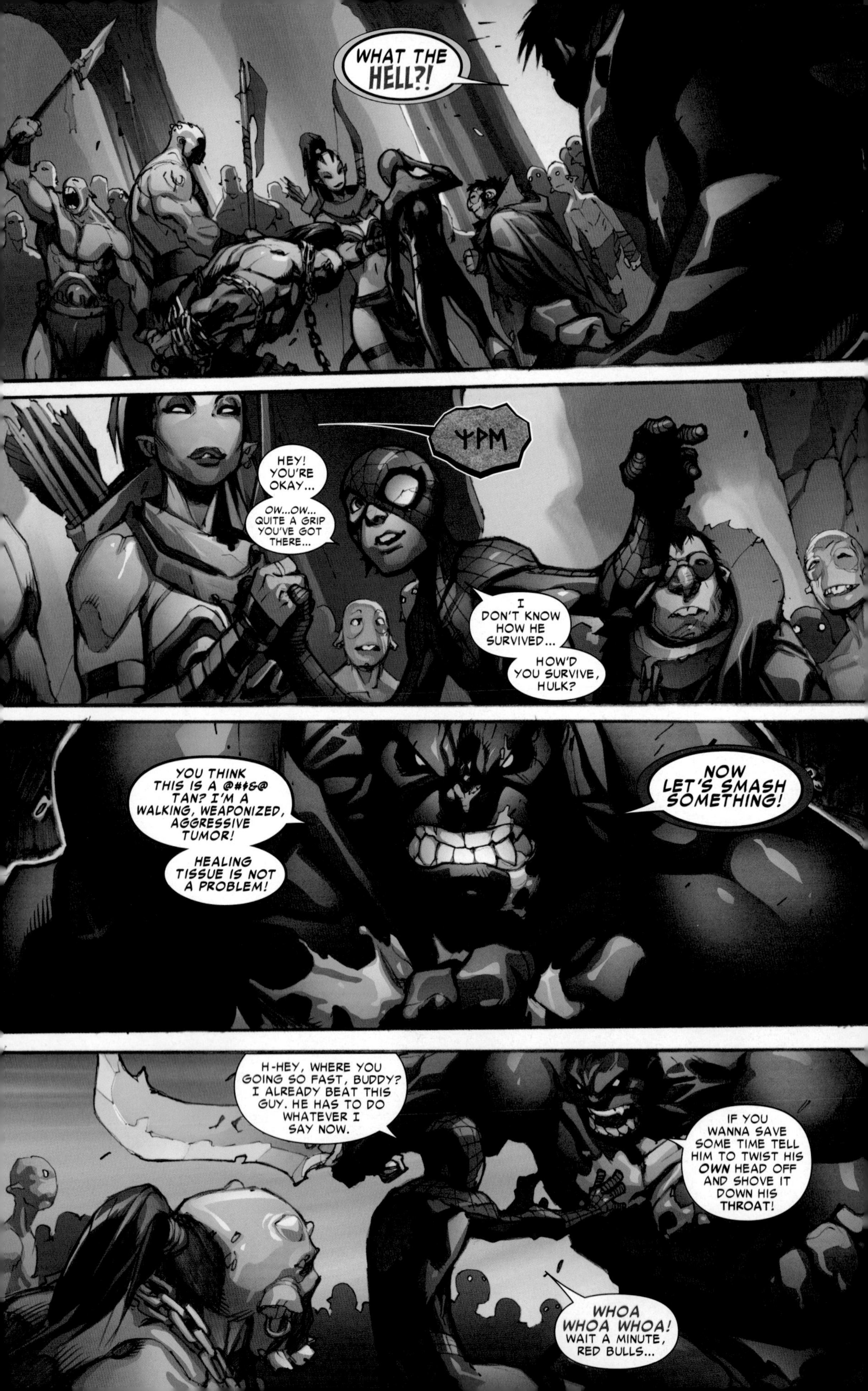
WHAT THE HELL?!
HEY! YOU'RE OKAY...
OW...OW... QUITE A GRIP YOU'VE GOT THERE...
ᛉᚹᛗ
I DON'T KNOW HOW HE SURVIVED...
HOW'D YOU SURVIVE, HULK?
YOU THINK THIS IS A @#$&@ TAN? I'M A WALKING, WEAPONIZED, AGGRESSIVE TUMOR!
HEALING TISSUE IS NOT A PROBLEM!
NOW LET'S SMASH SOMETHING!
H-HEY, WHERE YOU GOING SO FAST, BUDDY? I ALREADY BEAT THIS GUY. HE HAS TO DO WHATEVER I SAY NOW.
IF YOU WANNA SAVE SOME TIME TELL HIM TO TWIST HIS OWN HEAD OFF AND SHOVE IT DOWN HIS THROAT!
WHOA WHOA WHOA! WAIT A MINUTE, RED BULLS...

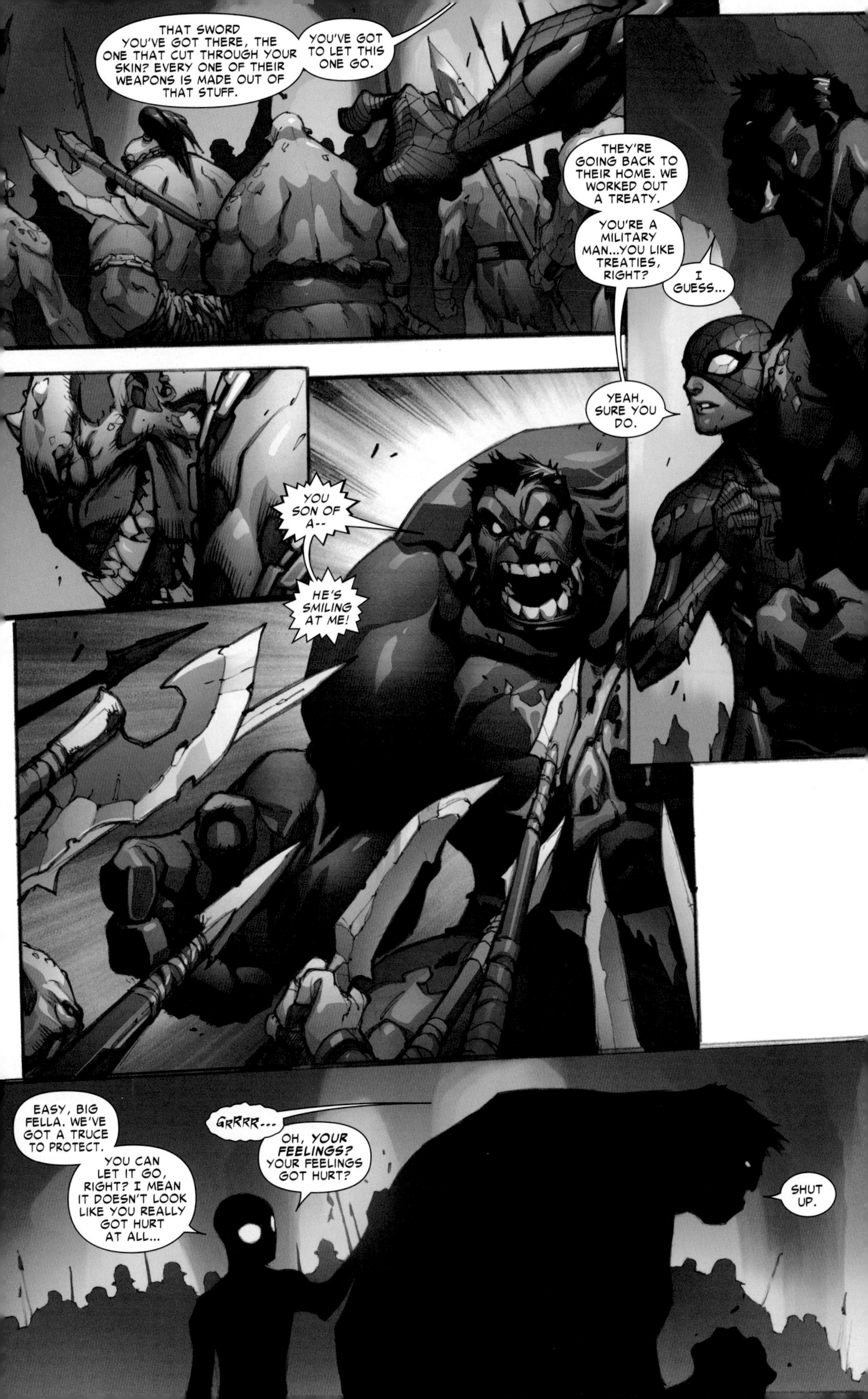
THAT SWORD YOU'VE GOT THERE, THE ONE THAT CUT THROUGH YOUR SKIN? EVERY ONE OF THEIR WEAPONS IS MADE OUT OF THAT STUFF.
YOU'VE GOT TO LET THIS ONE GO.
THEY'RE GOING BACK TO THEIR HOME. WE WORKED OUT A TREATY.
YOU'RE A MILITARY MAN...YOU LIKE TREATIES, RIGHT?
I GUESS...
YEAH, SURE YOU DO.
YOU SON OF A--
HE'S SMILING AT ME!
EASY, BIG FELLA. WE'VE GOT A TRUCE TO PROTECT.
YOU CAN LET IT GO, RIGHT? I MEAN IT DOESN'T LOOK LIKE YOU REALLY GOT HURT AT ALL...
GRRRR...
OH, YOUR FEELINGS? YOUR FEELINGS GOT HURT?
SHUT UP.

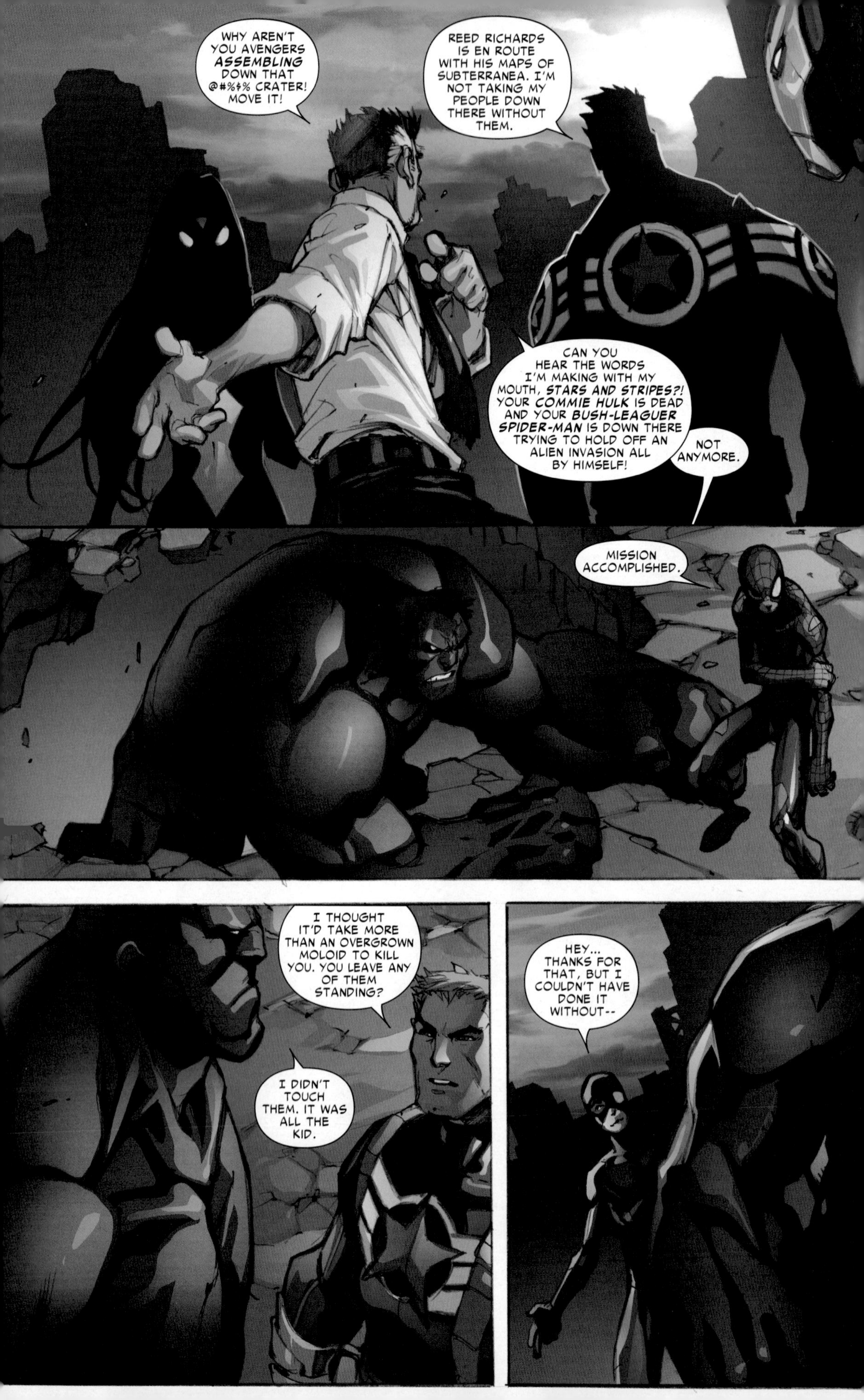
WHY AREN'T YOU AVENGERS ASSEMBLING DOWN THAT @#%$% CRATER! MOVE IT!
REED RICHARDS IS EN ROUTE WITH HIS MAPS OF SUBTERRANEA. I'M NOT TAKING MY PEOPLE DOWN THERE WITHOUT THEM.
CAN YOU HEAR THE WORDS I'M MAKING WITH MY MOUTH, STARS AND STRIPES?! YOUR COMMIE HULK IS DEAD AND YOUR BUSH-LEAGUER SPIDER-MAN IS DOWN THERE TRYING TO HOLD OFF AN ALIEN INVASION ALL BY HIMSELF!
NOT ANYMORE.
MISSION ACCOMPLISHED.
I THOUGHT IT'D TAKE MORE THAN AN OVERGROWN MOLOID TO KILL YOU. YOU LEAVE ANY OF THEM STANDING?
I DIDN'T TOUCH THEM. IT WAS ALL THE KID.
HEY... THANKS FOR THAT, BUT I COULDN'T HAVE DONE IT WITHOUT--

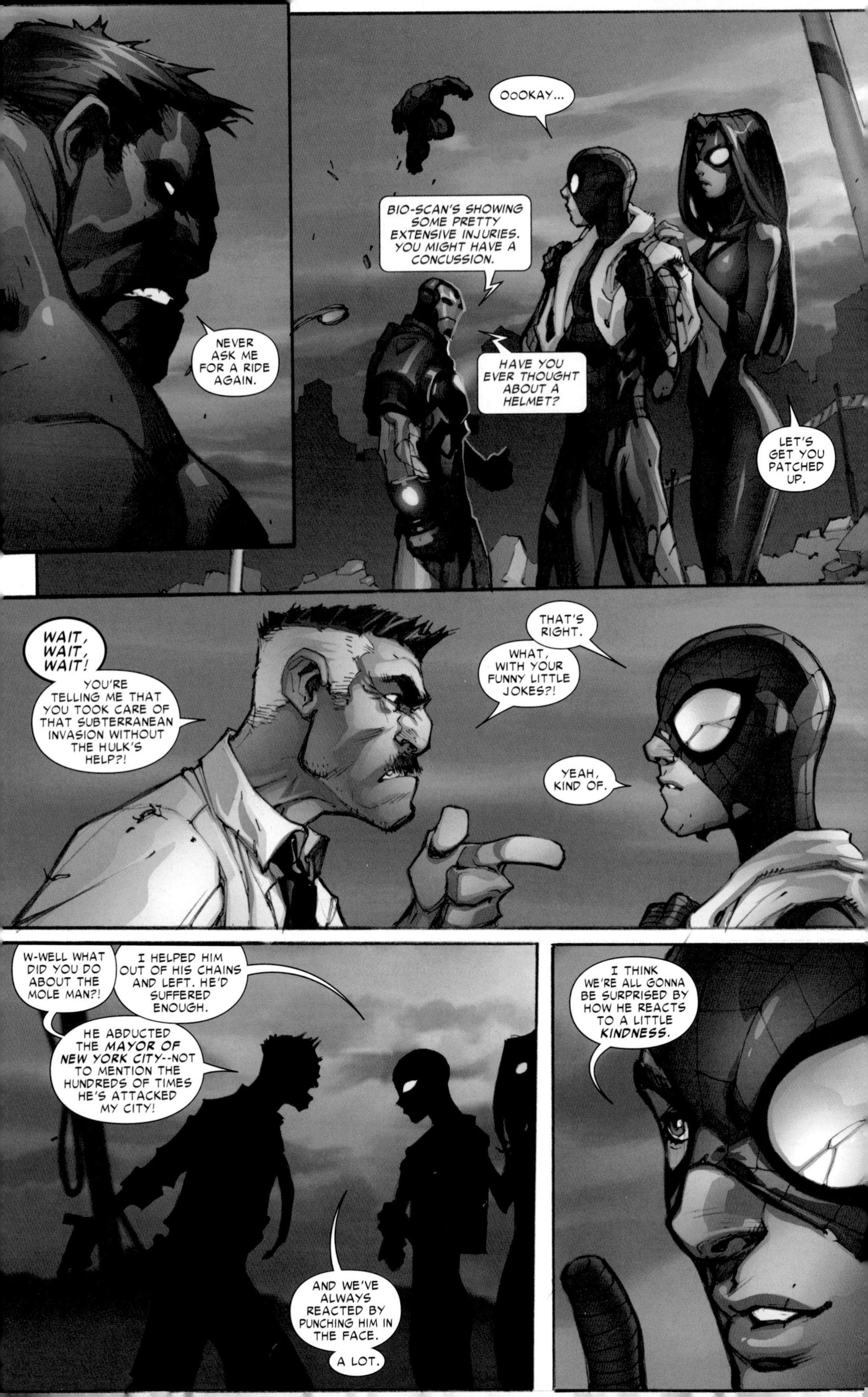
NEVER ASK ME FOR A RIDE AGAIN.
OOOKAY...
BIO-SCAN'S SHOWING SOME PRETTY EXTENSIVE INJURIES. YOU MIGHT HAVE A CONCUSSION.
HAVE YOU EVER THOUGHT ABOUT A HELMET?
LET'S GET YOU PATCHED UP.
WAIT, WAIT, WAIT!
YOU'RE TELLING ME THAT YOU TOOK CARE OF THAT SUBTERRANEAN INVASION WITHOUT THE HULK'S HELP?!
THAT'S RIGHT.
WHAT, WITH YOUR FUNNY LITTLE JOKES?!
YEAH, KIND OF.
W-WELL WHAT DID YOU DO ABOUT THE MOLE MAN?!
I HELPED HIM OUT OF HIS CHAINS AND LEFT. HE'D SUFFERED ENOUGH.
HE ABDUCTED THE MAYOR OF NEW YORK CITY--NOT TO MENTION THE HUNDREDS OF TIMES HE'S ATTACKED MY CITY!
AND WE'VE ALWAYS REACTED BY PUNCHING HIM IN THE FACE.
A LOT.
I THINK WE'RE ALL GONNA BE SURPRISED BY HOW HE REACTS TO A LITTLE KINDNESS.

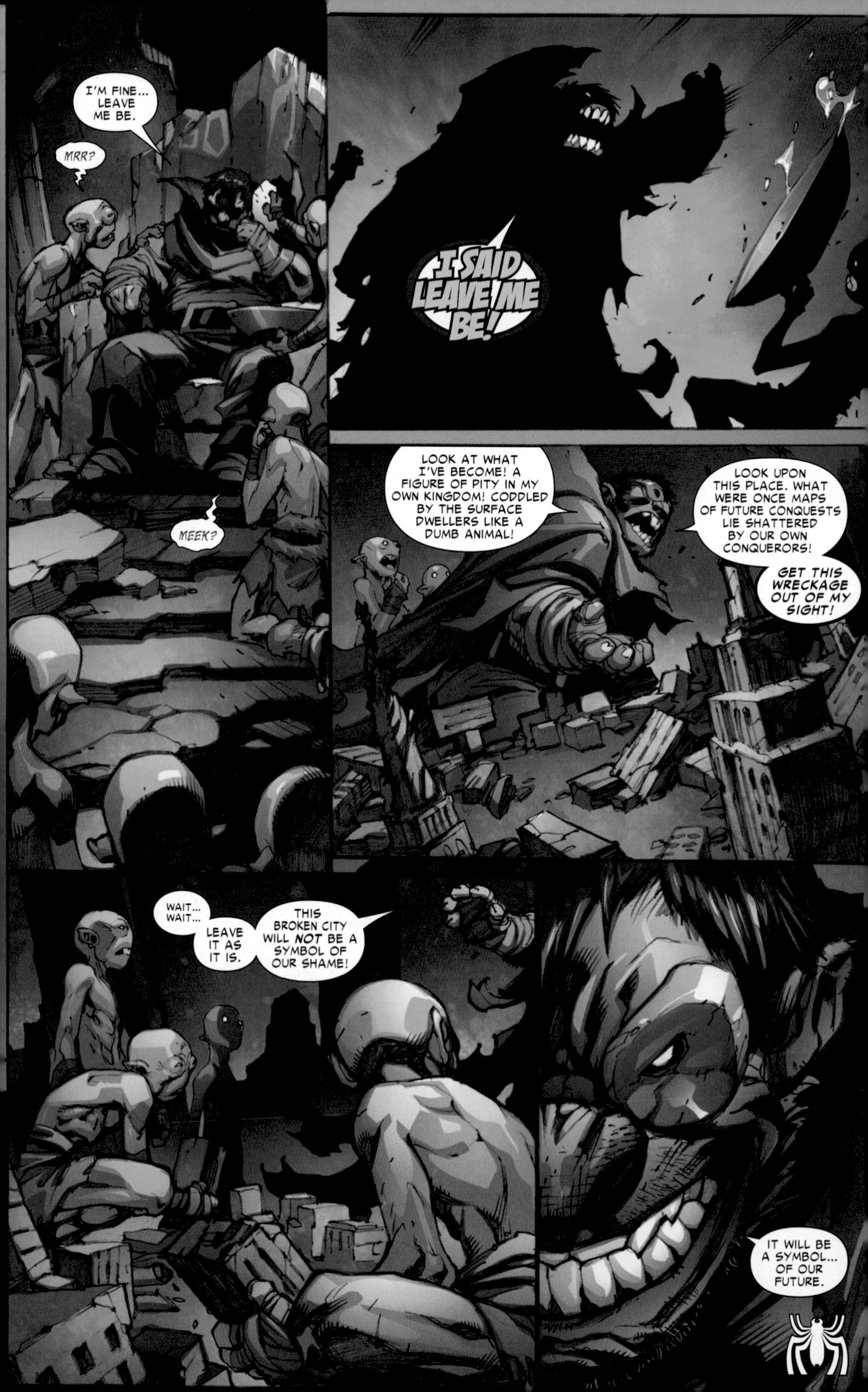

I'M FINE... LEAVE ME BE.
MRR?
MEEK?
I SAID LEAVE ME BE!
LOOK AT WHAT I'VE BECOME! A FIGURE OF PITY IN MY OWN KINGDOM! CODDLED BY THE SURFACE DWELLERS LIKE A DUMB ANIMAL!
LOOK UPON THIS PLACE. WHAT WERE ONCE MAPS OF FUTURE CONQUESTS LIE SHATTERED BY OUR OWN CONQUERORS!
GET THIS WRECKAGE OUT OF MY SIGHT!
WAIT... WAIT...
LEAVE IT AS IT IS.
THIS BROKEN CITY WILL NOT BE A SYMBOL OF OUR SHAME!
IT WILL BE A SYMBOL... OF OUR FUTURE.

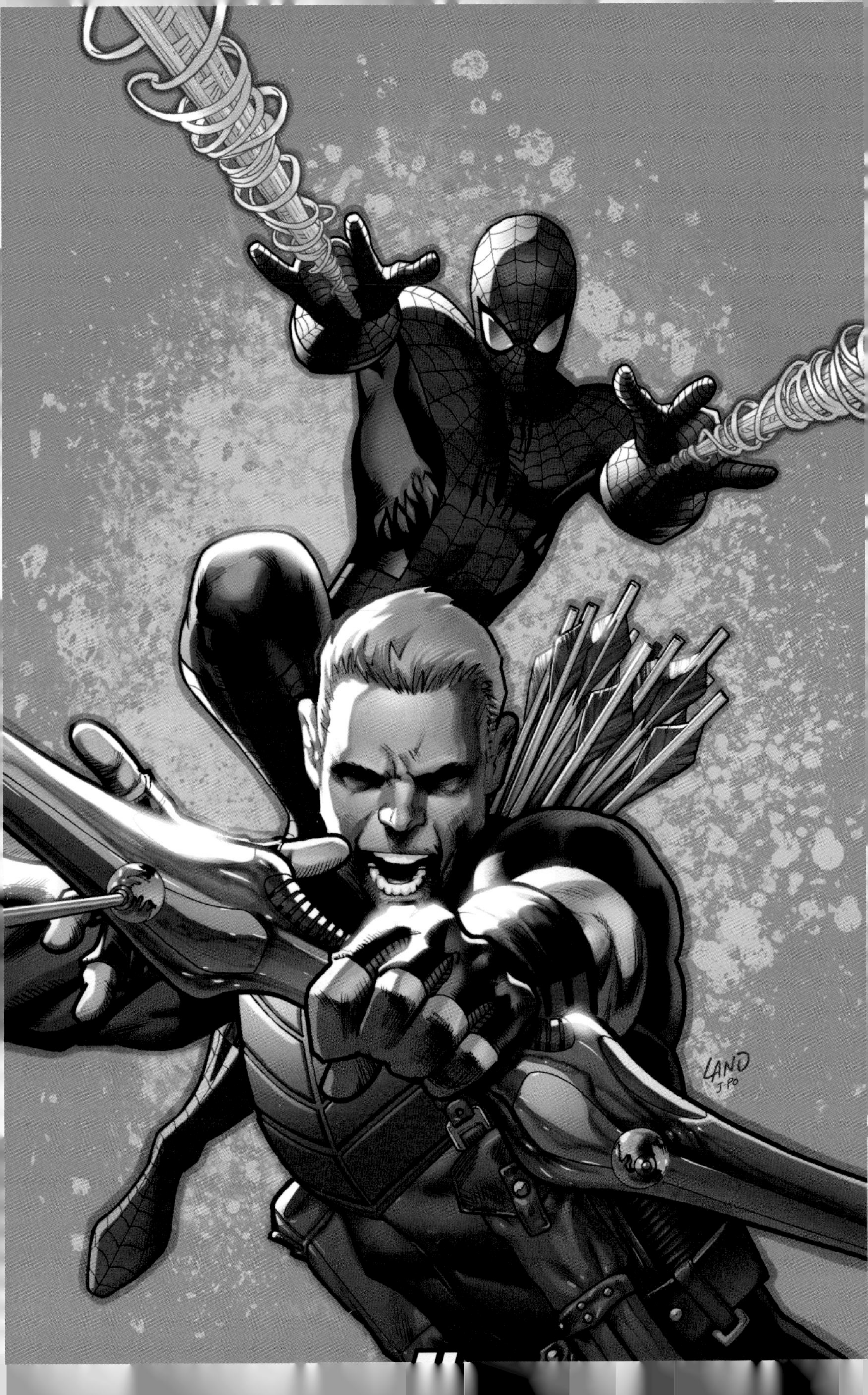
LAND
J-PO

While attending a demonstration in radiology, high school student Peter Parker was bitten by a spider which had accidentally been exposed to radioactive rays. Through a miracle of science, Peter soon found that he had gained the spider's powers...and had, in effect, become a human spider! Later he joined the Avengers (who have a movie coming out soon).

AVENGING SPIDER-MAN

After attending a demonstration in radiology, orphan Clint Barton was shot by a radioactive arrow and frozen in World War Two ice where he stayed until he was defrosted by Amazon Warriors during the super hero CIVIL WAR. Soon a hawk bit him in the eye and thus was born...

HAWKEYE*

AVENGING SPIDER-MAN

WRITER: **ZEB WELLS**   ARTIST: **GREG LAND**

INKER: **JAY LEISTEN**   COLOR ART: **WIL QUINTANA**

LETTERER: **VC's JOE CARAMAGNA**   COVER: **GREG LAND & JUSTIN PONSOR**

VARIANT COVER: **DALE KEOWN & PETER STEIGERWALD**

ASSISTANT EDITOR: **ELLIE PYLE**   EDITOR: **STEPHEN WACKER**

EXECUTIVE EDITOR: **TOM BREVOORT**   EDITOR IN CHIEF: **AXEL ALONSO**

CHIEF CREATIVE OFFICER: **JOE QUESADA**   PUBLISHER: **DAN BUCKLEY**   EXECUTIVE PRODUCER: **ALAN FINE**

*Sorry, folks. Wacker's an idiot who doesn't do a lot of research. ACTUALLY Clint Barton was orphaned at an early age and ran away to join the circus where he was trained to be an expert archer. While initially following a life of petty crime, Clint was inspired by the heroism of Iron Man to prove his skills to Earth's Mightiest Heroes and has become one of their most legendary members. How Wacker cannot know all this at this stage in his "career" is beyond me. -Zeb

Central Park, New York City.

TEEN DIVISION, ON YOUR MARK!

GET SET!

F--

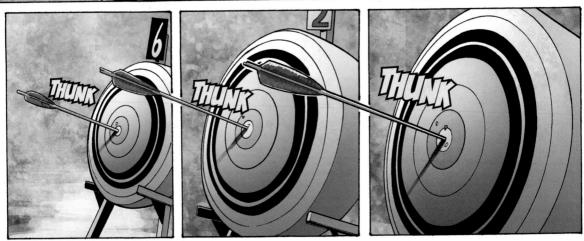

THUNK

THUNK

THUNK

WHO RELEASED?

NO ONE.

OH. STUPID AVENGERS.

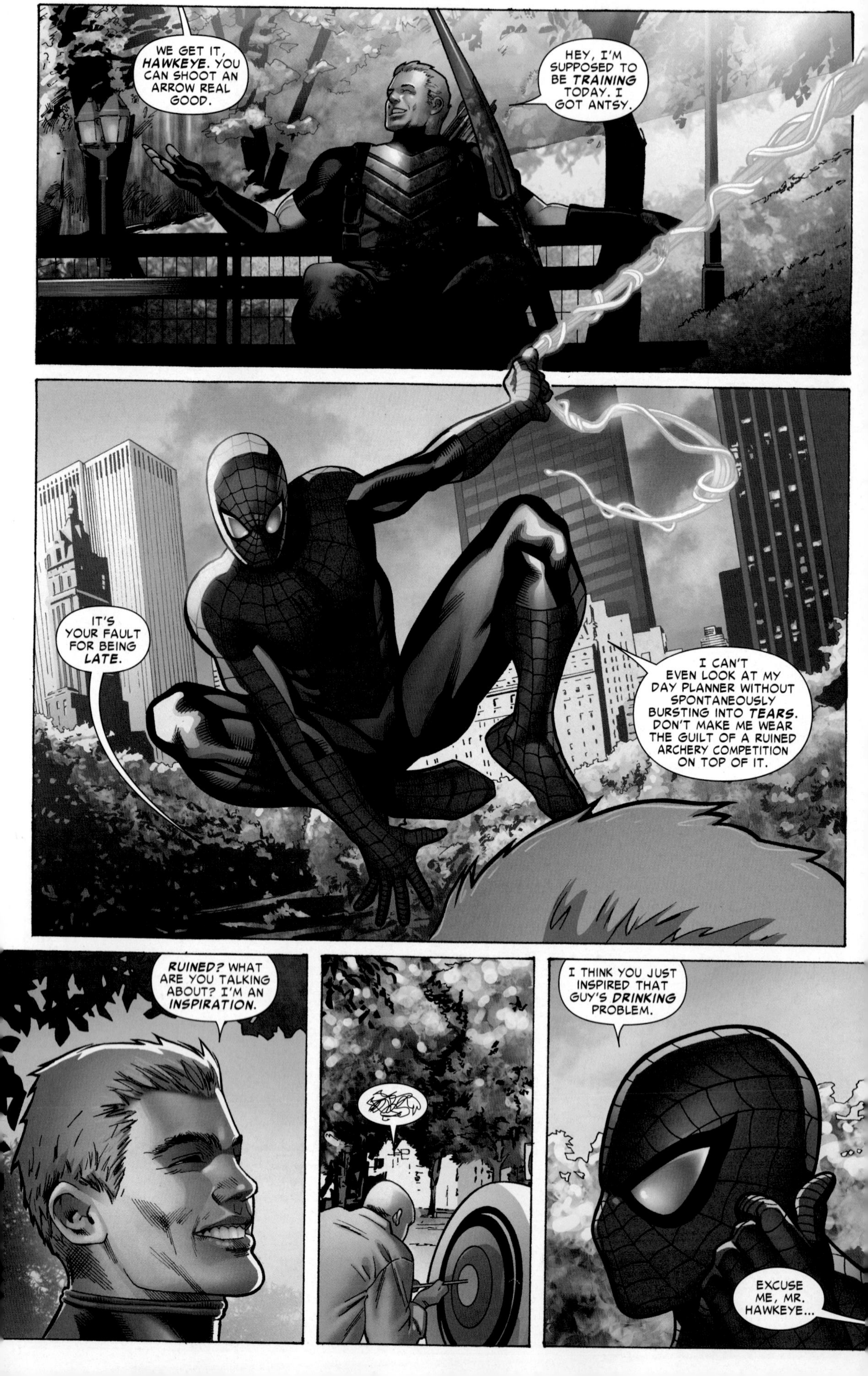
WE GET IT, HAWKEYE. YOU CAN SHOOT AN ARROW REAL GOOD.
HEY, I'M SUPPOSED TO BE TRAINING TODAY. I GOT ANTSY.
IT'S YOUR FAULT FOR BEING LATE.
I CAN'T EVEN LOOK AT MY DAY PLANNER WITHOUT SPONTANEOUSLY BURSTING INTO TEARS. DON'T MAKE ME WEAR THE GUILT OF A RUINED ARCHERY COMPETITION ON TOP OF IT.
RUINED? WHAT ARE YOU TALKING ABOUT? I'M AN INSPIRATION.
I THINK YOU JUST INSPIRED THAT GUY'S DRINKING PROBLEM.
EXCUSE ME, MR. HAWKEYE...

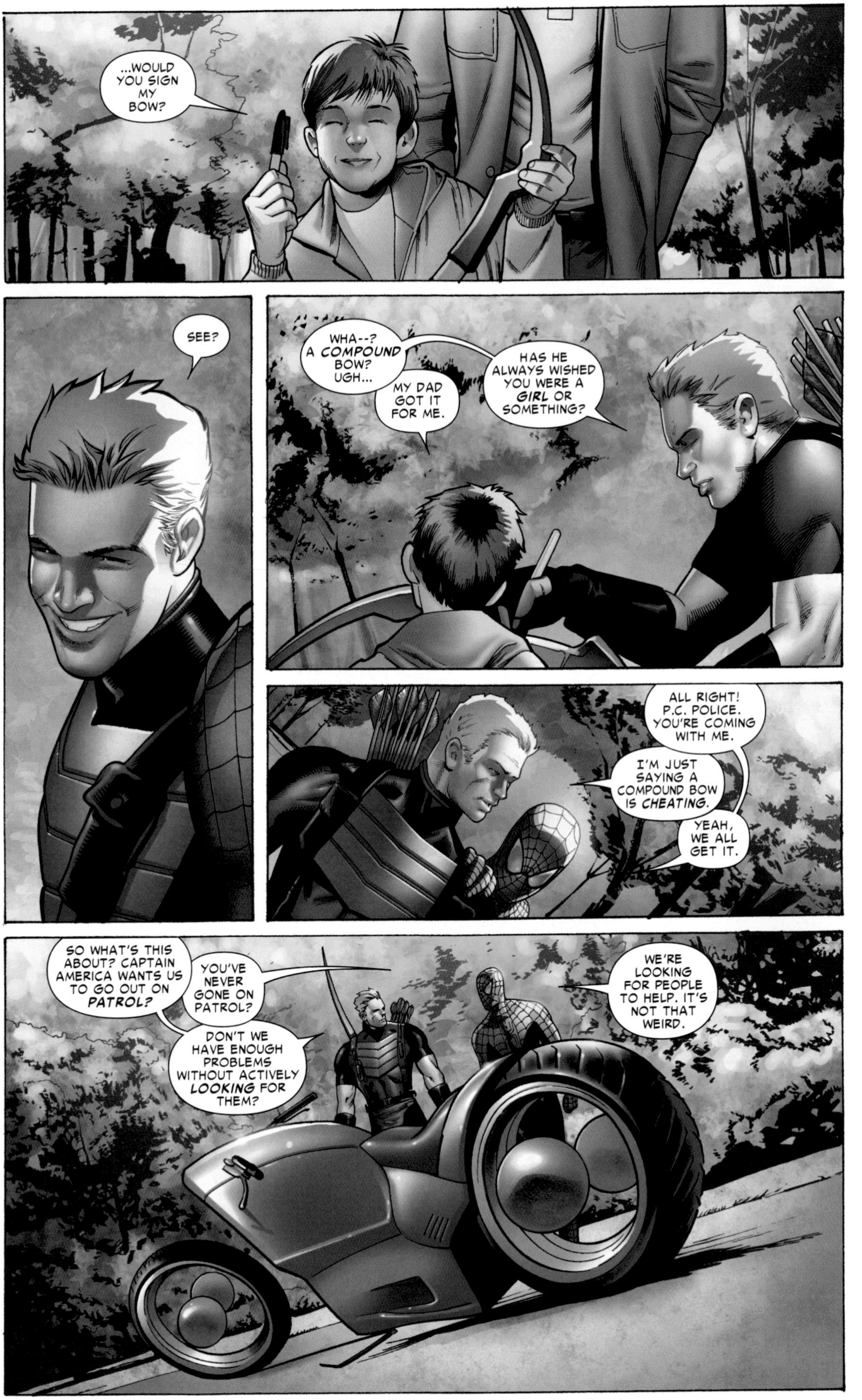

...WOULD YOU SIGN MY BOW?
SEE?
WHA--? A COMPOUND BOW? UGH...
MY DAD GOT IT FOR ME.
HAS HE ALWAYS WISHED YOU WERE A GIRL OR SOMETHING?
ALL RIGHT! P.C. POLICE. YOU'RE COMING WITH ME.
I'M JUST SAYING A COMPOUND BOW IS CHEATING.
YEAH, WE ALL GET IT.
SO WHAT'S THIS ABOUT? CAPTAIN AMERICA WANTS US TO GO OUT ON PATROL?
YOU'VE NEVER GONE ON PATROL?
DON'T WE HAVE ENOUGH PROBLEMS WITHOUT ACTIVELY LOOKING FOR THEM?
WE'RE LOOKING FOR PEOPLE TO HELP. IT'S NOT THAT WEIRD.

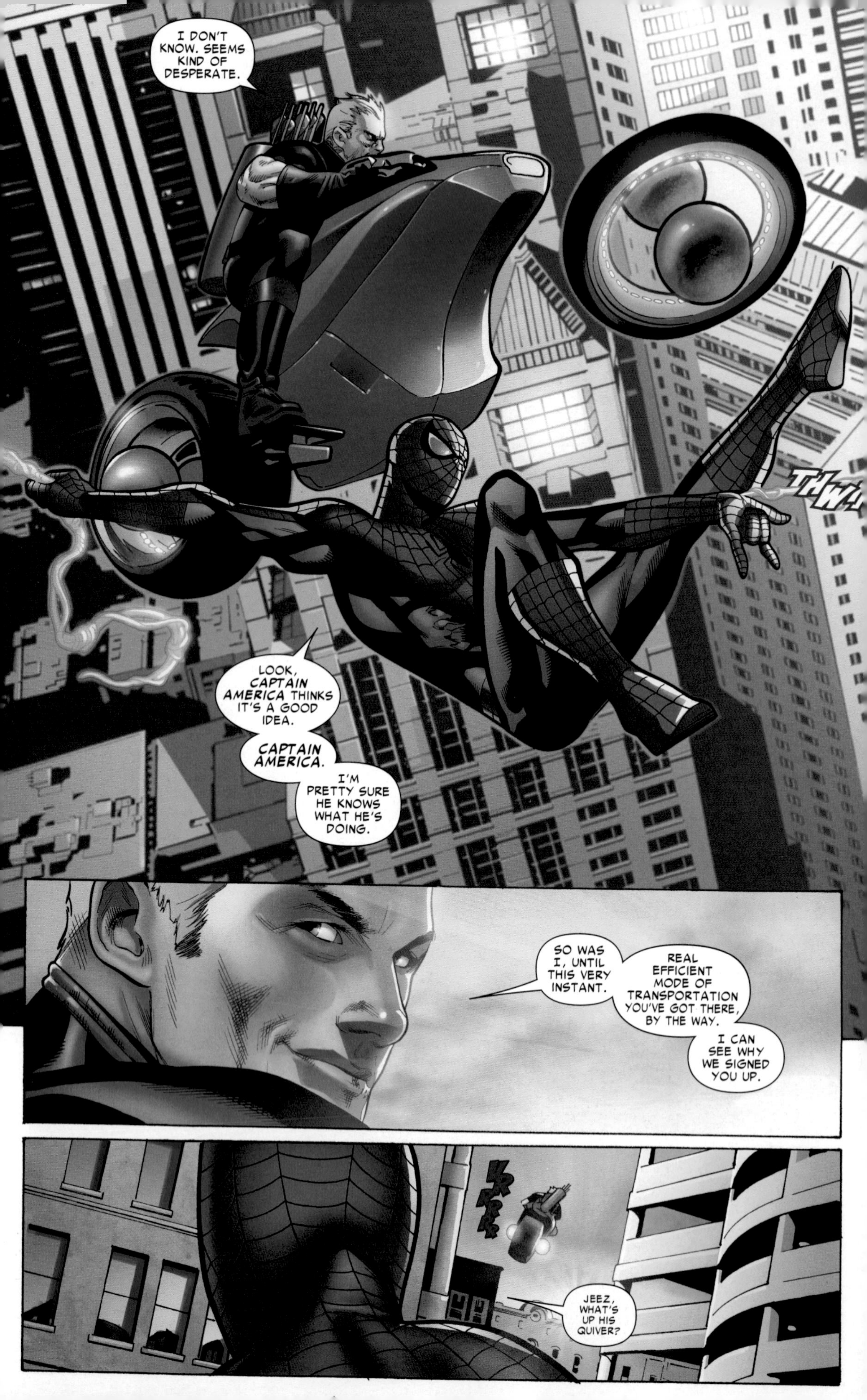
I DON'T KNOW. SEEMS KIND OF DESPERATE.
LOOK, CAPTAIN AMERICA THINKS IT'S A GOOD IDEA.
CAPTAIN AMERICA.
I'M PRETTY SURE HE KNOWS WHAT HE'S DOING.
SO WAS I, UNTIL THIS VERY INSTANT.
REAL EFFICIENT MODE OF TRANSPORTATION YOU'VE GOT THERE, BY THE WAY.
I CAN SEE WHY WE SIGNED YOU UP.
JEEZ, WHAT'S UP HIS QUIVER?

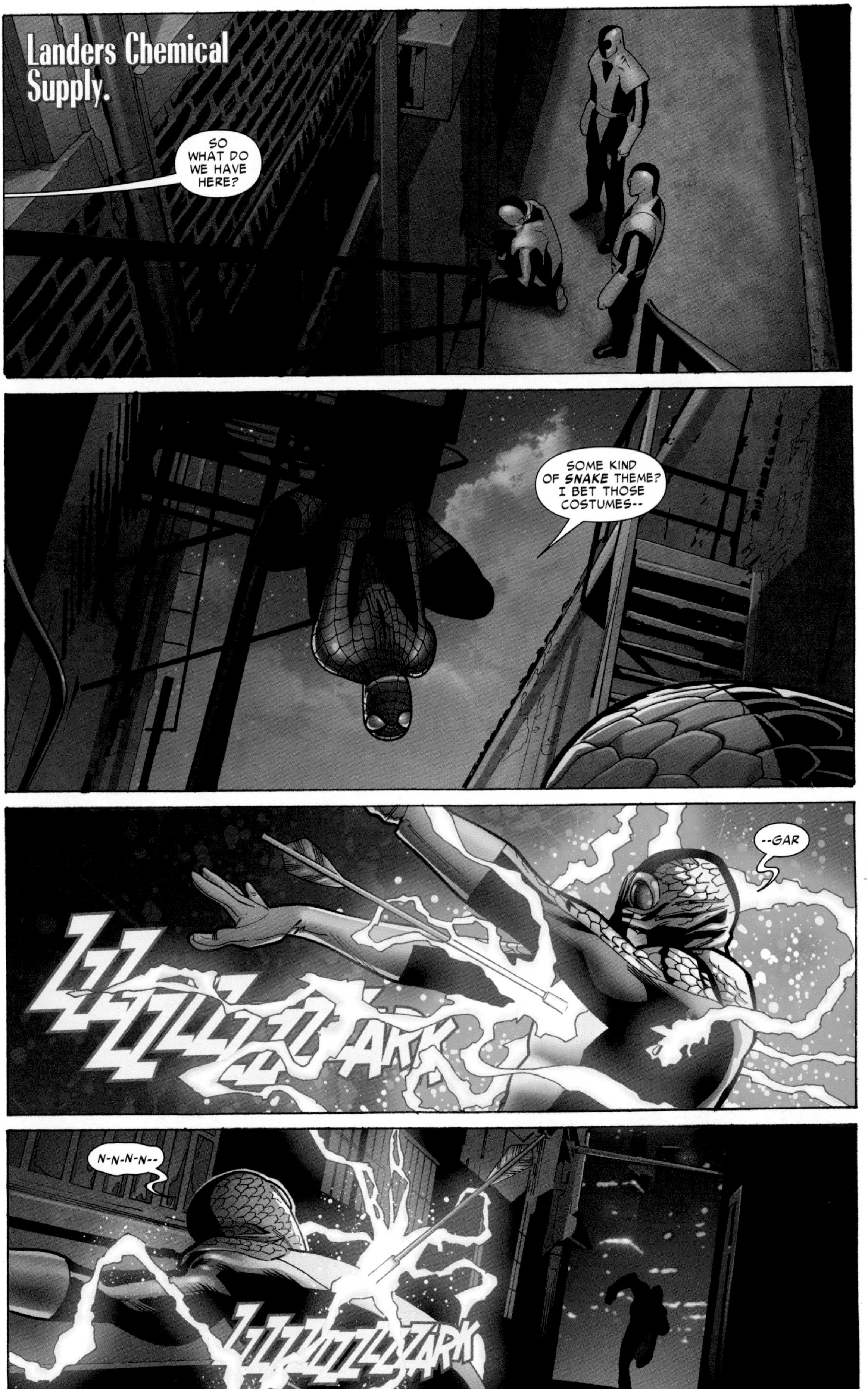
Landers Chemical Supply.
SO WHAT DO WE HAVE HERE?
SOME KIND OF SNAKE THEME? I BET THOSE COSTUMES--
--GAR
ZZZZZZZARK
N-N-N-N--
ZZZZZZZZZARK

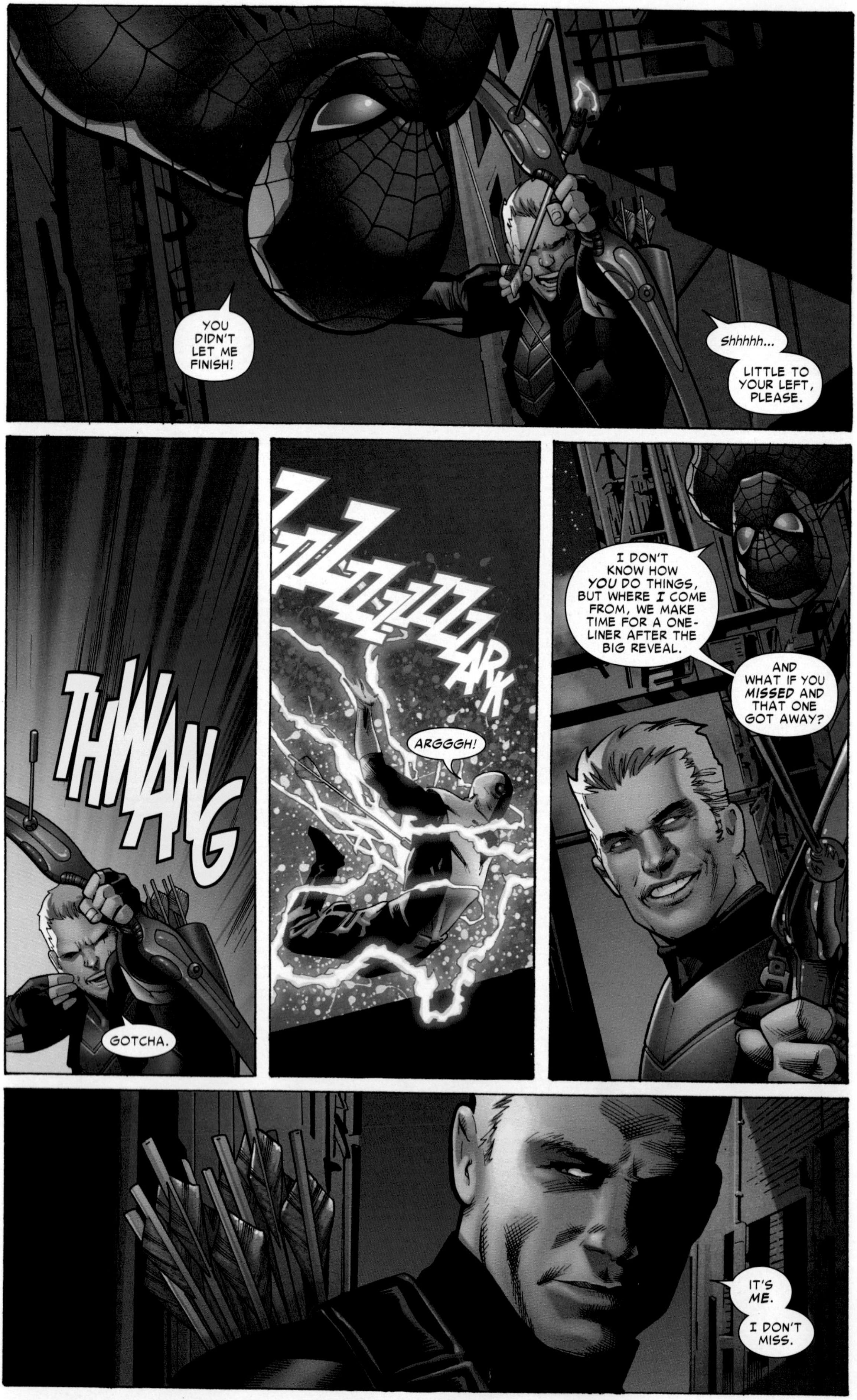
YOU DIDN'T LET ME FINISH!
Shhhhh...
LITTLE TO YOUR LEFT, PLEASE.
THWANG
GOTCHA.
ZZZZZZZZARK
ARGGGH!
I DON'T KNOW HOW YOU DO THINGS, BUT WHERE I COME FROM, WE MAKE TIME FOR A ONE-LINER AFTER THE BIG REVEAL.
AND WHAT IF YOU MISSED AND THAT ONE GOT AWAY?
IT'S ME.
I DON'T MISS.

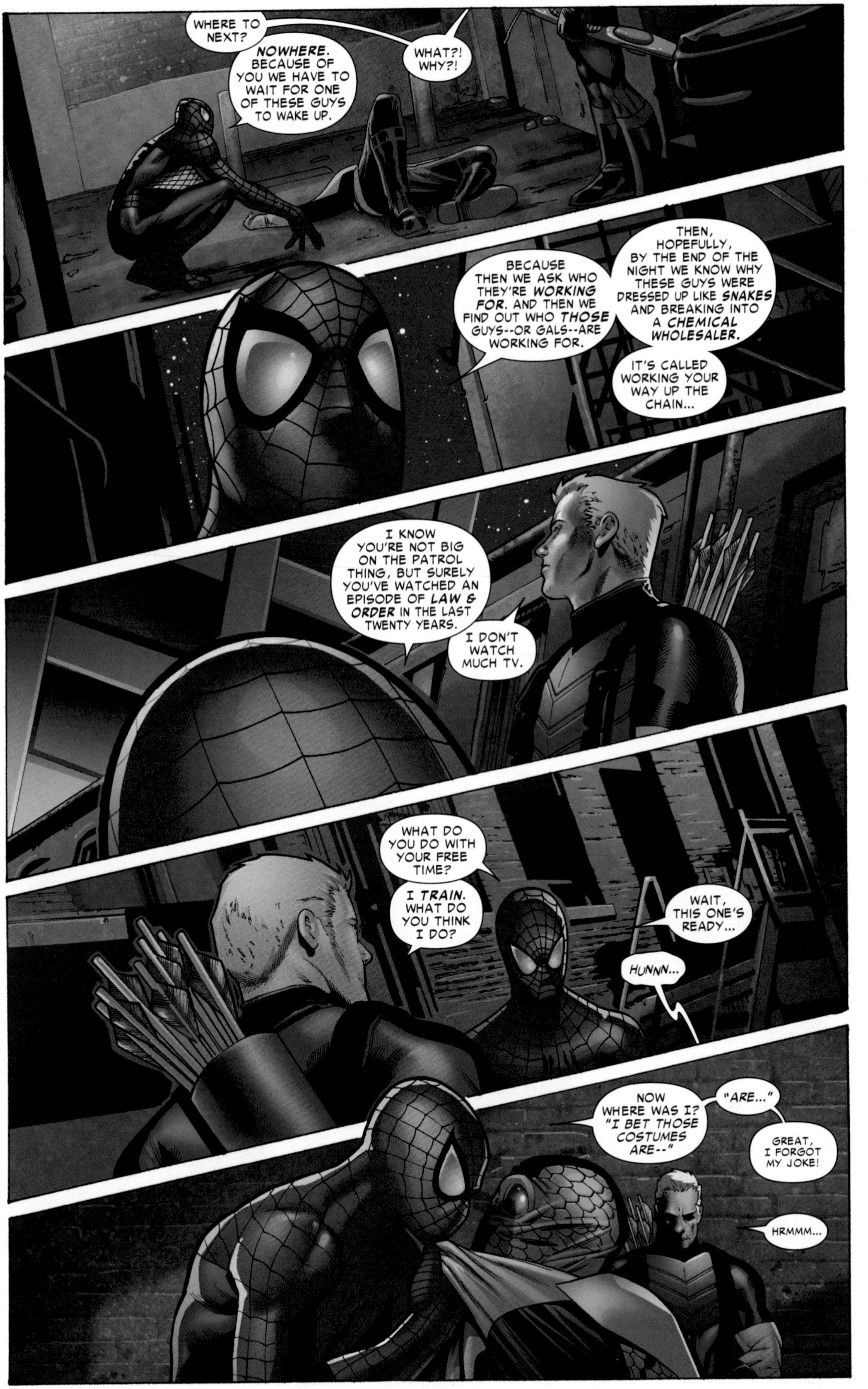
WHERE TO NEXT?
NOWHERE. BECAUSE OF YOU WE HAVE TO WAIT FOR ONE OF THESE GUYS TO WAKE UP.
WHAT?! WHY?!
BECAUSE THEN WE ASK WHO THEY'RE WORKING FOR. AND THEN WE FIND OUT WHO THOSE GUYS--OR GALS--ARE WORKING FOR.
THEN, HOPEFULLY, BY THE END OF THE NIGHT WE KNOW WHY THESE GUYS WERE DRESSED UP LIKE SNAKES AND BREAKING INTO A CHEMICAL WHOLESALER.
IT'S CALLED WORKING YOUR WAY UP THE CHAIN...
I KNOW YOU'RE NOT BIG ON THE PATROL THING, BUT SURELY YOU'VE WATCHED AN EPISODE OF LAW & ORDER IN THE LAST TWENTY YEARS.
I DON'T WATCH MUCH TV.
WHAT DO YOU DO WITH YOUR FREE TIME?
I TRAIN. WHAT DO YOU THINK I DO?
WAIT, THIS ONE'S READY...
HUNNN...
NOW WHERE WAS I? "I BET THOSE COSTUMES ARE--"
"ARE..."
GREAT, I FORGOT MY JOKE!
HRMMM...

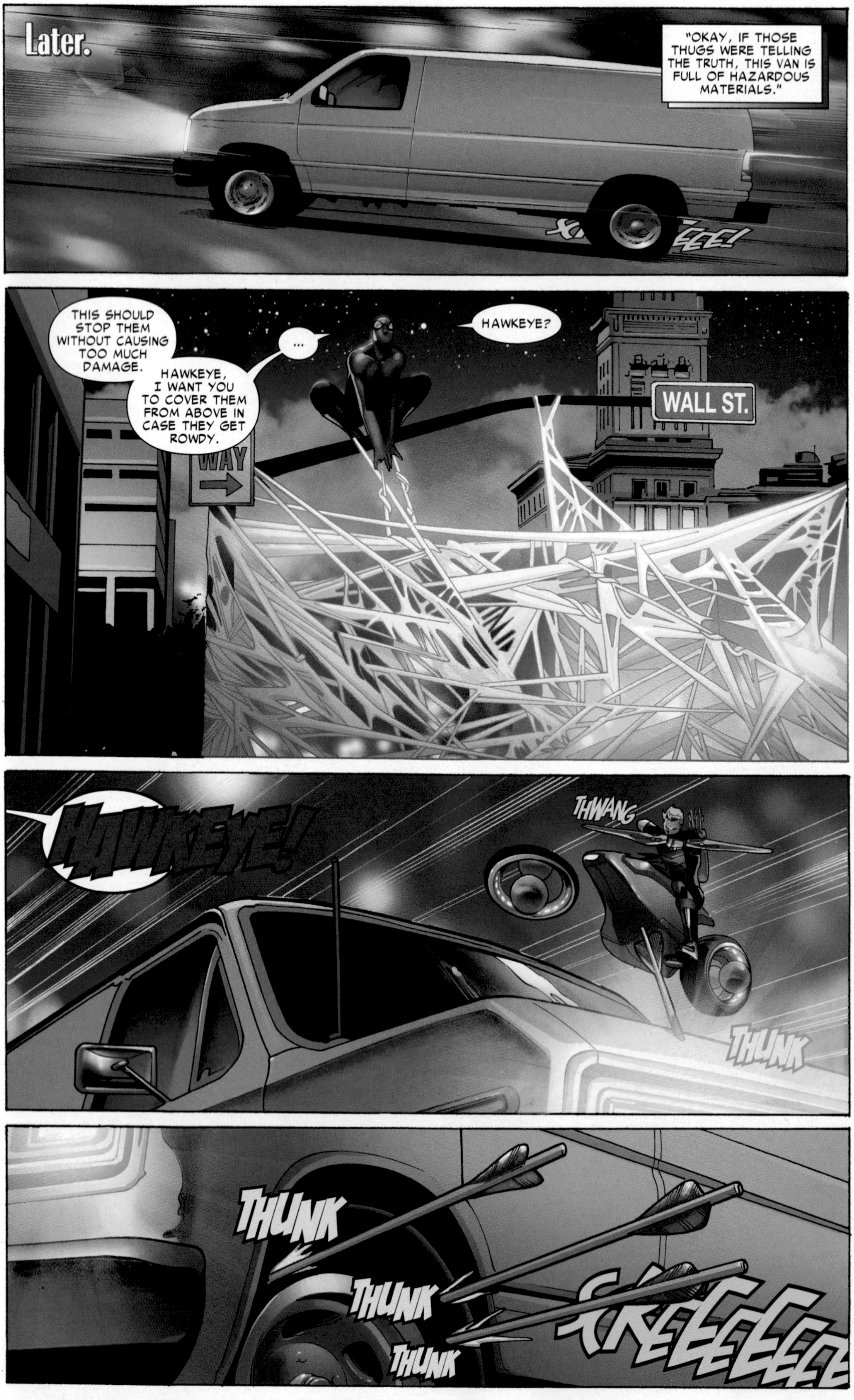
Later.
"OKAY, IF THOSE THUGS WERE TELLING THE TRUTH, THIS VAN IS FULL OF HAZARDOUS MATERIALS."
THIS SHOULD STOP THEM WITHOUT CAUSING TOO MUCH DAMAGE.
HAWKEYE, I WANT YOU TO COVER THEM FROM ABOVE IN CASE THEY GET ROWDY.
...
HAWKEYE?
WALL ST.
WAY
HAWKEYE!
THWANG
THUNK
THUNK
THUNK
THUNK

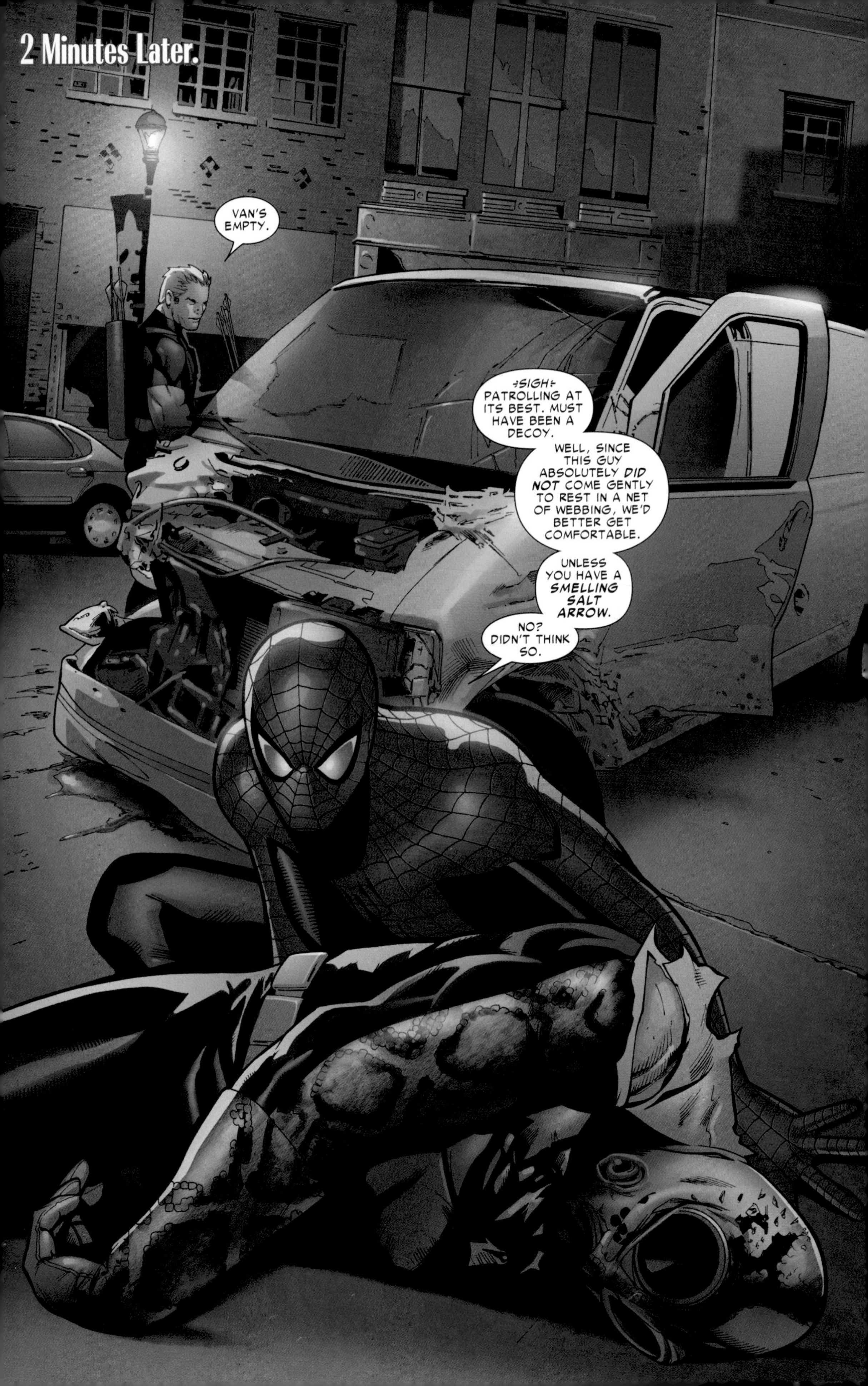
2 Minutes Later.
VAN'S EMPTY.
-SIGH- PATROLLING AT ITS BEST. MUST HAVE BEEN A DECOY.
WELL, SINCE THIS GUY ABSOLUTELY DID NOT COME GENTLY TO REST IN A NET OF WEBBING, WE'D BETTER GET COMFORTABLE.
UNLESS YOU HAVE A SMELLING SALT ARROW.
NO? DIDN'T THINK SO.

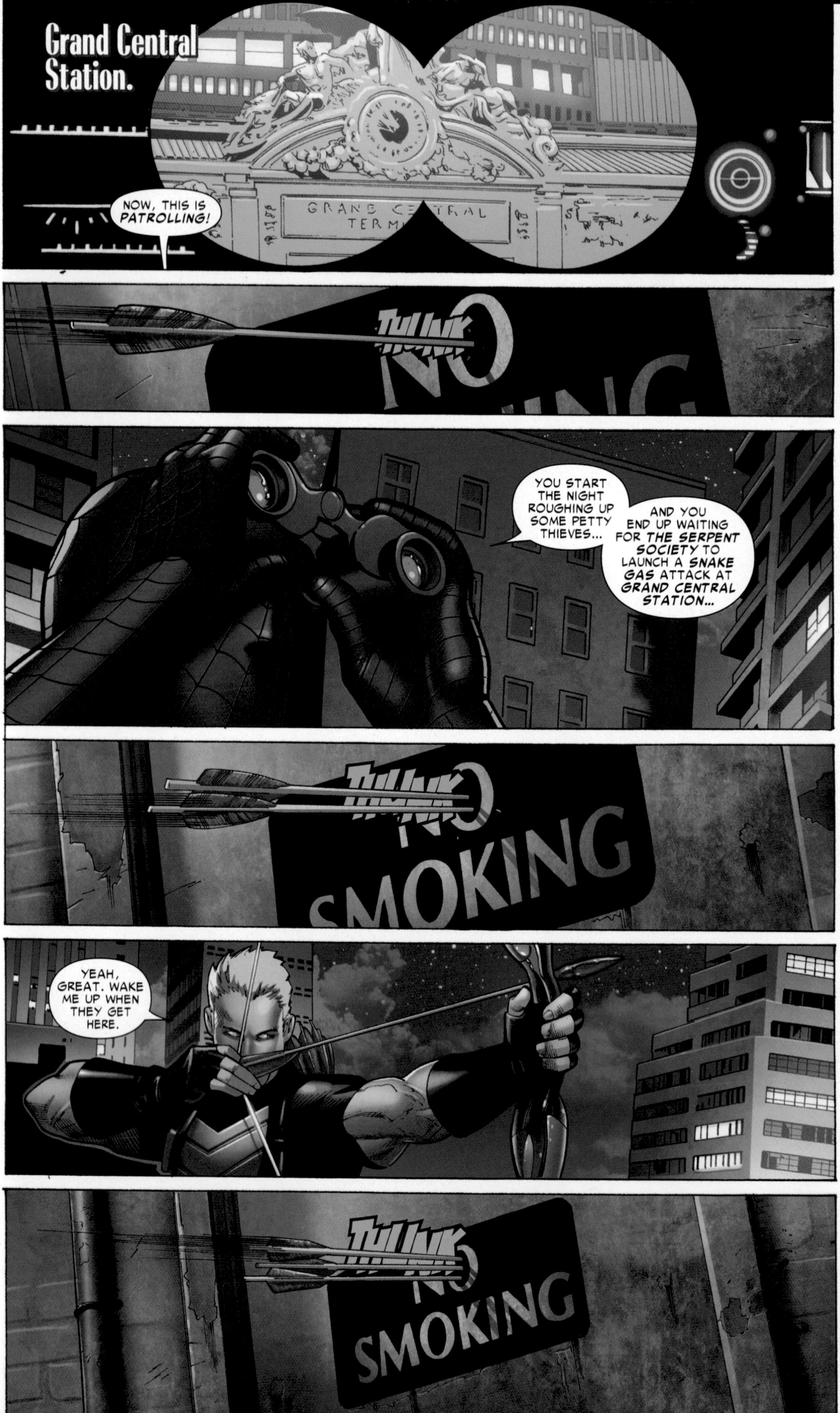
Grand Central Station.
GRAND CENTRAL TERM
NOW, THIS IS PATROLLING!
THUNK
NO
YOU START THE NIGHT ROUGHING UP SOME PETTY THIEVES...
AND YOU END UP WAITING FOR THE SERPENT SOCIETY TO LAUNCH A SNAKE GAS ATTACK AT GRAND CENTRAL STATION...
THUNK
NO SMOKING
YEAH, GREAT. WAKE ME UP WHEN THEY GET HERE.
THUNK
NO SMOKING

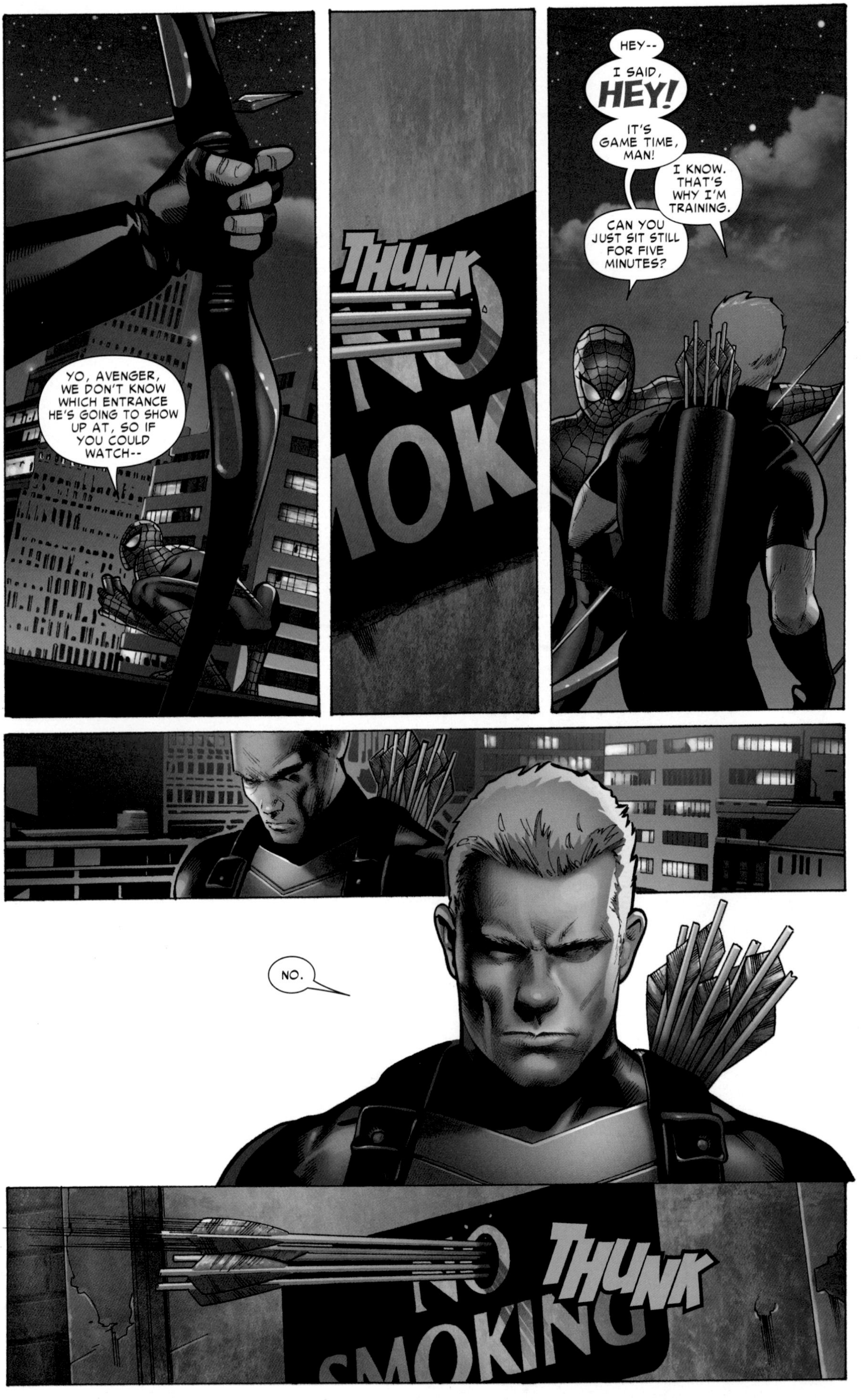
YO, AVENGER, WE DON'T KNOW WHICH ENTRANCE HE'S GOING TO SHOW UP AT, SO IF YOU COULD WATCH--
THUNK
HEY--
I SAID, HEY!
IT'S GAME TIME, MAN!
CAN YOU JUST SIT STILL FOR FIVE MINUTES?
I KNOW. THAT'S WHY I'M TRAINING.
NO.
NO SMOKING
THUNK

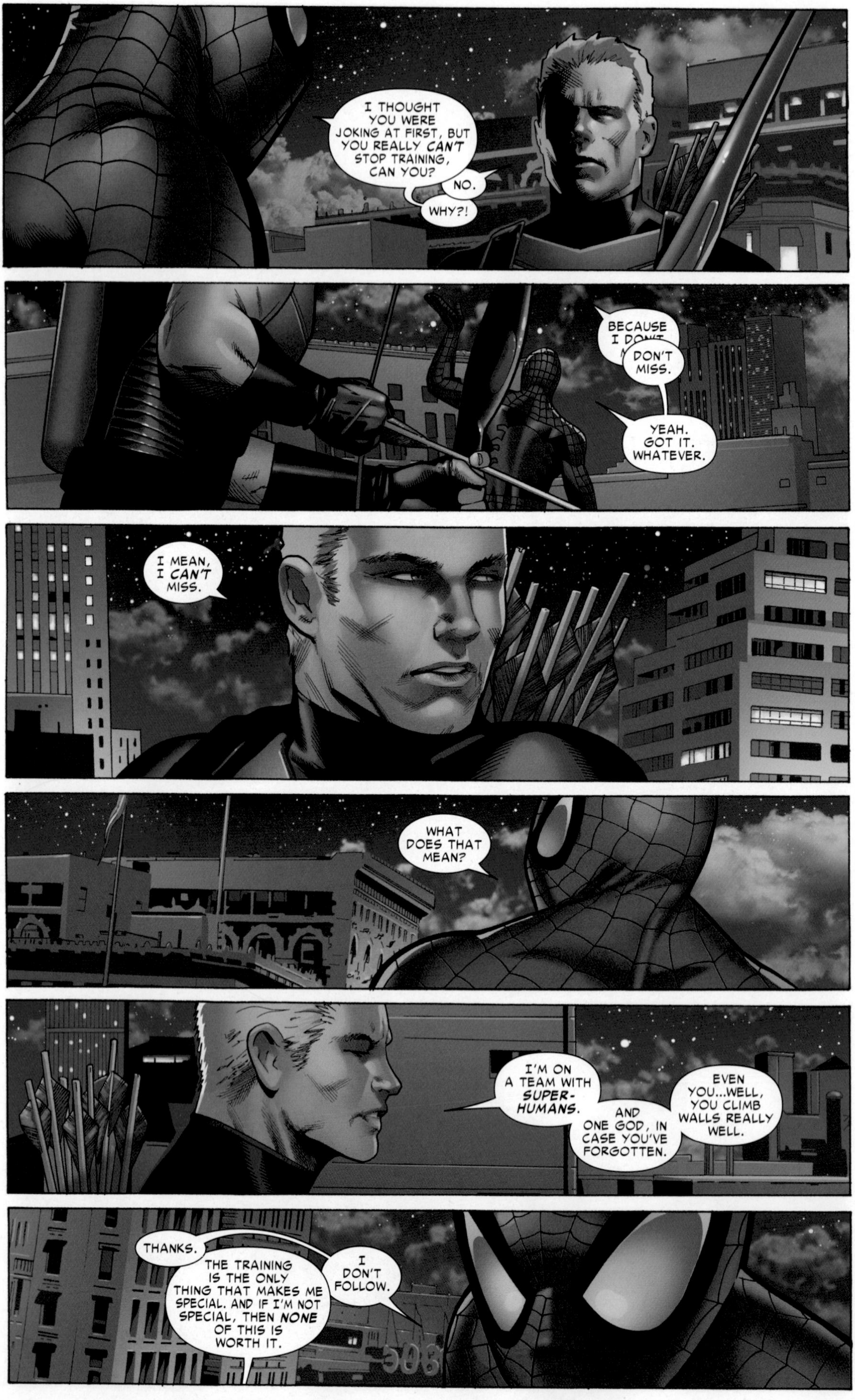

I THOUGHT YOU WERE JOKING AT FIRST, BUT YOU REALLY CAN'T STOP TRAINING, CAN YOU?
NO.
WHY?!
BECAUSE I DON'T
DON'T MISS.
YEAH. GOT IT. WHATEVER.
I MEAN, I CAN'T MISS.
WHAT DOES THAT MEAN?
I'M ON A TEAM WITH SUPER-HUMANS.
AND ONE GOD, IN CASE YOU'VE FORGOTTEN.
EVEN YOU...WELL, YOU CLIMB WALLS REALLY WELL.
THANKS.
I DON'T FOLLOW.
THE TRAINING IS THE ONLY THING THAT MAKES ME SPECIAL. AND IF I'M NOT SPECIAL, THEN NONE OF THIS IS WORTH IT.

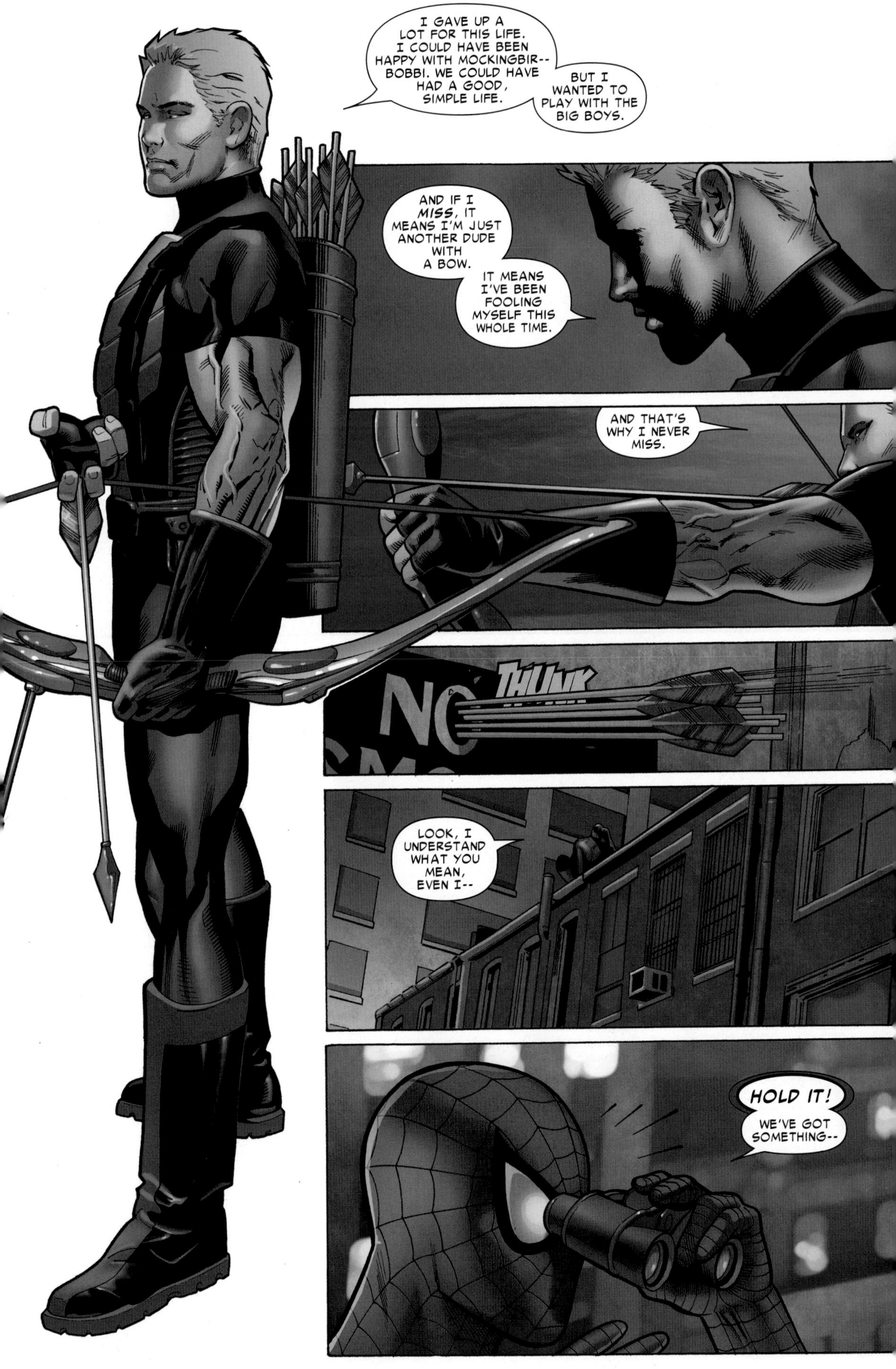
I GAVE UP A LOT FOR THIS LIFE. I COULD HAVE BEEN HAPPY WITH MOCKINGBIR-- BOBBI. WE COULD HAVE HAD A GOOD, SIMPLE LIFE.
BUT I WANTED TO PLAY WITH THE BIG BOYS.
AND IF I *MISS*, IT MEANS I'M JUST ANOTHER DUDE WITH A BOW.
IT MEANS I'VE BEEN FOOLING MYSELF THIS WHOLE TIME.
AND THAT'S WHY I NEVER MISS.
THUNK
LOOK, I UNDERSTAND WHAT YOU MEAN, EVEN I--
HOLD IT!
WE'VE GOT SOMETHING--

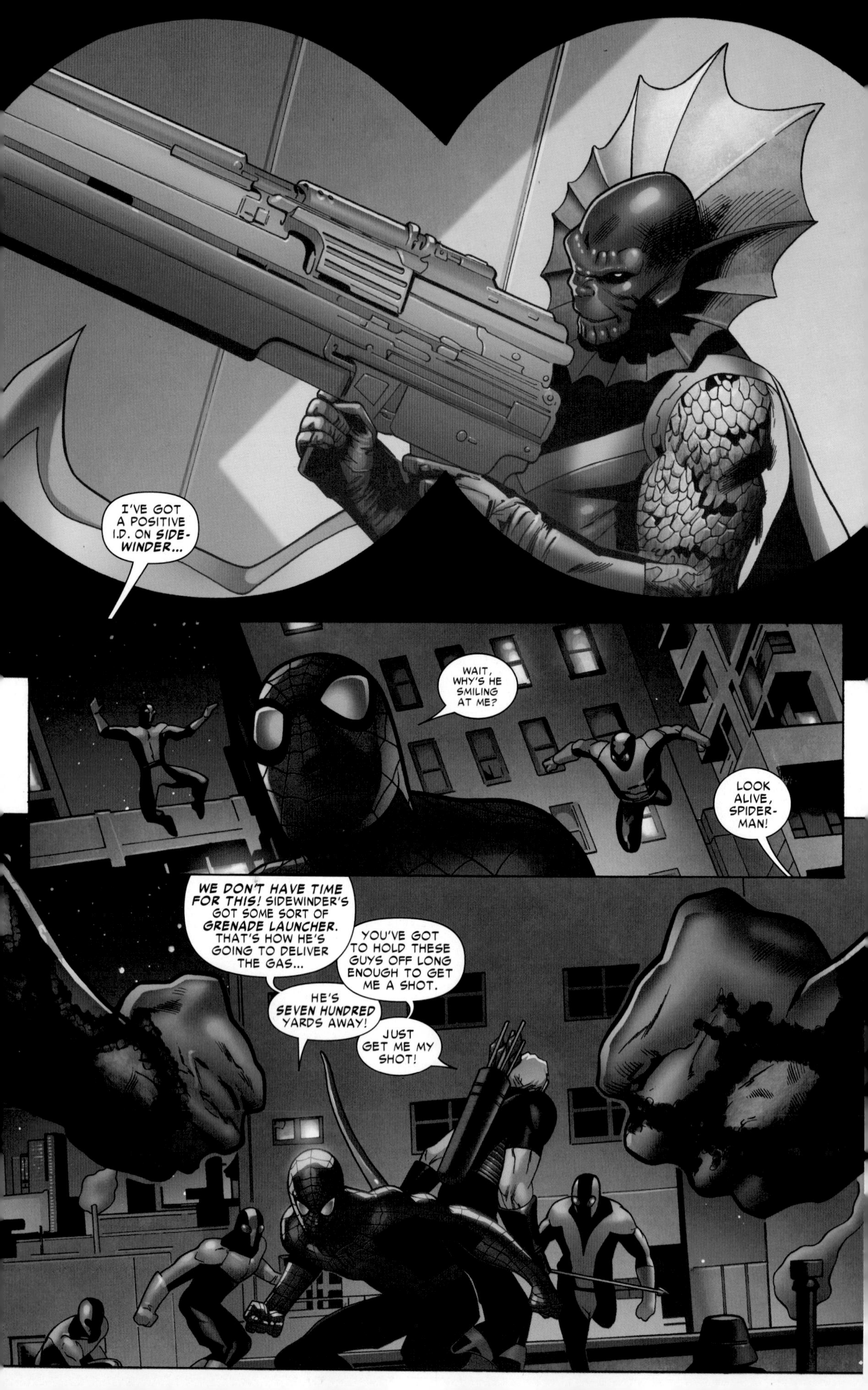
I'VE GOT A POSITIVE I.D. ON SIDE-WINDER...
WAIT, WHY'S HE SMILING AT ME?
LOOK ALIVE, SPIDER-MAN!
WE DON'T HAVE TIME FOR THIS! SIDEWINDER'S GOT SOME SORT OF GRENADE LAUNCHER. THAT'S HOW HE'S GOING TO DELIVER THE GAS...
YOU'VE GOT TO HOLD THESE GUYS OFF LONG ENOUGH TO GET ME A SHOT.
HE'S SEVEN HUNDRED YARDS AWAY!
JUST GET ME MY SHOT!

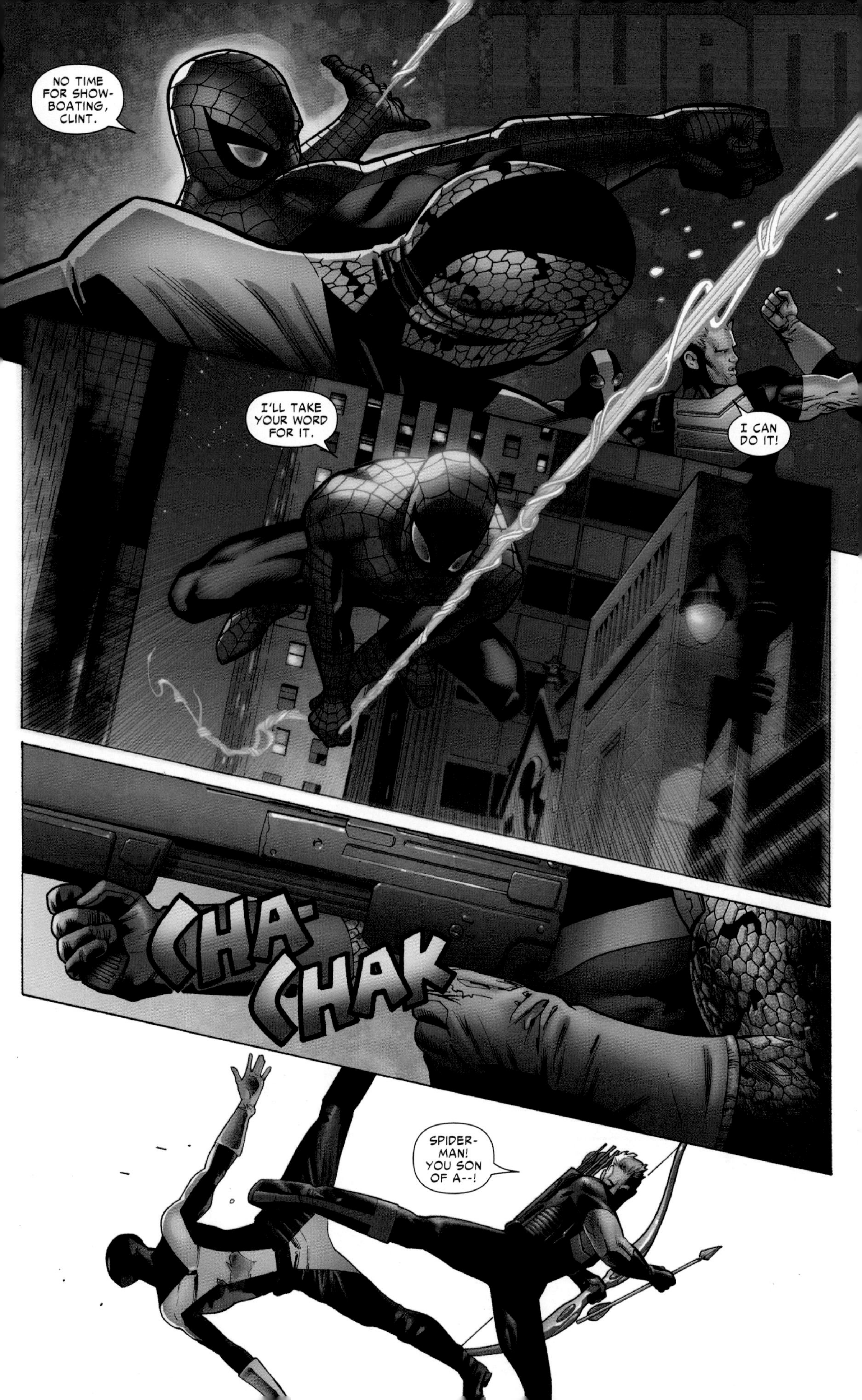
NO TIME FOR SHOW-BOATING, CLINT.
I'LL TAKE YOUR WORD FOR IT.
I CAN DO IT!
CHA-CHAK
SPIDER-MAN! YOU SON OF A--!

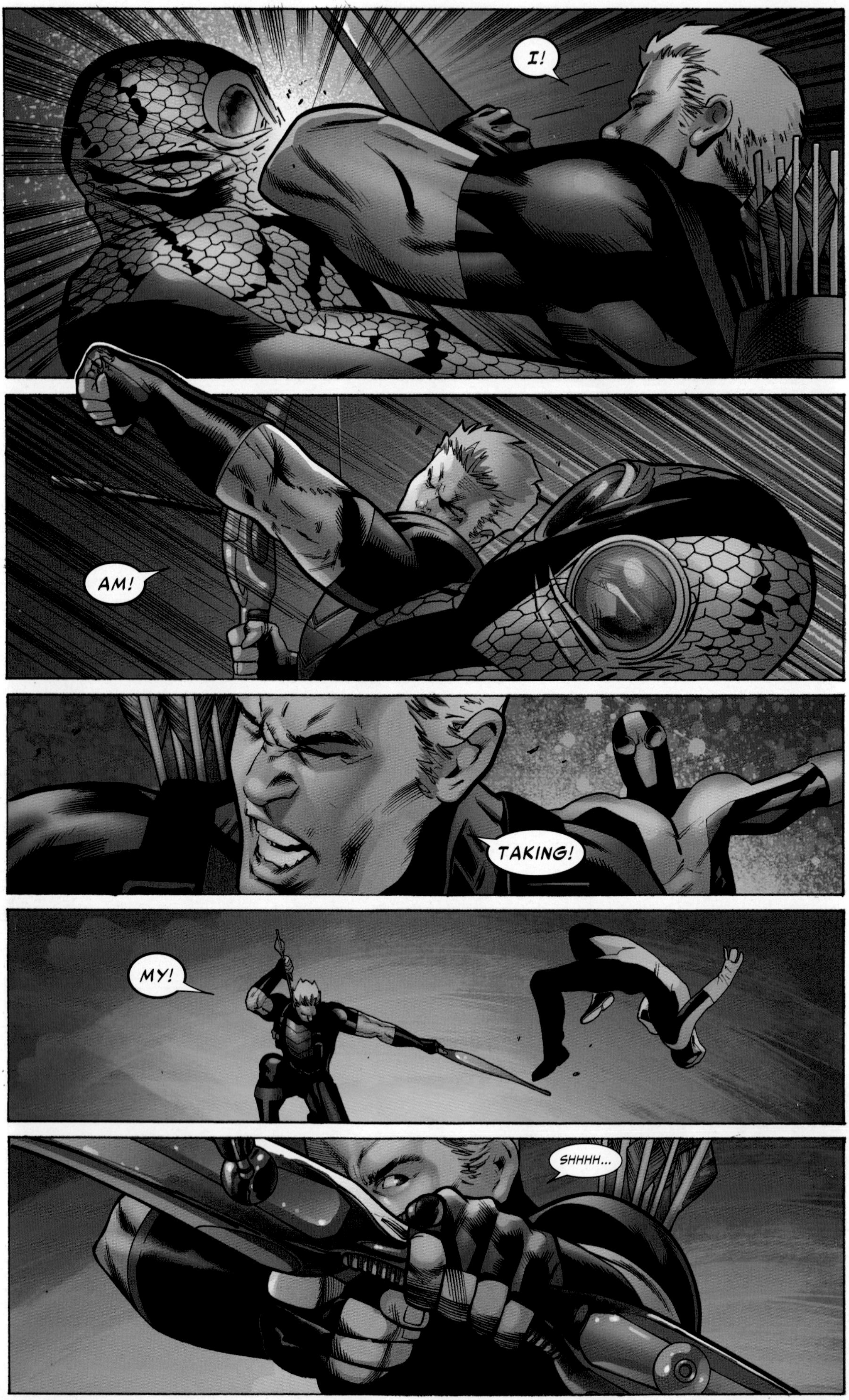
I!
AM!
TAKING!
MY!
SHHHH...

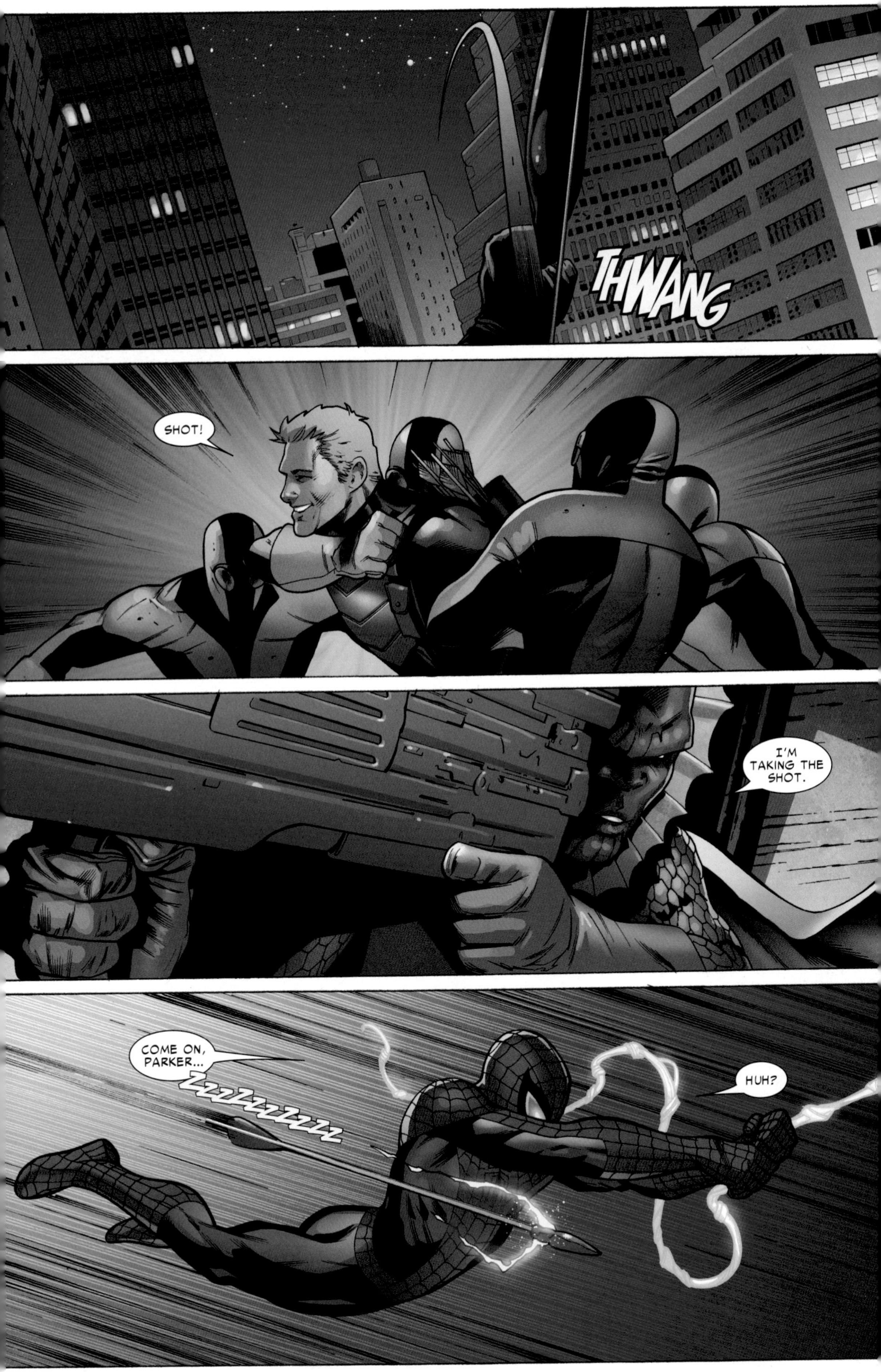
THWANG
SHOT!
I'M TAKING THE SHOT.
COME ON, PARKER...
ZZZZZZZZZZZ
HUH?

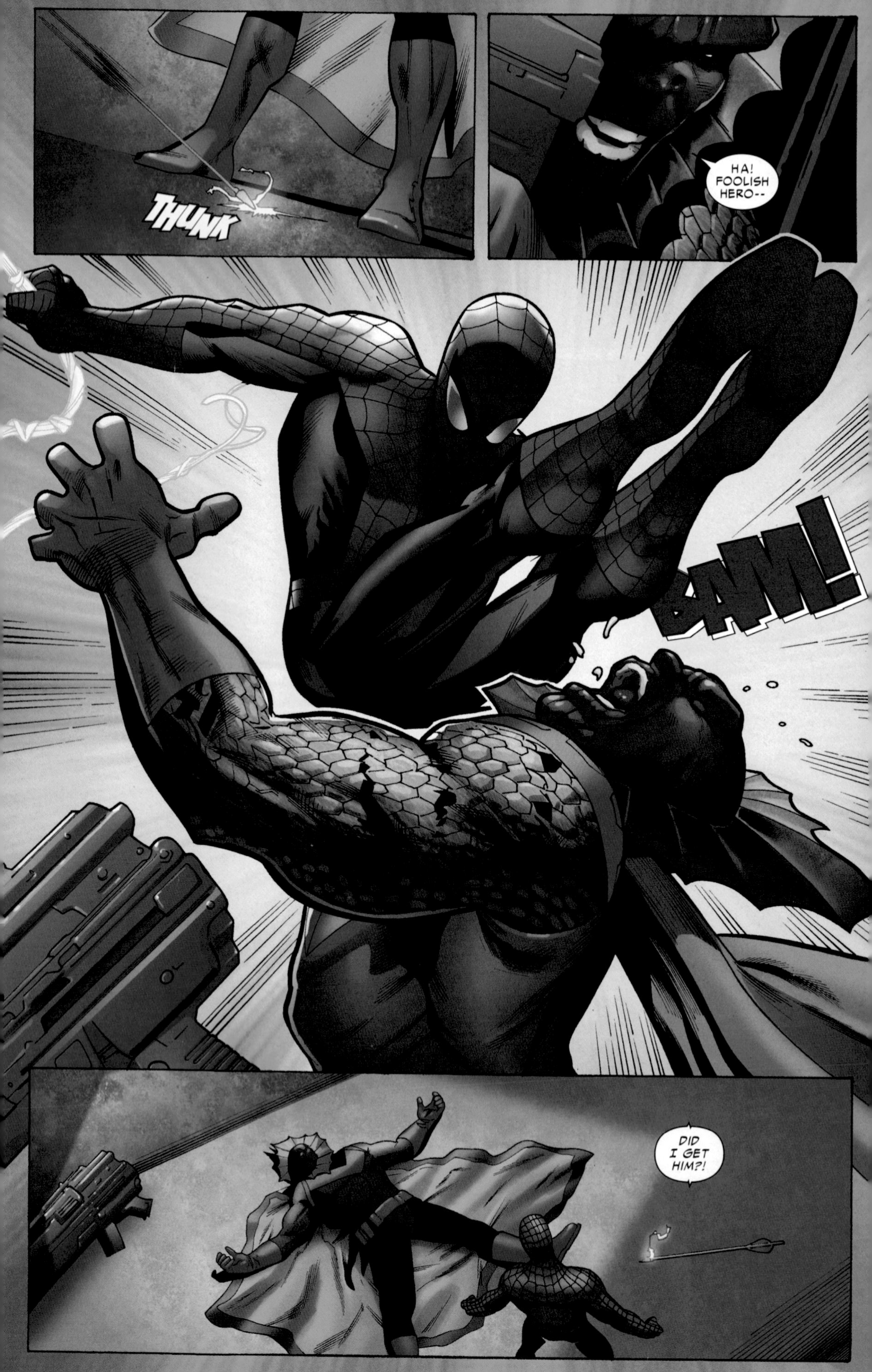
THUNK
HA! FOOLISH HERO--
BAM!
DID I GET HIM?!

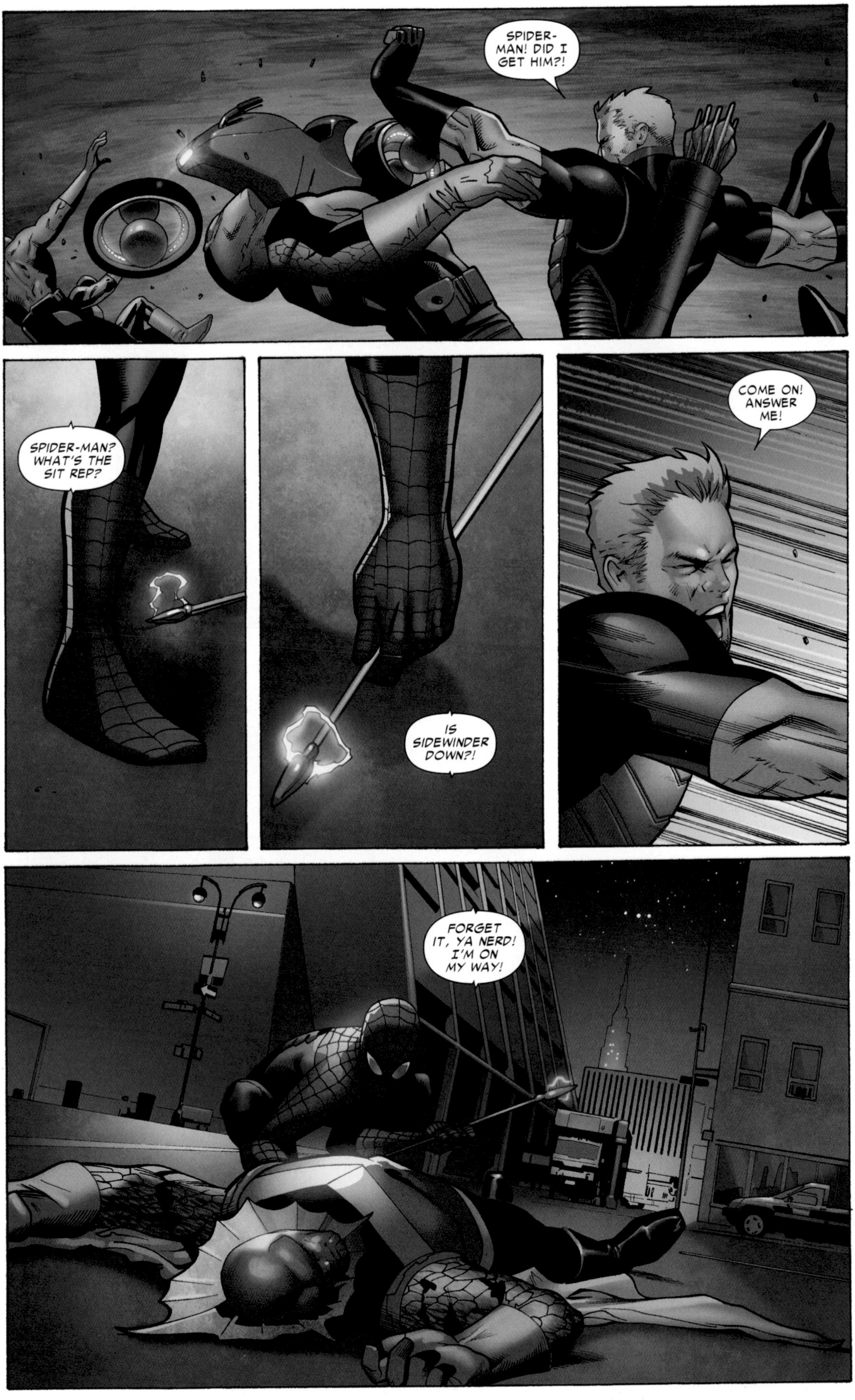
SPIDER-MAN! DID I GET HIM?!
SPIDER-MAN? WHAT'S THE SIT REP?
IS SIDEWINDER DOWN?!
COME ON! ANSWER ME!
FORGET IT, YA NERD! I'M ON MY WAY!

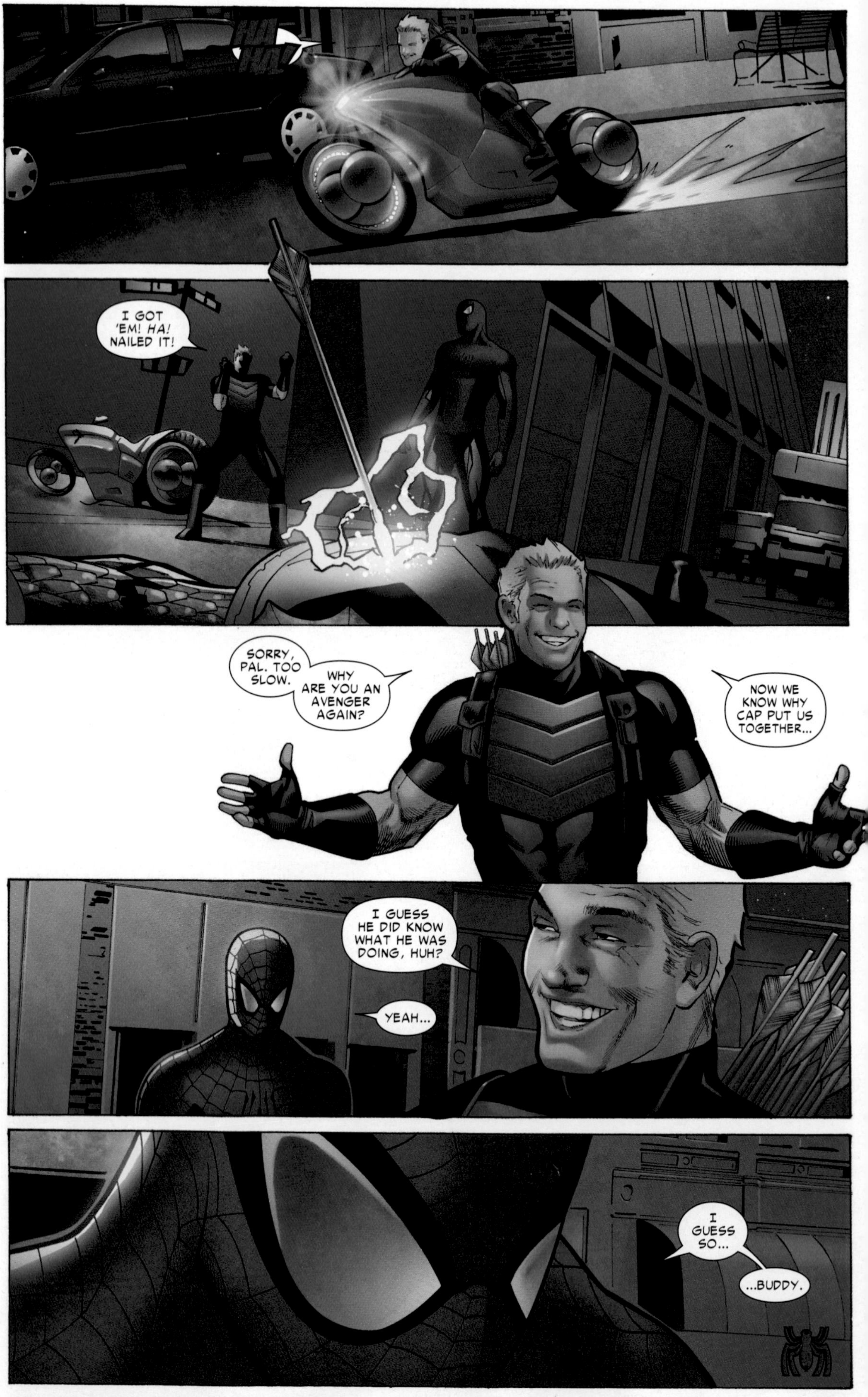
I GOT 'EM! HA! NAILED IT!
SORRY, PAL. TOO SLOW.
WHY ARE YOU AN AVENGER AGAIN?
NOW WE KNOW WHY CAP PUT US TOGETHER...
I GUESS HE DID KNOW WHAT HE WAS DOING, HUH?
YEAH...
I GUESS SO...
...BUDDY.

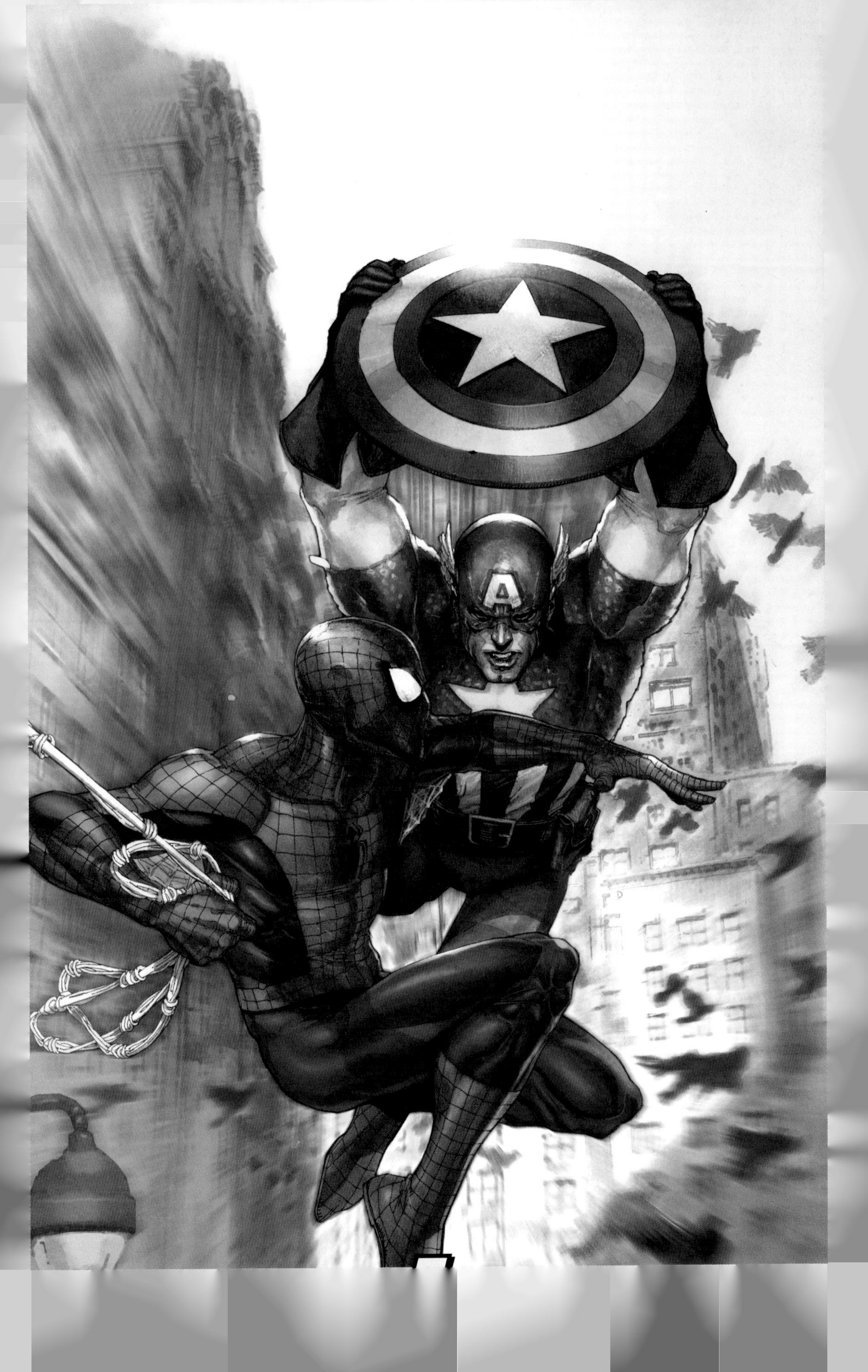

While attending a demonstration in radiology, high school student Peter Parker was bitten by a spider which had accidentally been exposed to radioactive rays. Through a miracle of science, Peter soon found that he had gained the spider's powers...and had, in effect, become a human spider! Later he joined the Avengers (who have a movie coming out soon). And now he is the...

AVENGING SPIDER-MAN

Steve Rogers was a frail, Zeb Wells-ish young man who wanted to serve his country during World War II. As part of a Super-Soldier program, he was injected with an experimental serum that enhanced him to the peak of human perfection. Thought to have disappeared during the war, he was later found frozen in the North Atlantic and-- who are we kidding look, you all saw the movie. Indestructible shield etc..etc... He leads the Avengers as--

CAPTAIN AMERICA

AVENGING SPIDER-MAN

PREVIOUSLY...

Hawkeye ~~and Spider-Man~~ stopped Sidewinder, of the Serpent Society, *the real hero* from snake-gassing Grand Central Station. Hawkeye was ~~kind of a jerk~~ but Spider-Man ~~had his back anyway~~ *didn't wet himself this time*. And isn't that what teamwork is all about?

WRITER: ~~ZEB WELLS~~ *HAWKEYE* ARTIST: ~~LEINIL FRANCIS YU~~ *HAWKEYE*

INKER: ~~GERRY ALANGUILAN~~ *HAWKEYE* COLOR ART: ~~SUNNY GHO~~ *HAWKEYE*

LETTERER: ~~VC's JOE CARAMAGNA~~ *HAWKEYE*

ASSISTANT EDITOR: *HAWKEYE* ~~ELLIE PYLE~~ EDITOR: ~~STEPHEN WACKER~~ *HAWKEYE*

EXECUTIVE EDITOR: *HAWKEYE* ~~TOM BREVOORT~~ EDITOR IN CHIEF: ~~AXEL ALONSO~~ *HAWKEYE*

CHIEF CREATIVE OFFICER: *HAWKEYE* ~~JOE QUESADA~~ PUBLISHER: ~~DAN BUCKLEY~~ *HAWKEYE* EXECUTIVE PRODUCER: ALAN FINE

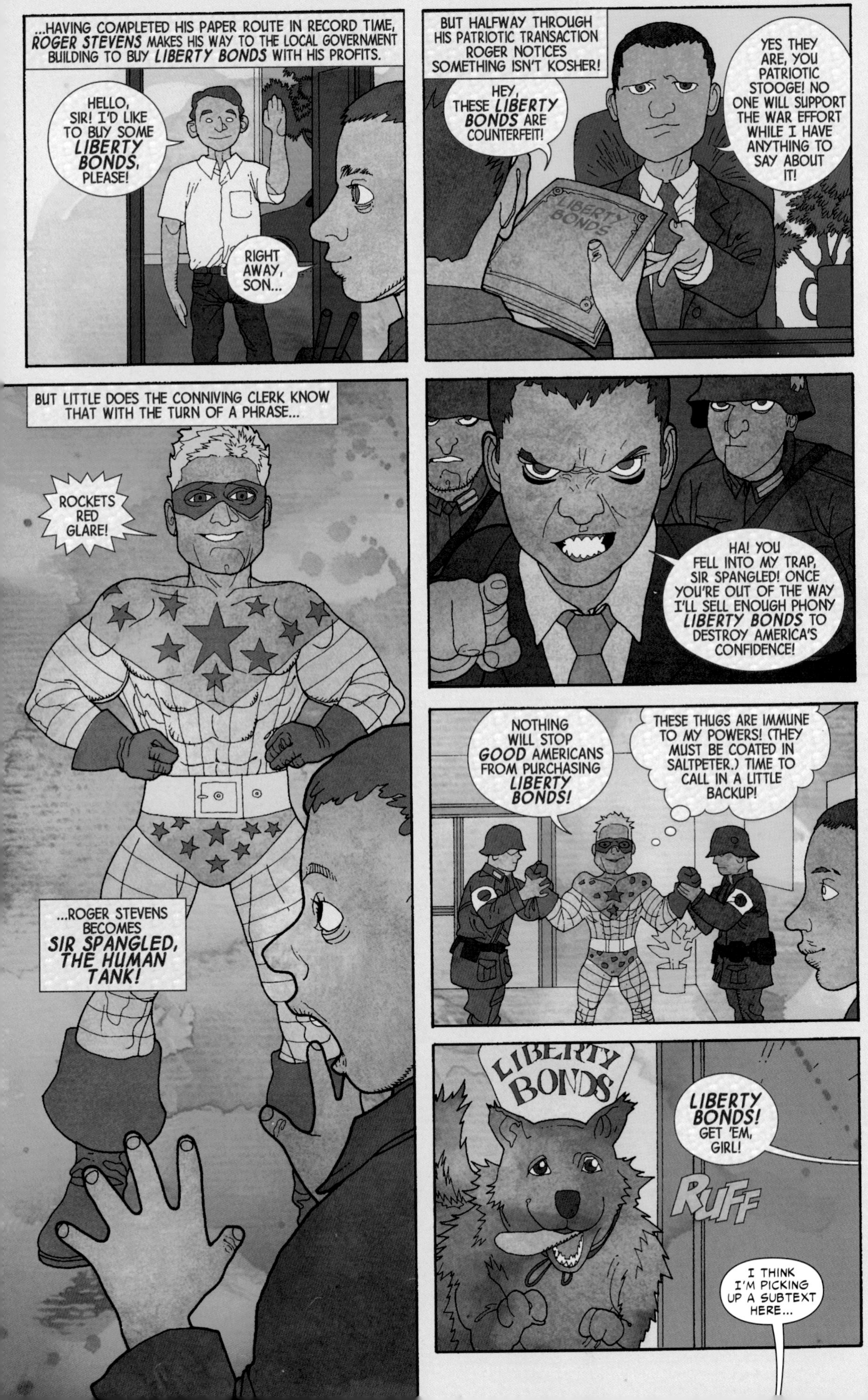
...HAVING COMPLETED HIS PAPER ROUTE IN RECORD TIME, ROGER STEVENS MAKES HIS WAY TO THE LOCAL GOVERNMENT BUILDING TO BUY LIBERTY BONDS WITH HIS PROFITS.
HELLO, SIR! I'D LIKE TO BUY SOME LIBERTY BONDS, PLEASE!
RIGHT AWAY, SON...
BUT HALFWAY THROUGH HIS PATRIOTIC TRANSACTION ROGER NOTICES SOMETHING ISN'T KOSHER!
HEY, THESE LIBERTY BONDS ARE COUNTERFEIT!
YES THEY ARE, YOU PATRIOTIC STOOGE! NO ONE WILL SUPPORT THE WAR EFFORT WHILE I HAVE ANYTHING TO SAY ABOUT IT!
LIBERTY BONDS
BUT LITTLE DOES THE CONNIVING CLERK KNOW THAT WITH THE TURN OF A PHRASE...
ROCKETS RED GLARE!
...ROGER STEVENS BECOMES SIR SPANGLED, THE HUMAN TANK!
HA! YOU FELL INTO MY TRAP, SIR SPANGLED! ONCE YOU'RE OUT OF THE WAY I'LL SELL ENOUGH PHONY LIBERTY BONDS TO DESTROY AMERICA'S CONFIDENCE!
NOTHING WILL STOP GOOD AMERICANS FROM PURCHASING LIBERTY BONDS!
THESE THUGS ARE IMMUNE TO MY POWERS! (THEY MUST BE COATED IN SALTPETER.) TIME TO CALL IN A LITTLE BACKUP!
LIBERTY BONDS
LIBERTY BONDS! GET 'EM, GIRL!
RUFF
I THINK I'M PICKING UP A SUBTEXT HERE...

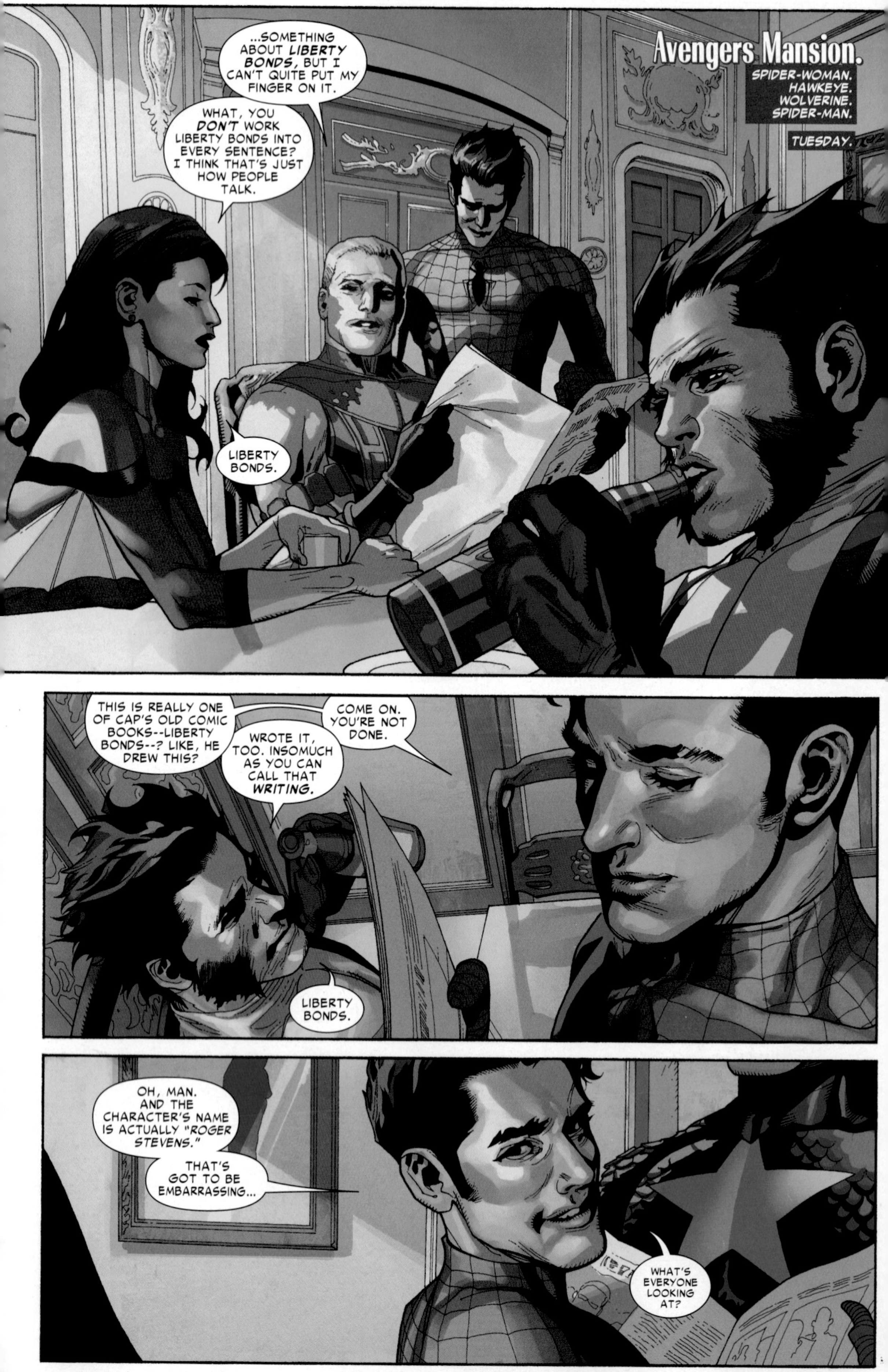
Avengers Mansion.
SPIDER-WOMAN. HAWKEYE. WOLVERINE. SPIDER-MAN.
TUESDAY.
...SOMETHING ABOUT LIBERTY BONDS, BUT I CAN'T QUITE PUT MY FINGER ON IT.
WHAT, YOU DON'T WORK LIBERTY BONDS INTO EVERY SENTENCE? I THINK THAT'S JUST HOW PEOPLE TALK.
LIBERTY BONDS.
THIS IS REALLY ONE OF CAP'S OLD COMIC BOOKS--LIBERTY BONDS--? LIKE, HE DREW THIS?
WROTE IT, TOO. INSOMUCH AS YOU CAN CALL THAT WRITING.
COME ON. YOU'RE NOT DONE.
LIBERTY BONDS.
OH, MAN. AND THE CHARACTER'S NAME IS ACTUALLY "ROGER STEVENS."
THAT'S GOT TO BE EMBARRASSING...
WHAT'S EVERYONE LOOKING AT?

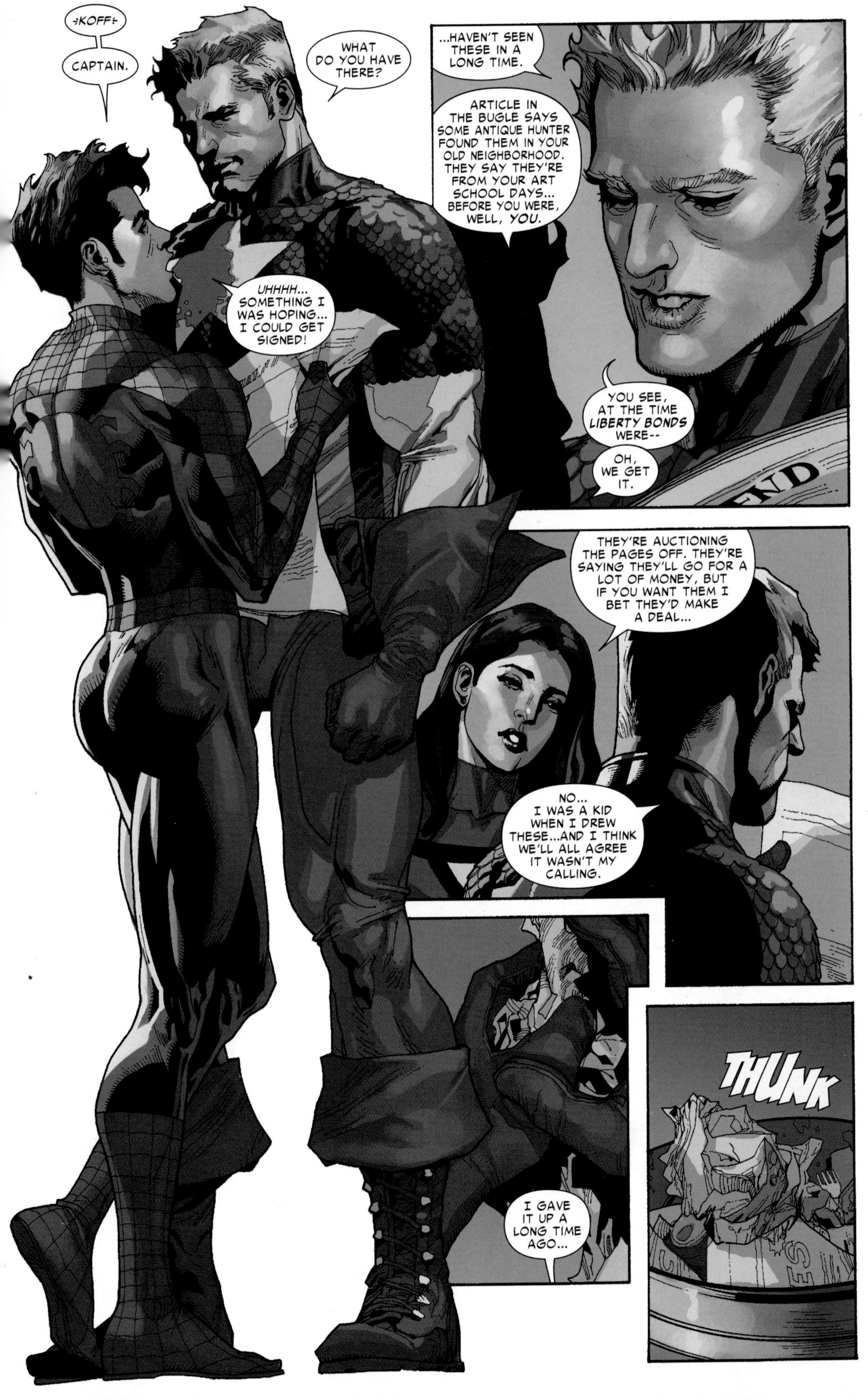

-KOFF-
CAPTAIN.
WHAT DO YOU HAVE THERE?
UHHHH... SOMETHING I WAS HOPING... I COULD GET SIGNED!
...HAVEN'T SEEN THESE IN A LONG TIME.
ARTICLE IN THE BUGLE SAYS SOME ANTIQUE HUNTER FOUND THEM IN YOUR OLD NEIGHBORHOOD. THEY SAY THEY'RE FROM YOUR ART SCHOOL DAYS... BEFORE YOU WERE, WELL, *YOU.*
YOU SEE, AT THE TIME *LIBERTY BONDS* WERE--
OH, WE GET IT.
THEY'RE AUCTIONING THE PAGES OFF. THEY'RE SAYING THEY'LL GO FOR A LOT OF MONEY, BUT IF YOU WANT THEM I BET THEY'D MAKE A DEAL...
NO... I WAS A KID WHEN I DREW THESE...AND I THINK WE'LL ALL AGREE IT WASN'T MY CALLING.
I GAVE IT UP A LONG TIME AGO...
THUNK

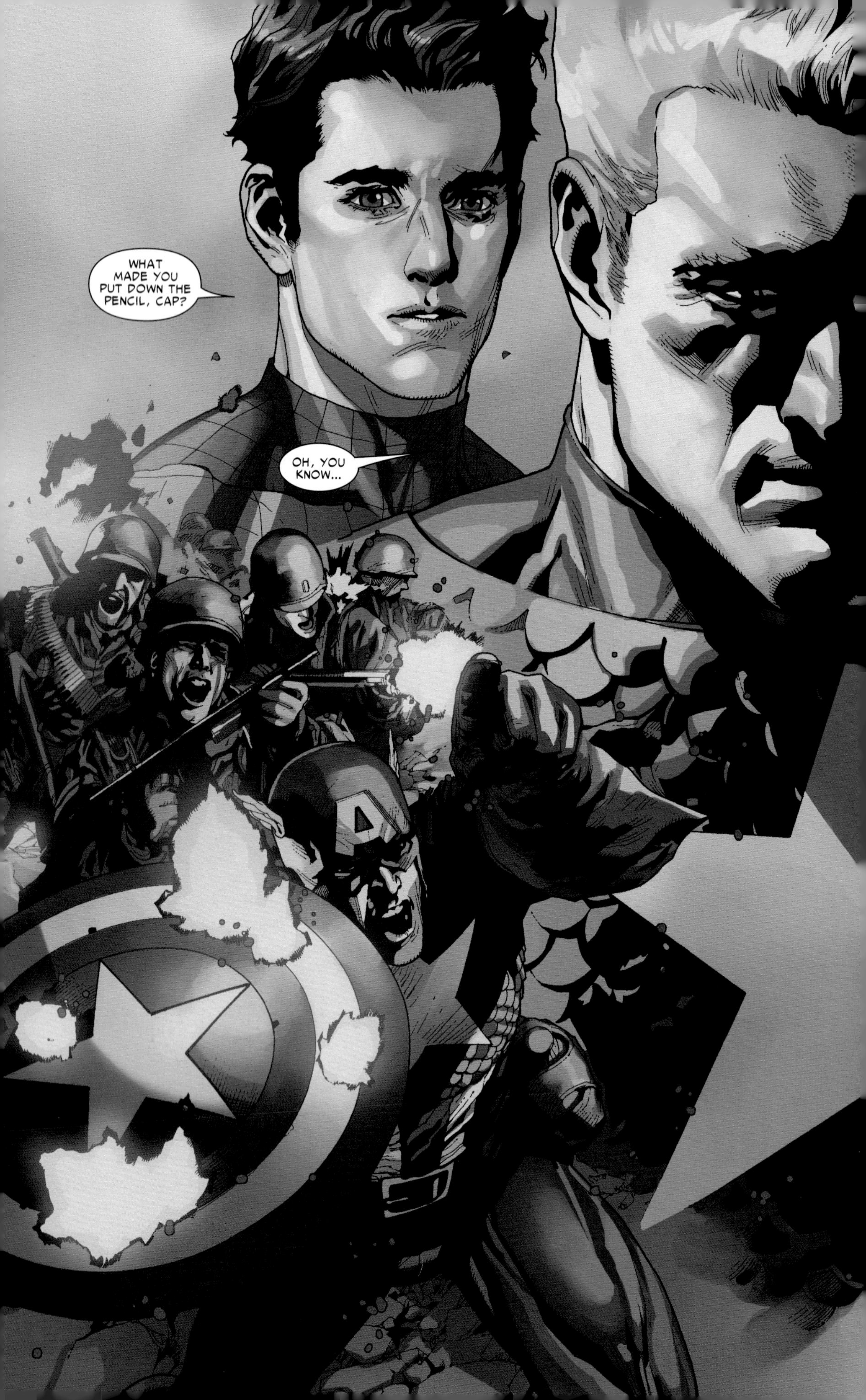
WHAT MADE YOU PUT DOWN THE PENCIL, CAP?
OH, YOU KNOW...

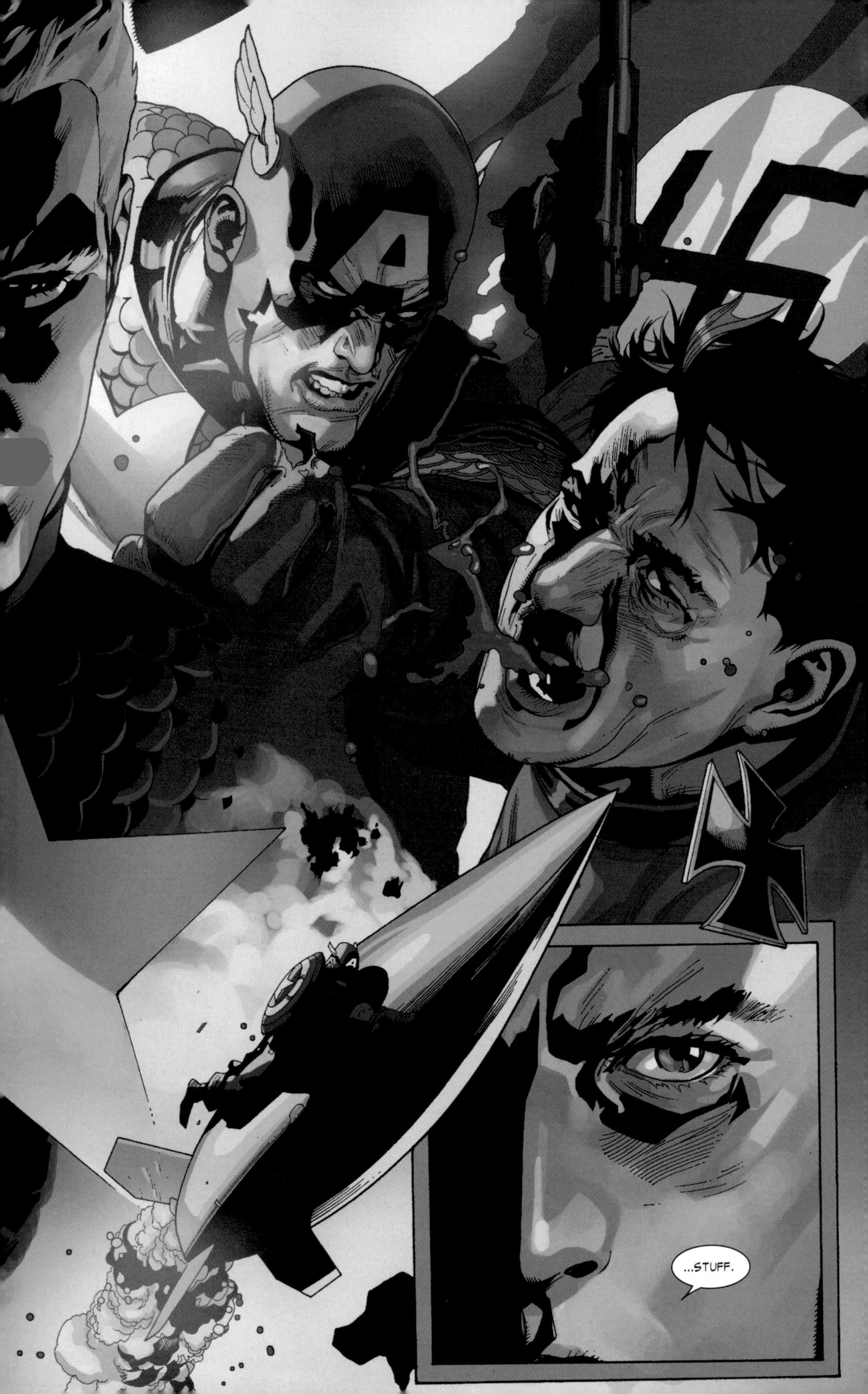
...STUFF.

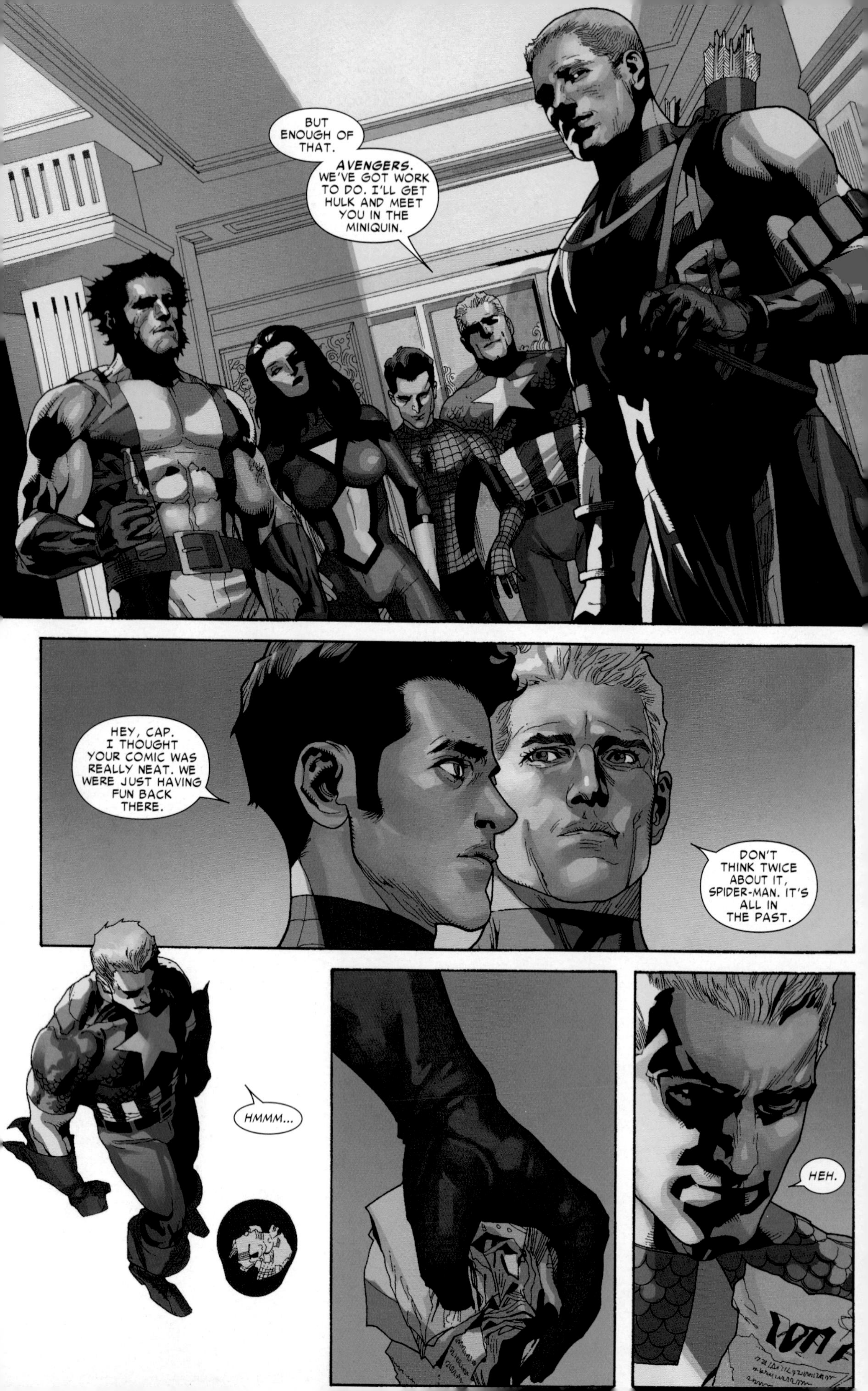
BUT ENOUGH OF THAT.
AVENGERS. WE'VE GOT WORK TO DO. I'LL GET HULK AND MEET YOU IN THE MINIQUIN.
HEY, CAP. I THOUGHT YOUR COMIC WAS REALLY NEAT. WE WERE JUST HAVING FUN BACK THERE.
DON'T THINK TWICE ABOUT IT, SPIDER-MAN. IT'S ALL IN THE PAST.
HMMM...
HEH.

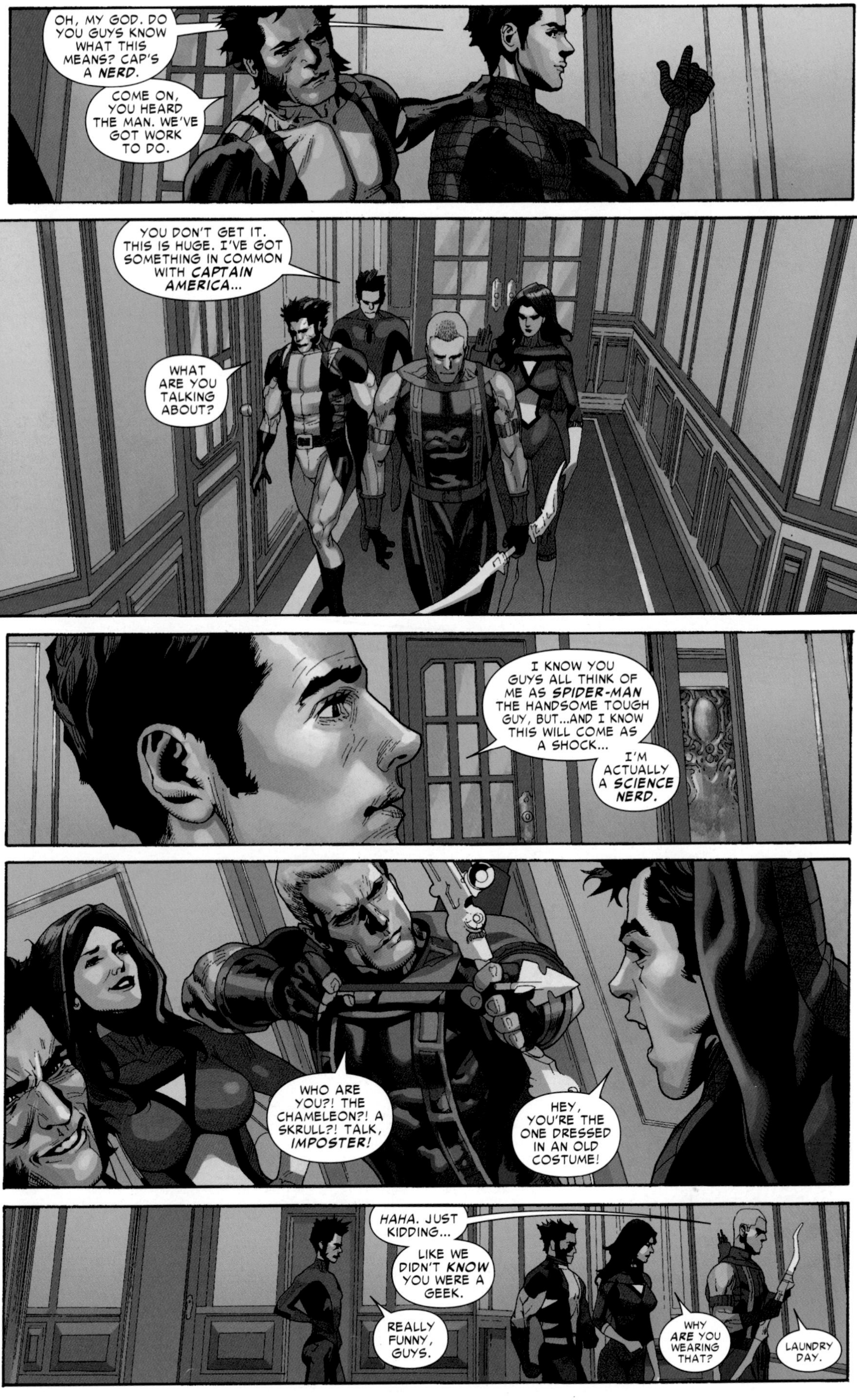

OH, MY GOD. DO YOU GUYS KNOW WHAT THIS MEANS? CAP'S A **NERD**.
COME ON, YOU HEARD THE MAN. WE'VE GOT WORK TO DO.
YOU DON'T GET IT. THIS IS HUGE. I'VE GOT SOMETHING IN COMMON WITH **CAPTAIN AMERICA**...
WHAT ARE YOU TALKING ABOUT?
I KNOW YOU GUYS ALL THINK OF ME AS **SPIDER-MAN** THE HANDSOME TOUGH GUY, BUT...AND I KNOW THIS WILL COME AS A SHOCK...
I'M ACTUALLY A **SCIENCE NERD.**
WHO ARE YOU?! THE CHAMELEON?! A SKRULL?! TALK, ***IMPOSTER!***
HEY, YOU'RE THE ONE DRESSED IN AN OLD COSTUME!
HAHA. JUST KIDDING...
LIKE WE DIDN'T ***KNOW*** YOU WERE A GEEK.
REALLY FUNNY, GUYS.
WHY ***ARE*** YOU WEARING THAT?
LAUNDRY DAY.

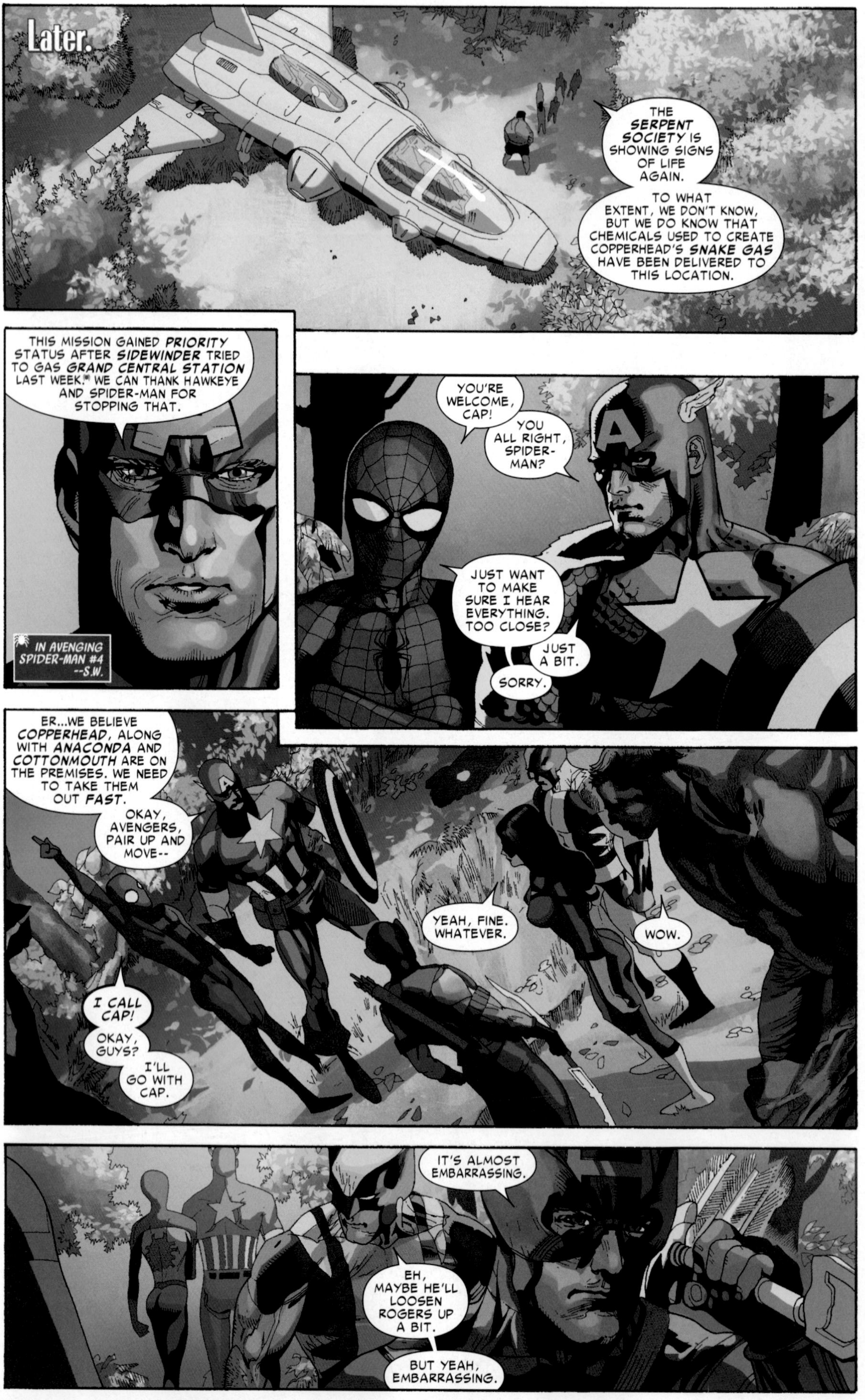
Later.
THE SERPENT SOCIETY IS SHOWING SIGNS OF LIFE AGAIN.
TO WHAT EXTENT, WE DON'T KNOW, BUT WE DO KNOW THAT CHEMICALS USED TO CREATE COPPERHEAD'S SNAKE GAS HAVE BEEN DELIVERED TO THIS LOCATION.
THIS MISSION GAINED PRIORITY STATUS AFTER SIDEWINDER TRIED TO GAS GRAND CENTRAL STATION LAST WEEK.* WE CAN THANK HAWKEYE AND SPIDER-MAN FOR STOPPING THAT.
*IN AVENGING SPIDER-MAN #4 --S.W.
YOU'RE WELCOME, CAP!
YOU ALL RIGHT, SPIDER-MAN?
JUST WANT TO MAKE SURE I HEAR EVERYTHING. TOO CLOSE?
JUST A BIT.
SORRY.
ER...WE BELIEVE COPPERHEAD, ALONG WITH ANACONDA AND COTTONMOUTH ARE ON THE PREMISES. WE NEED TO TAKE THEM OUT FAST.
OKAY, AVENGERS, PAIR UP AND MOVE--
I CALL CAP!
OKAY, GUYS?
I'LL GO WITH CAP.
YEAH, FINE. WHATEVER.
WOW.
IT'S ALMOST EMBARRASSING.
EH, MAYBE HE'LL LOOSEN ROGERS UP A BIT.
BUT YEAH, EMBARRASSING.

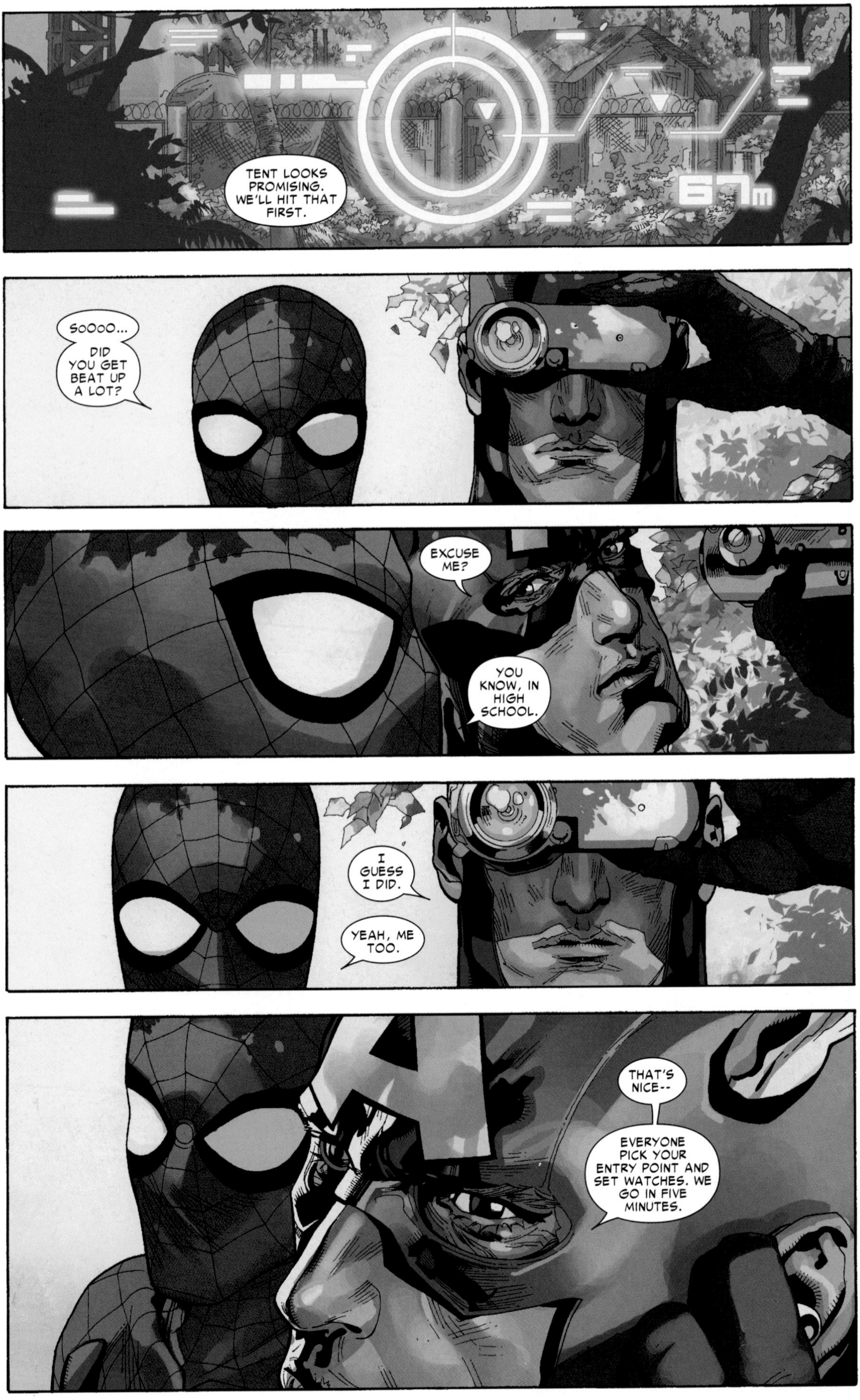

TENT LOOKS PROMISING. WE'LL HIT THAT FIRST.
67m
SOOOO...
DID YOU GET BEAT UP A LOT?
EXCUSE ME?
YOU KNOW, IN HIGH SCHOOL.
I GUESS I DID.
YEAH, ME TOO.
THAT'S NICE--
EVERYONE PICK YOUR ENTRY POINT AND SET WATCHES. WE GO IN FIVE MINUTES.

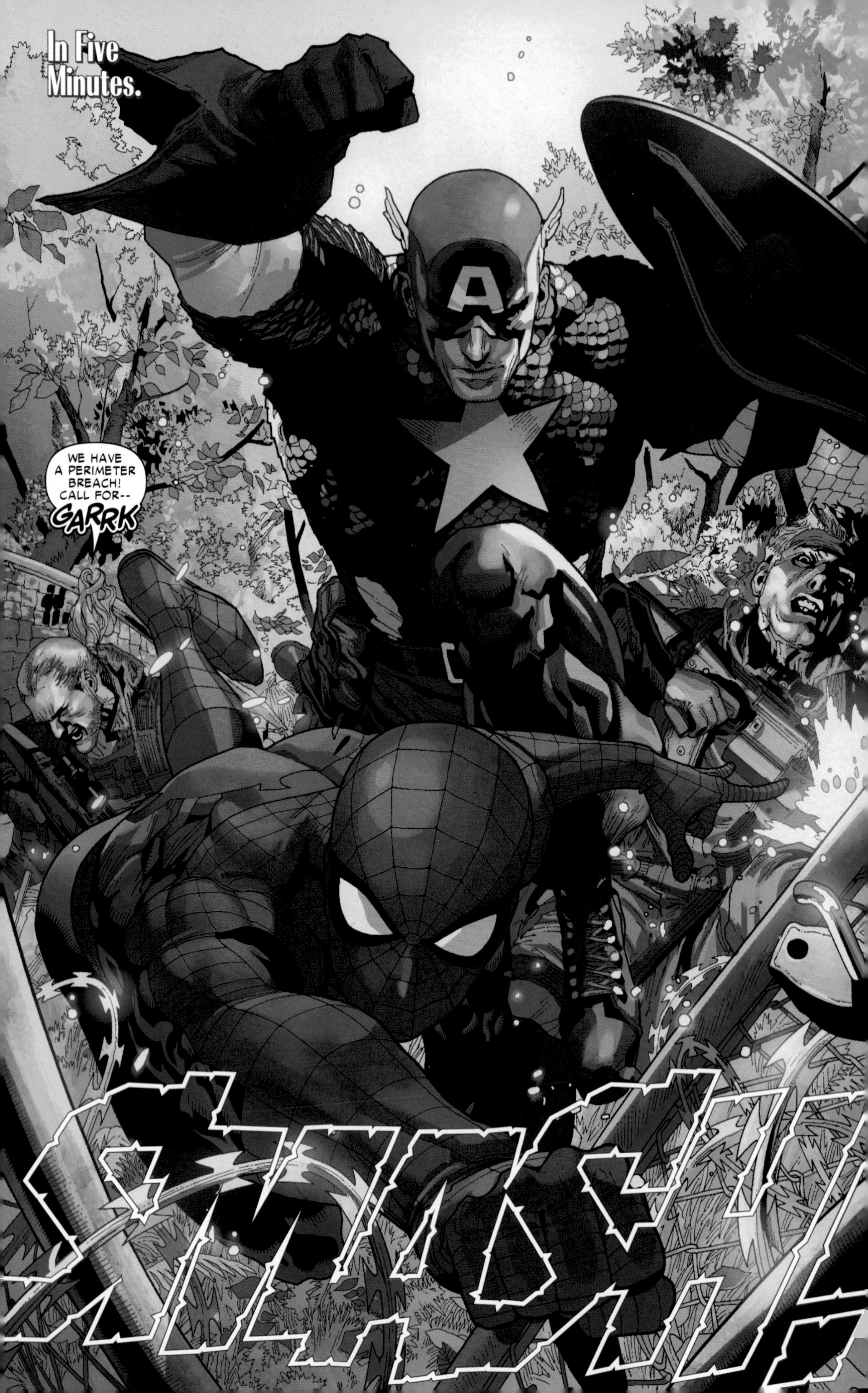
In Five Minutes.
WE HAVE A PERIMETER BREACH! CALL FOR-- GARRK

THWIP

IT SOUNDED LIKE HE SAID, "CALL FOR GARRK."

WHO'S THIS "GARRK" GUY? HE SOUNDS PRETTY COOL.

GOT IT.

CLANG

CLANG

THUK

GUHHH--!

HNNK--!

I WAS A SCIENCE NERD, WHICH ISN'T THE SAME AS A COMIC GEEK, BUT THE VENN DIAGRAMS DEFINITELY HAVE SOME OVERLAP.

ALL I'M SAYING IS WE PROBABLY HAVE A LOT IN COMMON.

YOU SEEM TO BE TALKING A LOT.

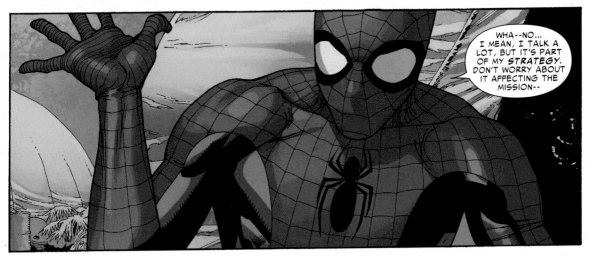

WHA--NO... I MEAN, I TALK A LOT, BUT IT'S PART OF MY STRATEGY. DON'T WORRY ABOUT IT AFFECTING THE MISSION--

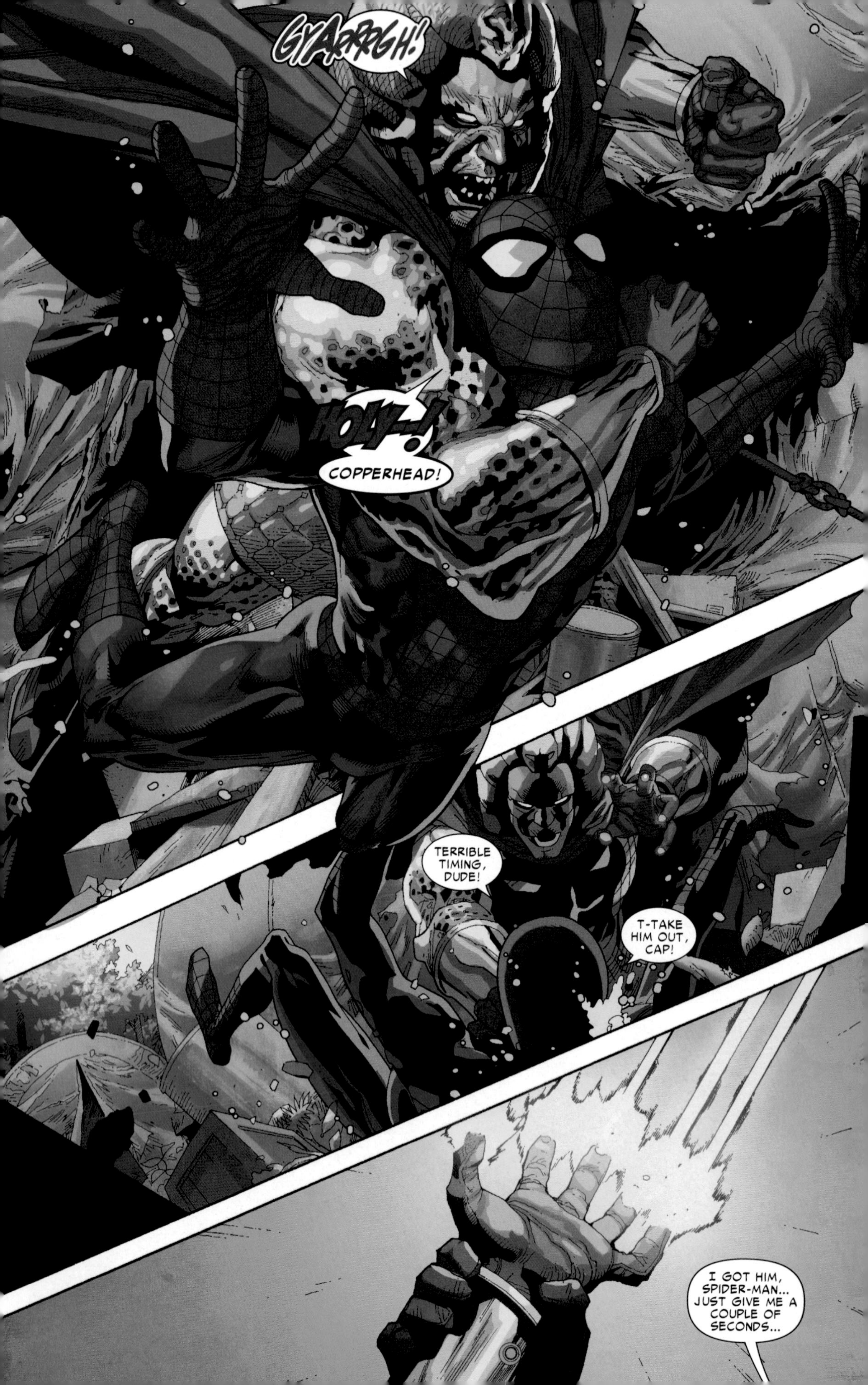
GYARRRGH!
HOLY--!
COPPERHEAD!
TERRIBLE TIMING, DUDE!
T-TAKE HIM OUT, CAP!
I GOT HIM, SPIDER-MAN... JUST GIVE ME A COUPLE OF SECONDS...

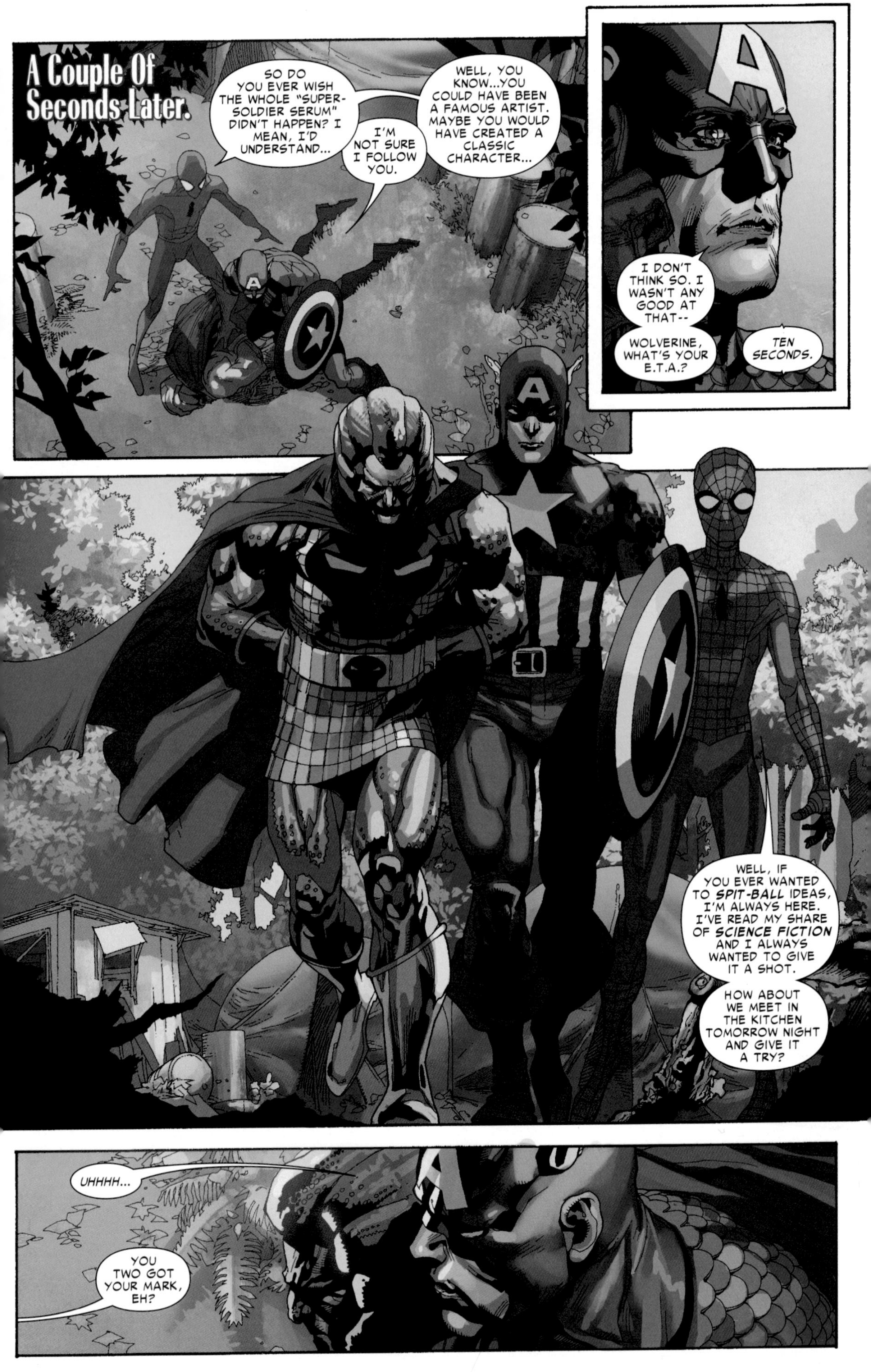
A Couple Of Seconds Later.
SO DO YOU EVER WISH THE WHOLE "SUPER-SOLDIER SERUM" DIDN'T HAPPEN? I MEAN, I'D UNDERSTAND...
I'M NOT SURE I FOLLOW YOU.
WELL, YOU KNOW...YOU COULD HAVE BEEN A FAMOUS ARTIST. MAYBE YOU WOULD HAVE CREATED A CLASSIC CHARACTER...
I DON'T THINK SO. I WASN'T ANY GOOD AT THAT--
WOLVERINE, WHAT'S YOUR E.T.A.?
TEN SECONDS.
WELL, IF YOU EVER WANTED TO SPIT-BALL IDEAS, I'M ALWAYS HERE. I'VE READ MY SHARE OF SCIENCE FICTION AND I ALWAYS WANTED TO GIVE IT A SHOT.
HOW ABOUT WE MEET IN THE KITCHEN TOMORROW NIGHT AND GIVE IT A TRY?
UHHHH...
YOU TWO GOT YOUR MARK, EH?

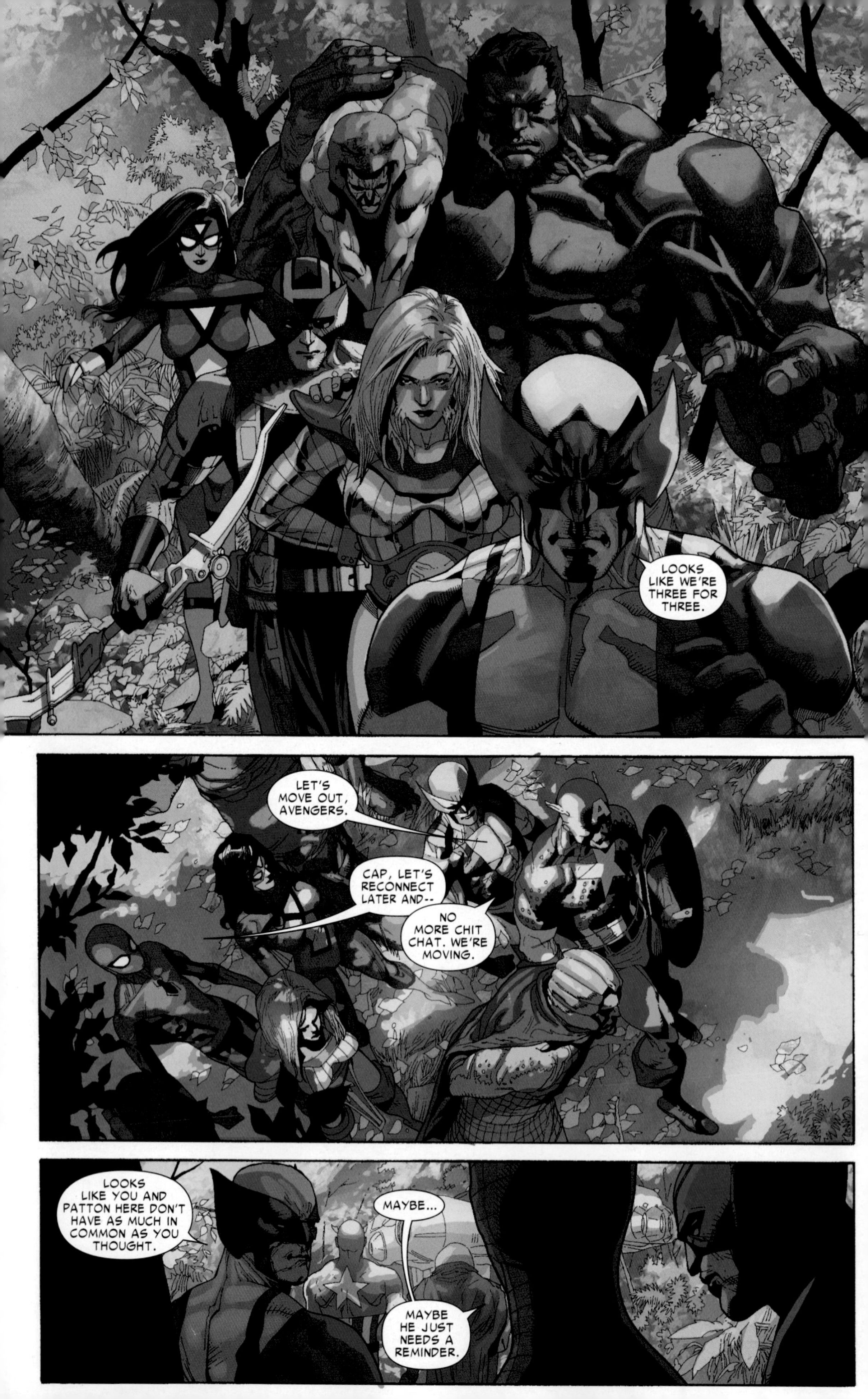
LOOKS LIKE WE'RE THREE FOR THREE.
LET'S MOVE OUT, AVENGERS.
CAP, LET'S RECONNECT LATER AND--
NO MORE CHIT CHAT. WE'RE MOVING.
LOOKS LIKE YOU AND PATTON HERE DON'T HAVE AS MUCH IN COMMON AS YOU THOUGHT.
MAYBE...
MAYBE HE JUST NEEDS A REMINDER.

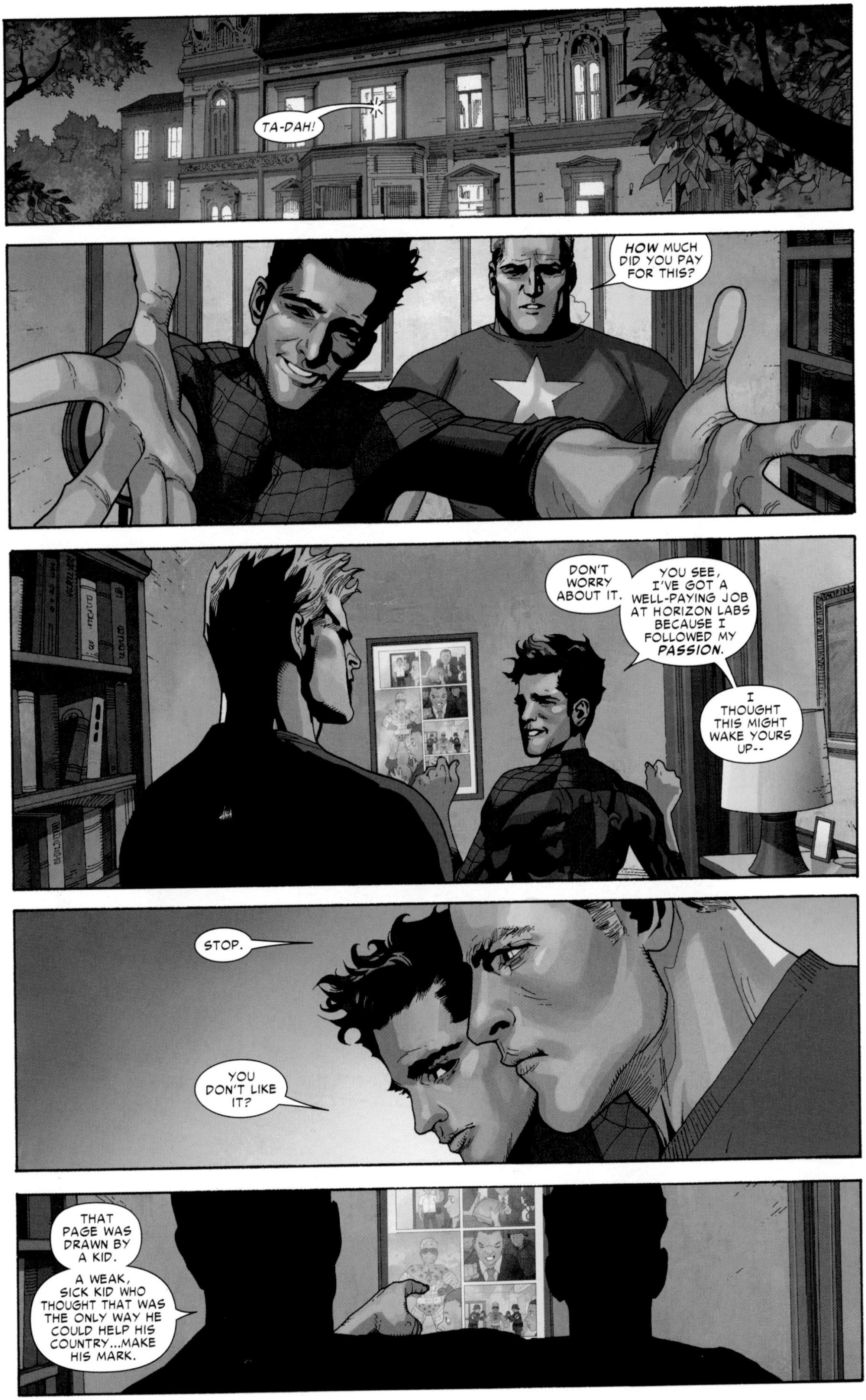
TA-DAH!
HOW MUCH DID YOU PAY FOR THIS?
DON'T WORRY ABOUT IT.
YOU SEE, I'VE GOT A WELL-PAYING JOB AT HORIZON LABS BECAUSE I FOLLOWED MY PASSION.
I THOUGHT THIS MIGHT WAKE YOURS UP--
STOP.
YOU DON'T LIKE IT?
THAT PAGE WAS DRAWN BY A KID.
A WEAK, SICK KID WHO THOUGHT THAT WAS THE ONLY WAY HE COULD HELP HIS COUNTRY...MAKE HIS MARK.

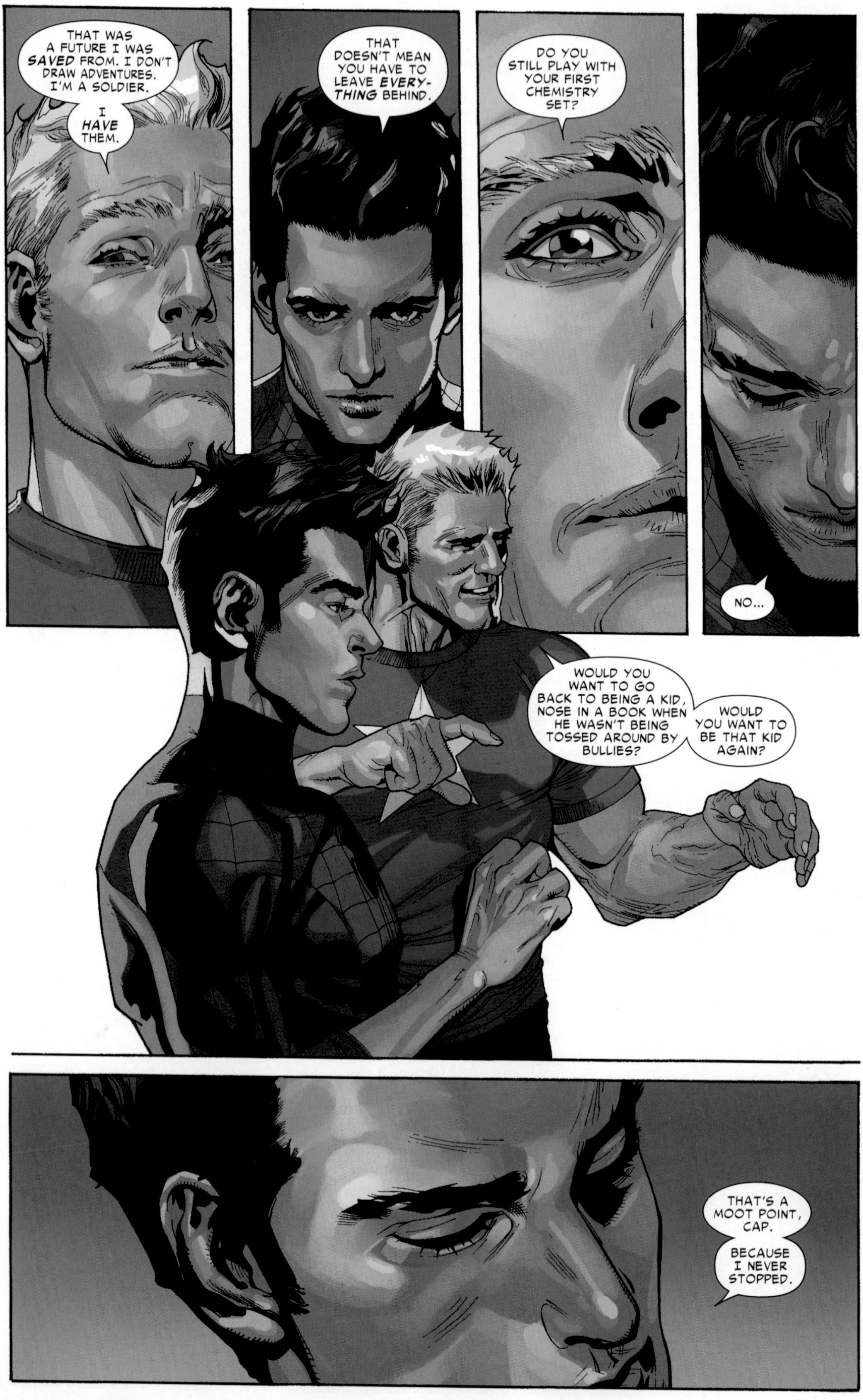
THAT WAS A FUTURE I WAS SAVED FROM. I DON'T DRAW ADVENTURES. I'M A SOLDIER.
I HAVE THEM.
THAT DOESN'T MEAN YOU HAVE TO LEAVE EVERY-THING BEHIND.
DO YOU STILL PLAY WITH YOUR FIRST CHEMISTRY SET?
NO...
WOULD YOU WANT TO GO BACK TO BEING A KID, NOSE IN A BOOK WHEN HE WASN'T BEING TOSSED AROUND BY BULLIES?
WOULD YOU WANT TO BE THAT KID AGAIN?
THAT'S A MOOT POINT, CAP.
BECAUSE I NEVER STOPPED.

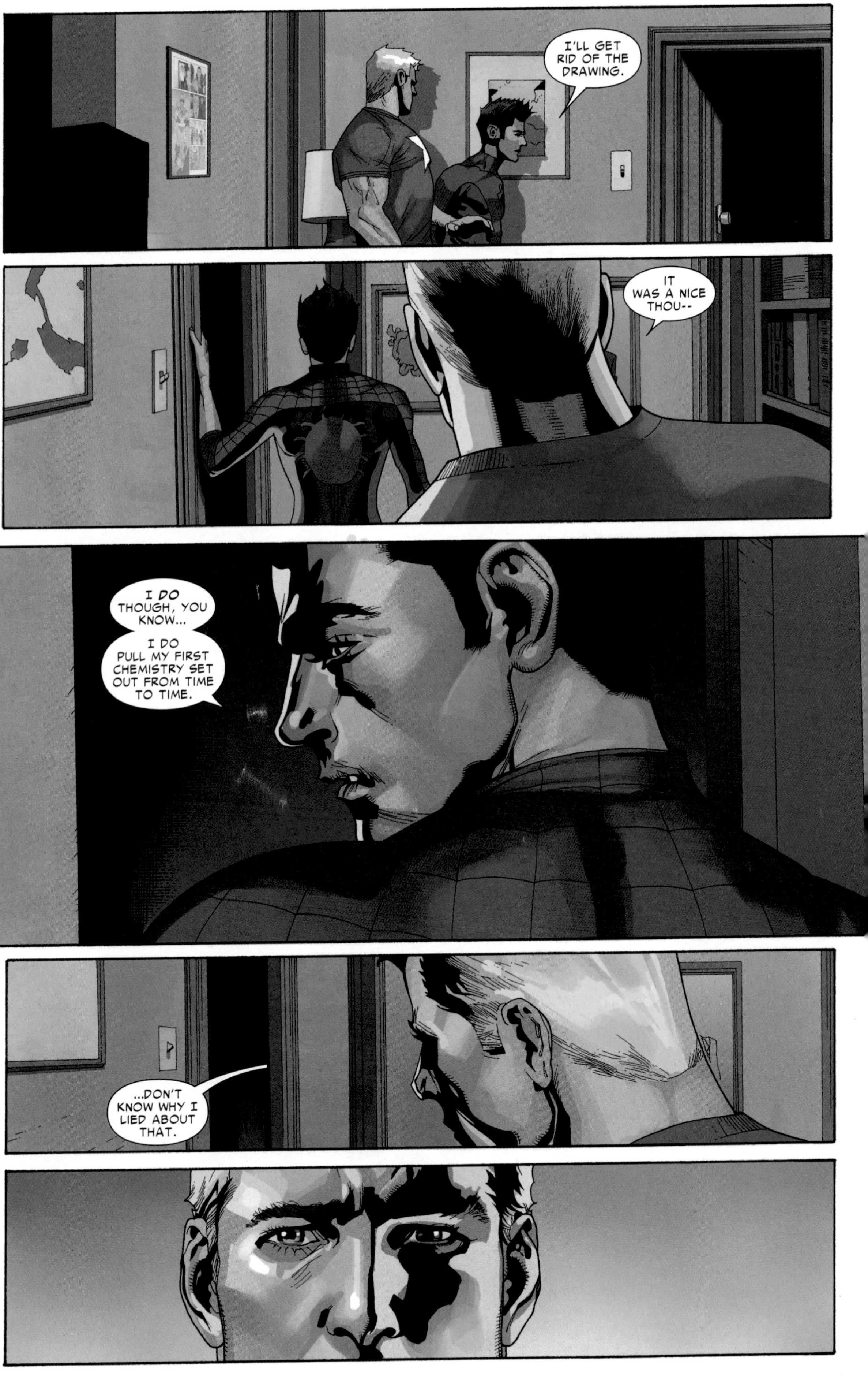

I'LL GET RID OF THE DRAWING.
IT WAS A NICE THOU--
I DO THOUGH, YOU KNOW...
I DO PULL MY FIRST CHEMISTRY SET OUT FROM TIME TO TIME.
...DON'T KNOW WHY I LIED ABOUT THAT.

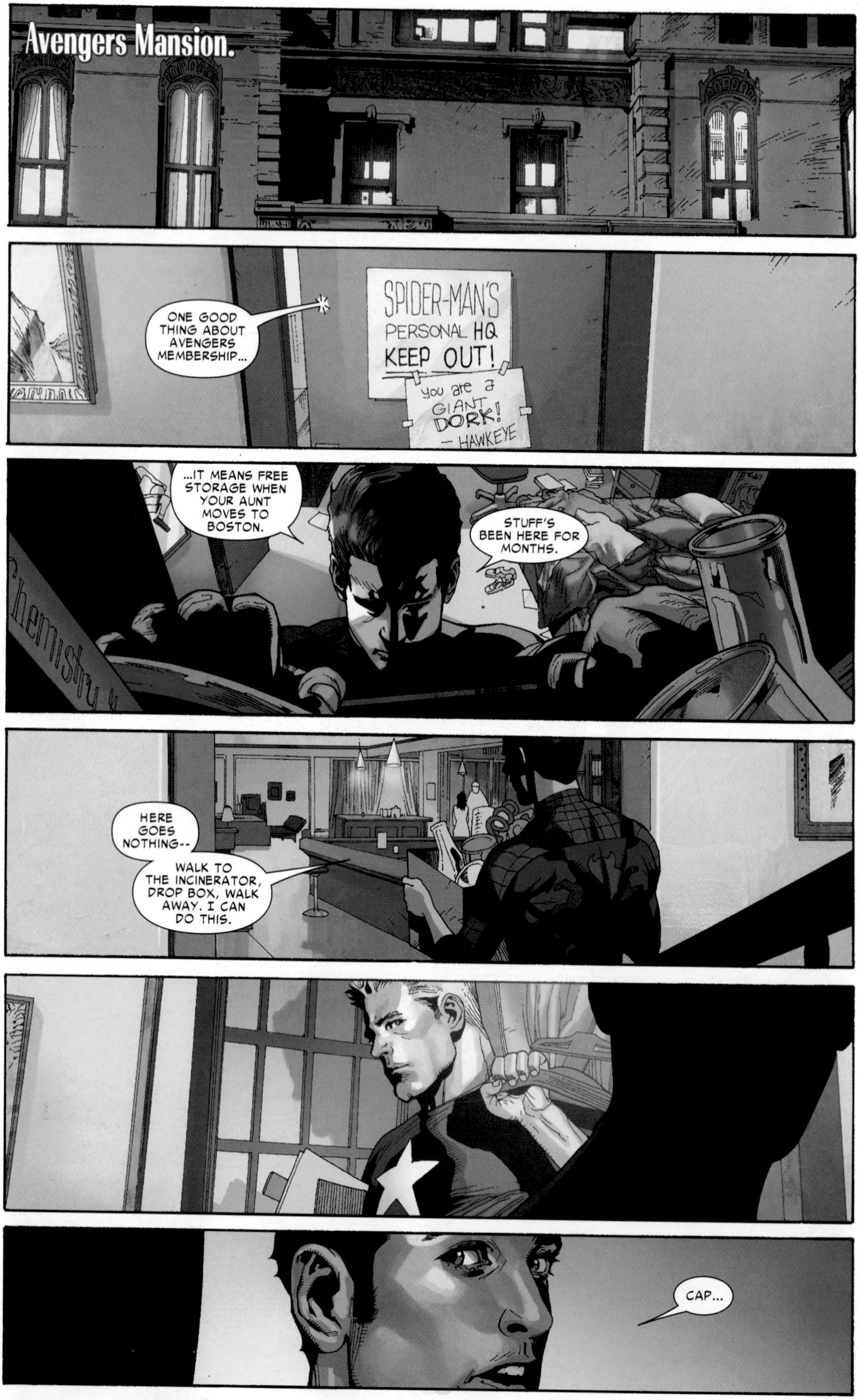

Avengers Mansion.
ONE GOOD THING ABOUT AVENGERS MEMBERSHIP...
SPIDER-MAN'S PERSONAL HQ KEEP OUT!
you are a GIANT DORK! — HAWKEYE
...IT MEANS FREE STORAGE WHEN YOUR AUNT MOVES TO BOSTON.
STUFF'S BEEN HERE FOR MONTHS.
HERE GOES NOTHING--
WALK TO THE INCINERATOR, DROP BOX, WALK AWAY. I CAN DO THIS.
CAP...

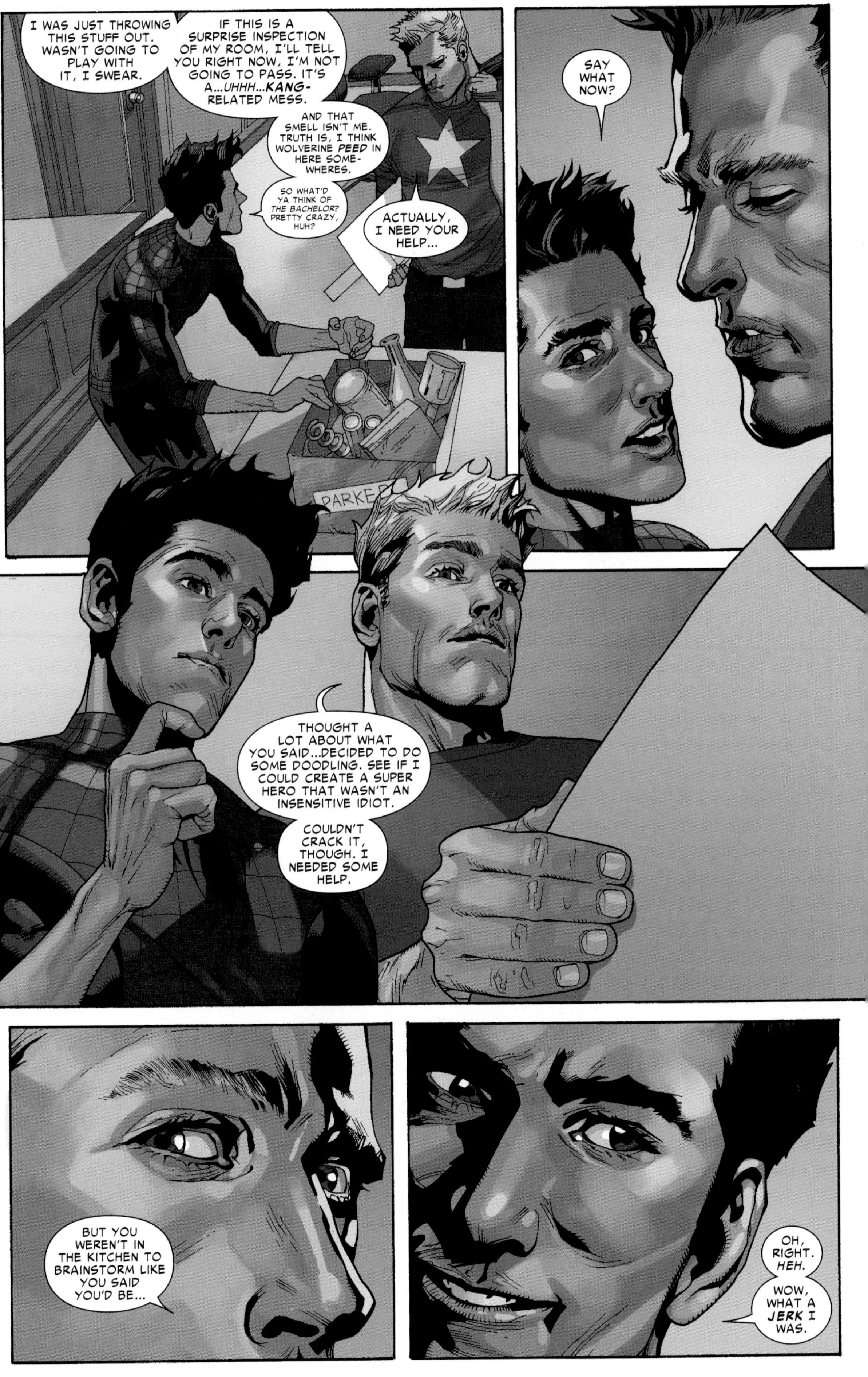
I WAS JUST THROWING THIS STUFF OUT. WASN'T GOING TO PLAY WITH IT, I SWEAR.
IF THIS IS A SURPRISE INSPECTION OF MY ROOM, I'LL TELL YOU RIGHT NOW, I'M NOT GOING TO PASS. IT'S A...*UHHH*...***KANG***-RELATED MESS.
AND THAT SMELL ISN'T ME. TRUTH IS, I THINK WOLVERINE ***PEED*** IN HERE SOME-WHERES.
SO WHAT'D YA THINK OF *THE BACHELOR*? PRETTY CRAZY, HUH?
ACTUALLY, I NEED YOUR HELP...
PARKER
SAY WHAT NOW?
THOUGHT A LOT ABOUT WHAT YOU SAID...DECIDED TO DO SOME DOODLING. SEE IF I COULD CREATE A SUPER HERO THAT WASN'T AN INSENSITIVE IDIOT.
COULDN'T CRACK IT, THOUGH. I NEEDED SOME HELP.
BUT YOU WEREN'T IN THE KITCHEN TO BRAINSTORM LIKE YOU SAID YOU'D BE...
OH, RIGHT. *HEH*.
WOW, WHAT A ***JERK*** I WAS.

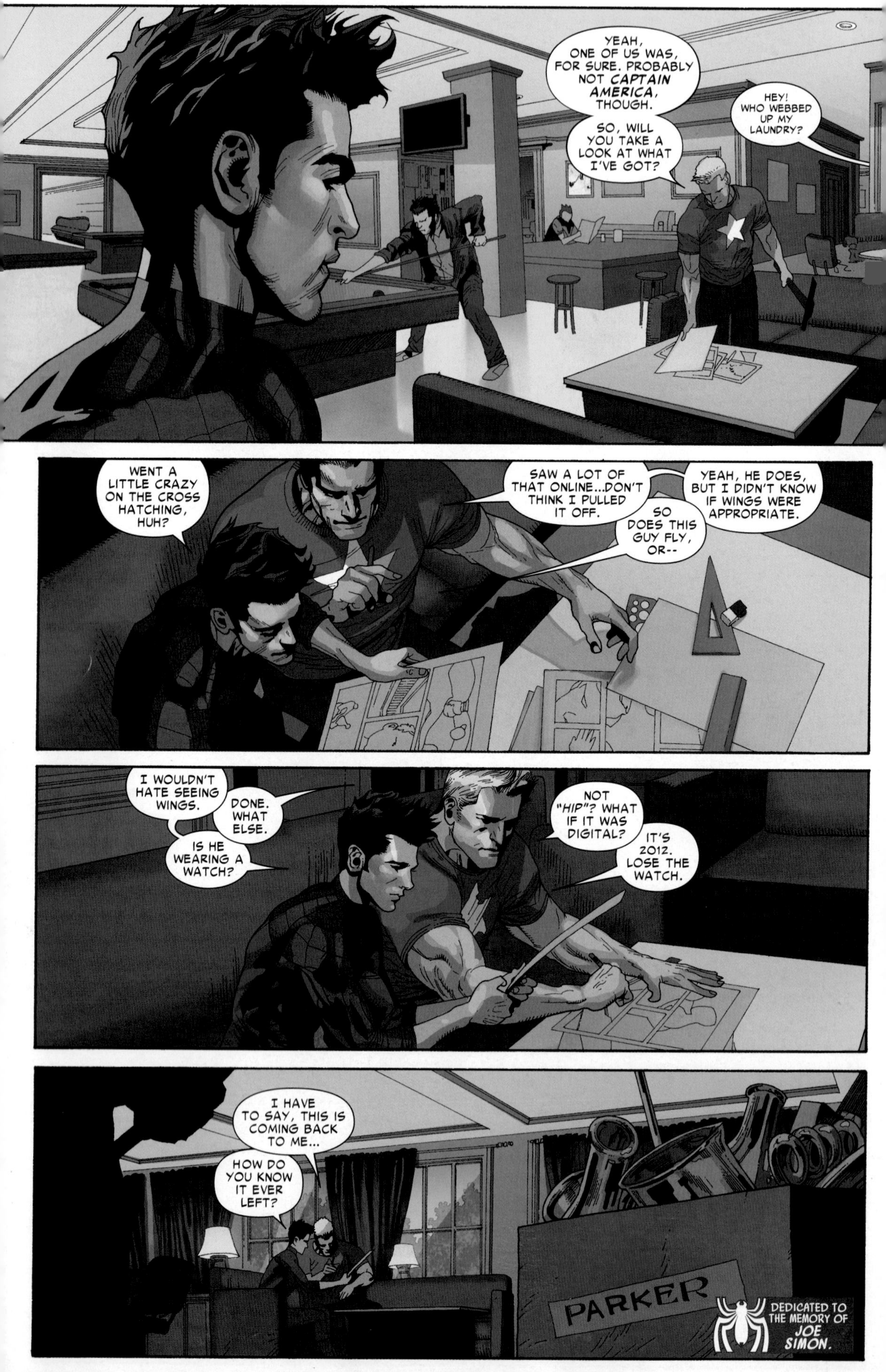
YEAH, ONE OF US WAS, FOR SURE. PROBABLY NOT CAPTAIN AMERICA, THOUGH.
SO, WILL YOU TAKE A LOOK AT WHAT I'VE GOT?
HEY! WHO WEBBED UP MY LAUNDRY?
WENT A LITTLE CRAZY ON THE CROSS HATCHING, HUH?
SAW A LOT OF THAT ONLINE...DON'T THINK I PULLED IT OFF.
SO DOES THIS GUY FLY, OR--
YEAH, HE DOES, BUT I DIDN'T KNOW IF WINGS WERE APPROPRIATE.
I WOULDN'T HATE SEEING WINGS.
DONE. WHAT ELSE.
IS HE WEARING A WATCH?
NOT "HIP"? WHAT IF IT WAS DIGITAL?
IT'S 2012. LOSE THE WATCH.
I HAVE TO SAY, THIS IS COMING BACK TO ME...
HOW DO YOU KNOW IT EVER LEFT?
PARKER
DEDICATED TO THE MEMORY OF JOE SIMON.

#1 VARIANT BY
**HUMBERTO RAMOS
& EDGAR DELGADO**

#1 VARIANT BY
**J. SCOTT CAMPBELL &
EDGAR DELGADO**

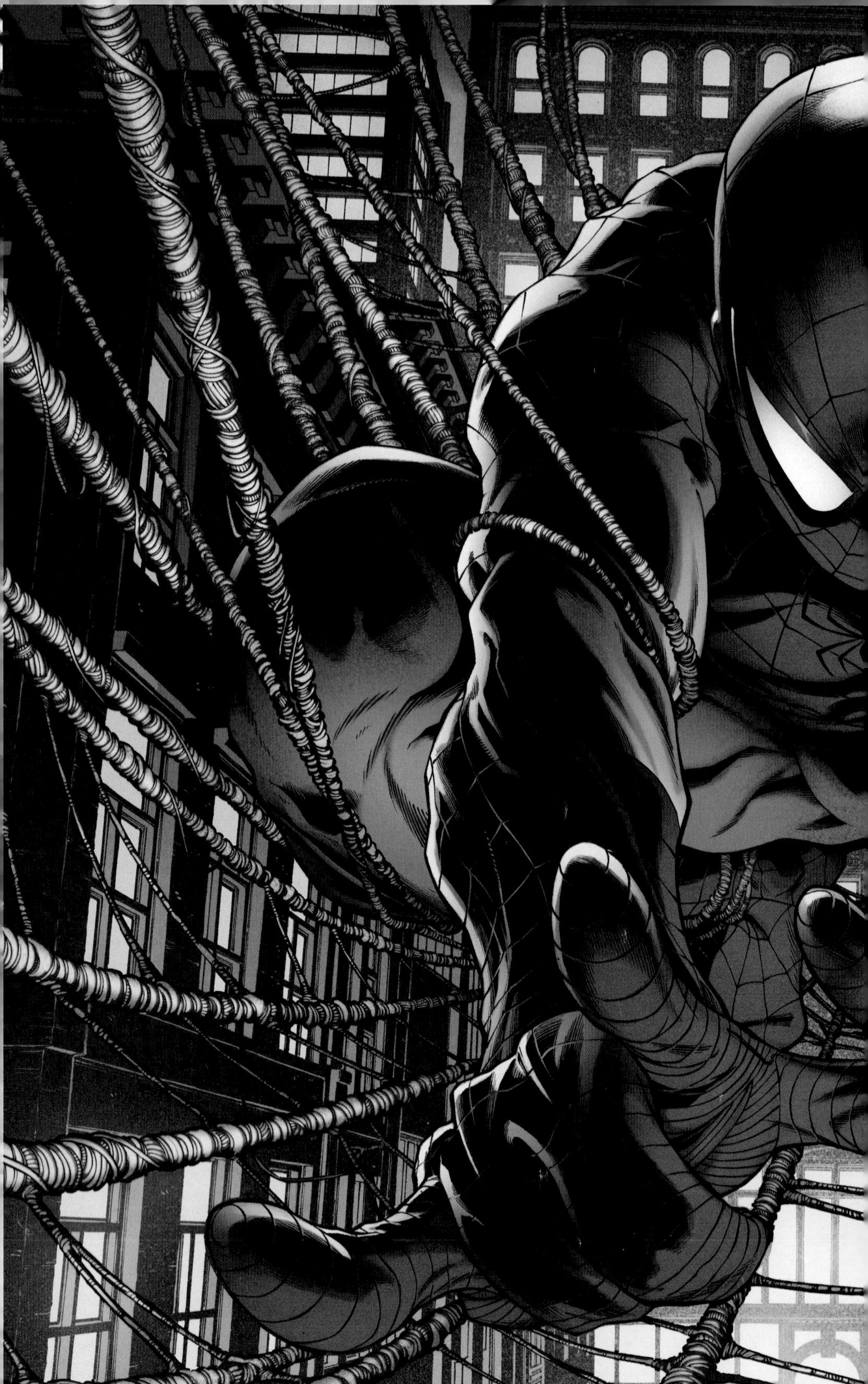

#1 VARIANT BY JOE QUESADA, DANNY MIKI & RICHARD ISANOVE

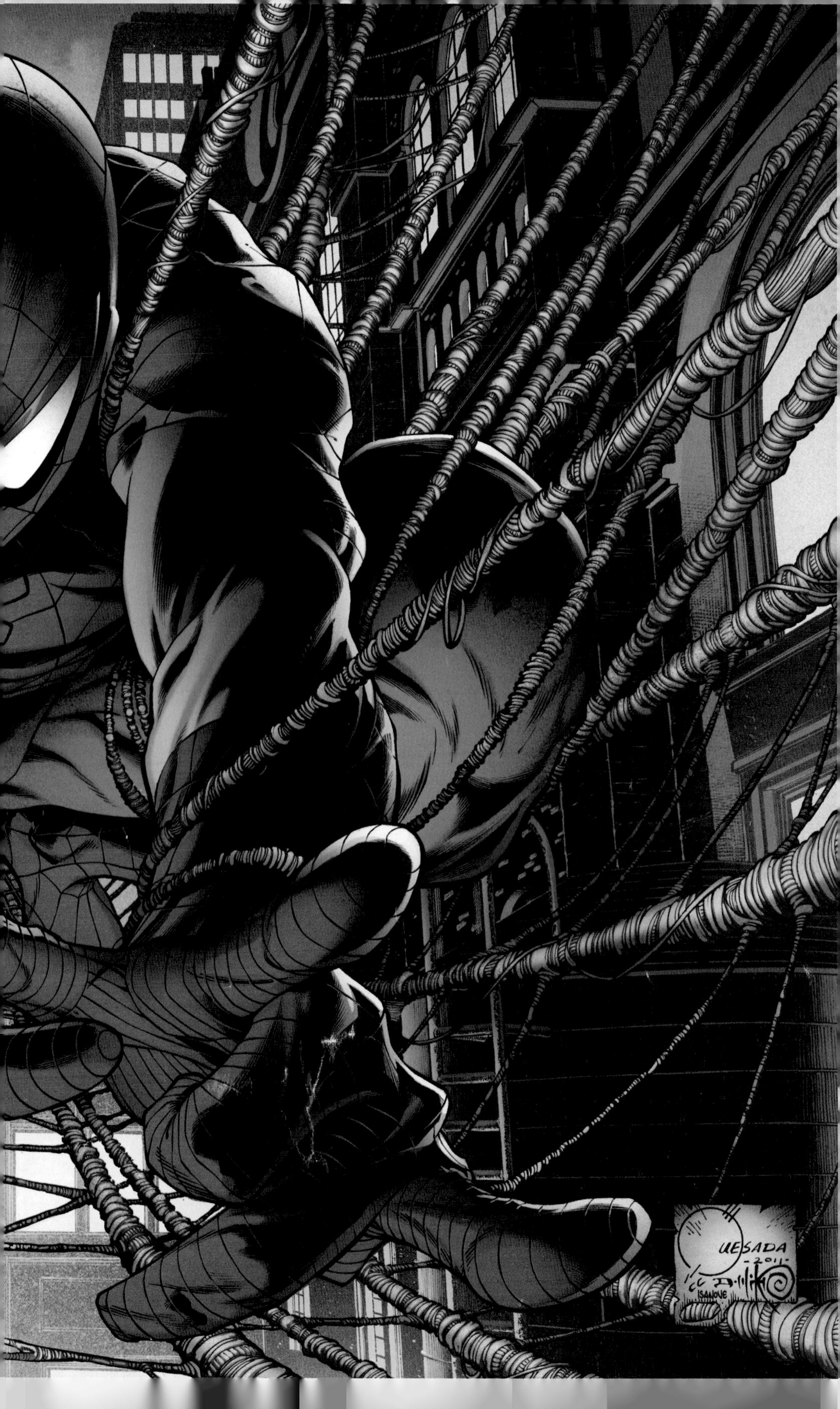

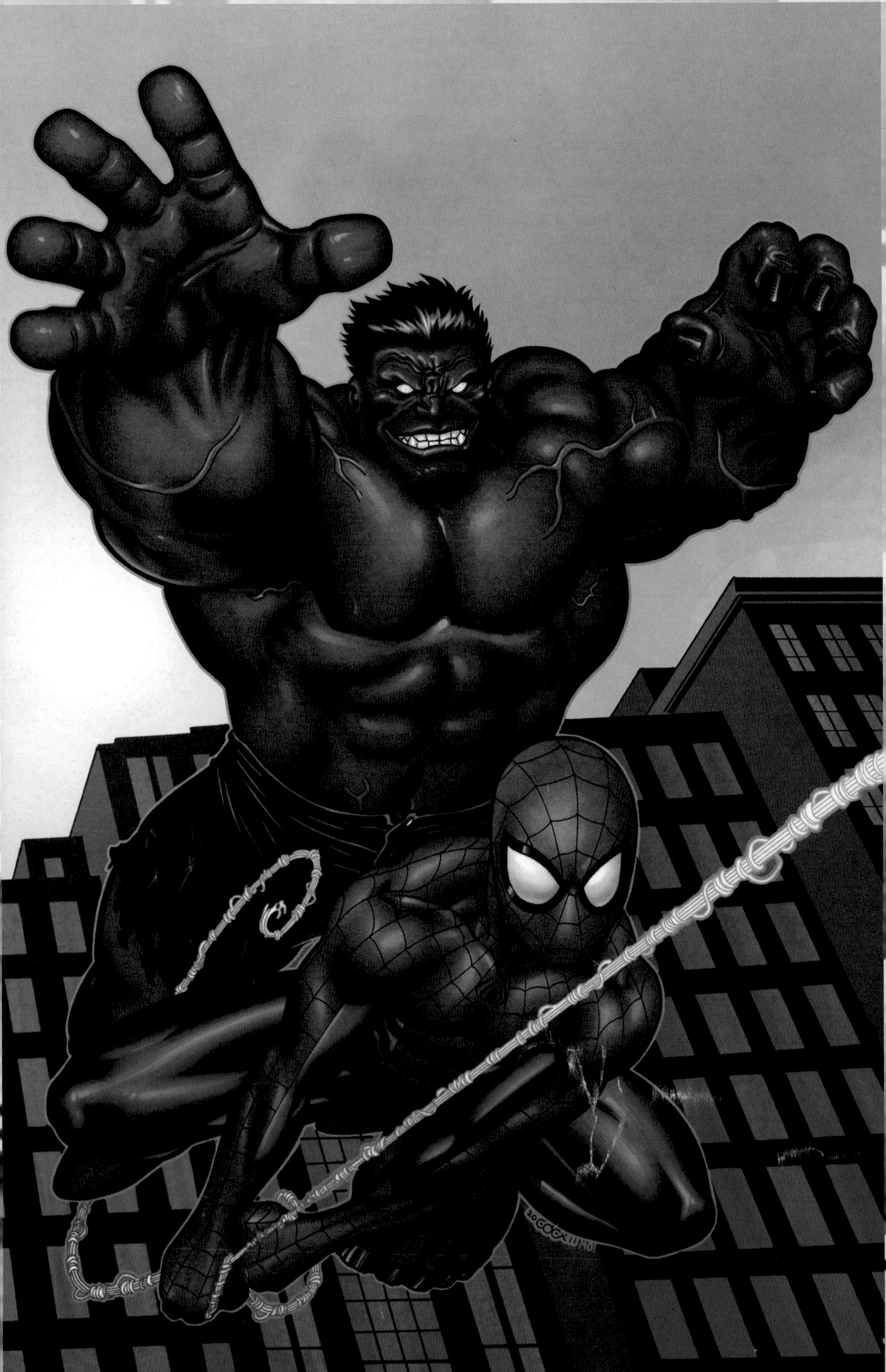

#2 VARIANT BY ED McGUINNESS, DEXTER VINES & MORRY HOLLOWELL

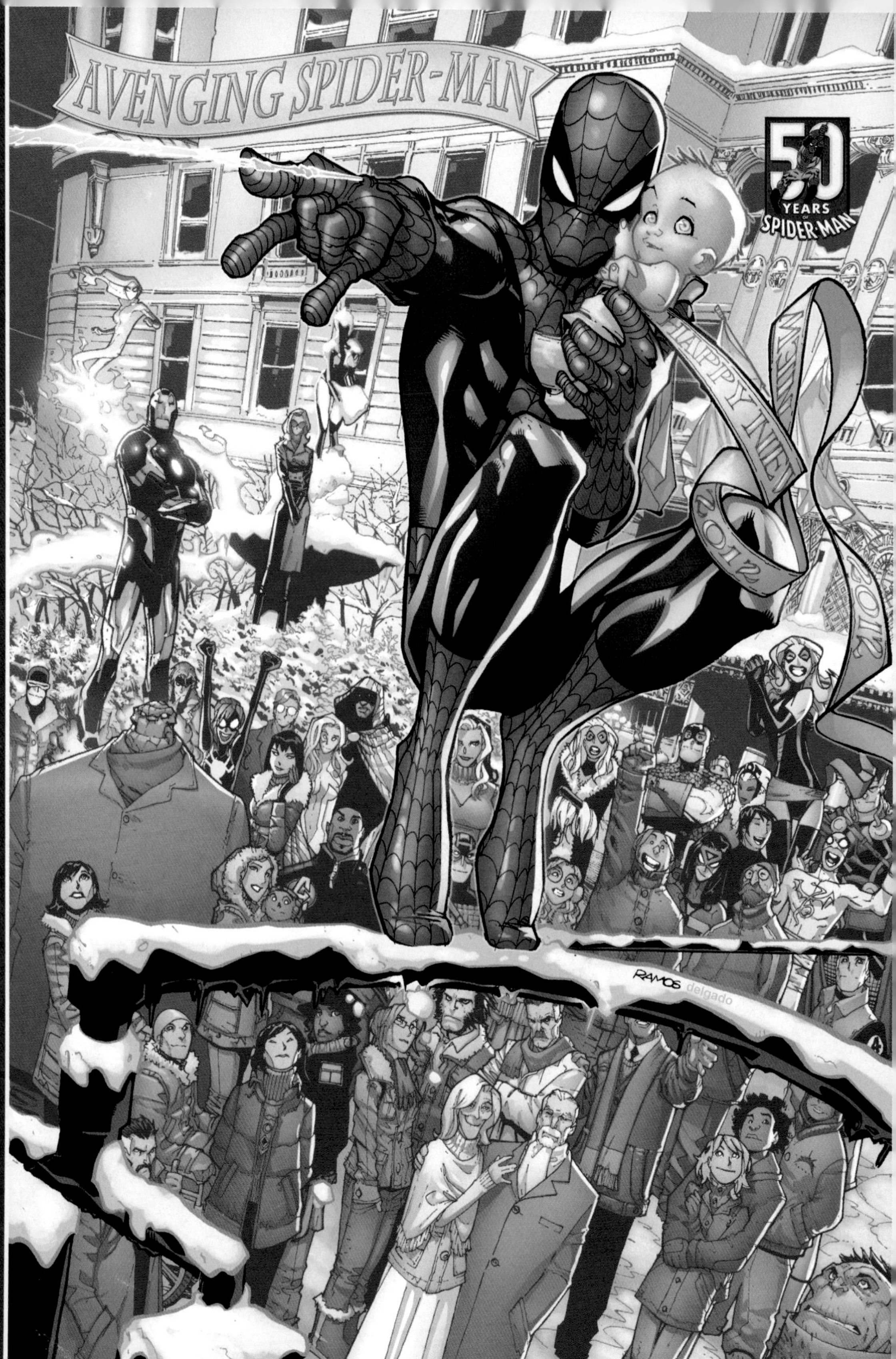
AVENGING SPIDER-MAN
50 YEARS OF SPIDER-MAN
HAPPY NEW
2012
2012
RAMOS delgado

#3 SPIDER-MAN 50TH ANNIVERSARY VARIANT BY **HUMBERTO RAMOS & EDGAR DELGADO**

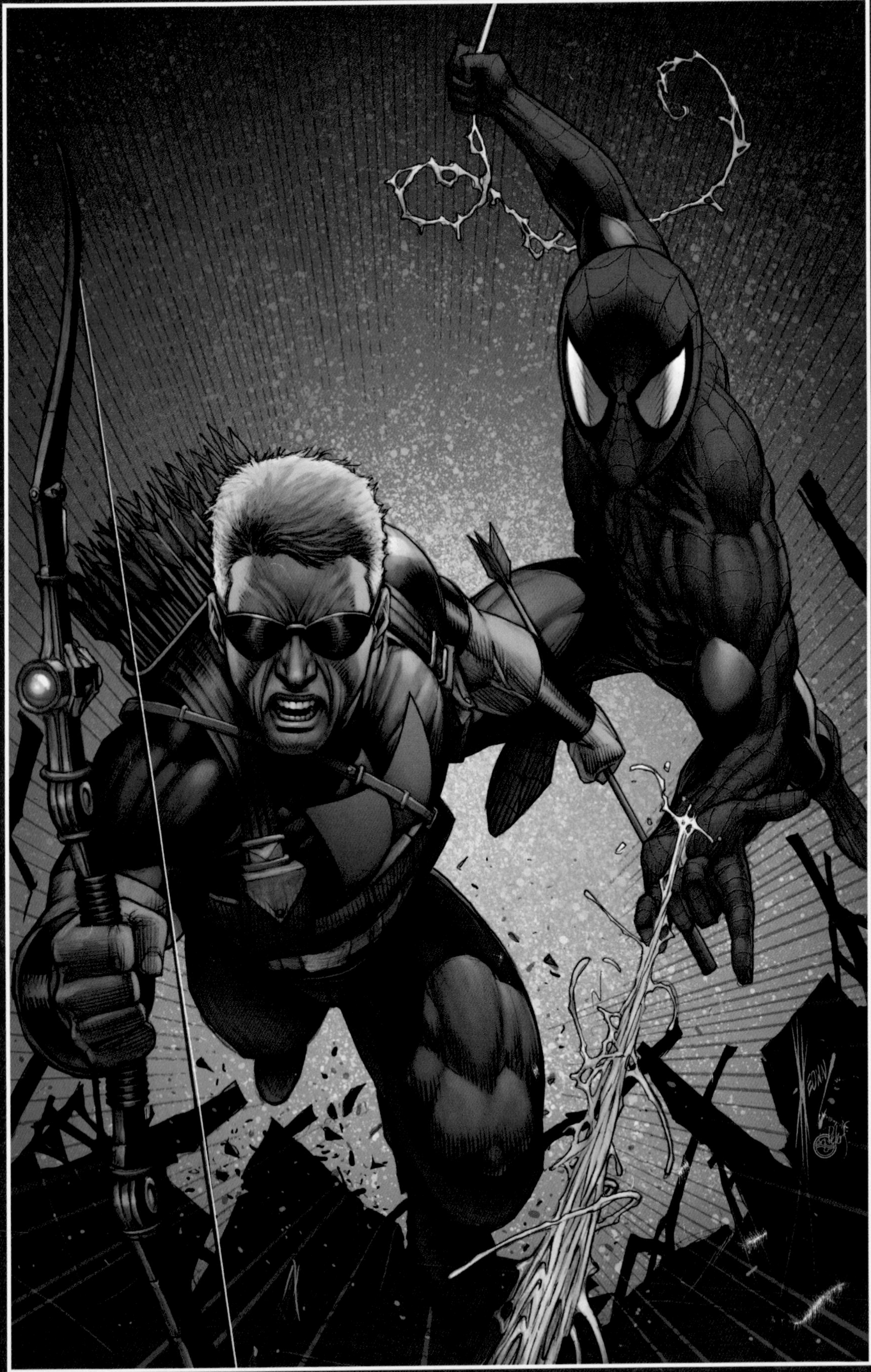

#4 VARIANT BY **DALE KEOWN & P[illegible]R STEIGERWALD**